From Tyranny to Anarchy

FROM TYRANNY TO ANARCHY

The Somali Experience

Hussein M. Adam

The Red Sea Press, Inc.
Publishers & Distributors of Third World Books

P. O. Box 1892
Trenton, NJ 08607

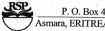

P. O. Box 48
Asmara, ERITREA

The Red Sea Press, Inc.
Publishers & Distributors of Third World Books

P. O. Box 1892   P. O. Box 48
Trenton, NJ 08607   Asmara, ERITREA

Book and Cover design: Saverance Publishing Services
(www.saverancepublishing.com)

Library of Congress Cataloging-in-Publication Data

Hussein Mohamed Adam.
  From tyranny to anarchy : the Somali experience / Hussein M. Adam.
    p. cm.
  Includes bibliographical references and index.
  ISBN 1-56902-287-9 (hard cover) -- ISBN 1-56902-288-7 (pbk.)
  1. Somalia--Politics and government--1960-1991. 2. Somalia--Politics and government--1991- I. Title.
  DT407.H865 2007
  967.7305--dc22
                        2007033994

I dedicate this book to my family: to my wife Fadumo A. Adam who, unfortunately, has been in a coma since September 2002; and to all my children—Ayaan, Farhan, Ubah, Guled, Zahra, Mohamed and Roble.

CONTENTS

ACKNOWLEDGEMENTS

This book could not have been produced without the grant from the Holy Cross Committee on Fellowships, Research and Publications.

I am grateful to the following people for their friendship and support: Richard Ford, Charles Geshekter, Lee Cassanelli, John Johnson, Mohamed Hassan Farah, and Abdirahman Osman Raghe. I am grateful to Professor Ali Mazrui for his inspiration.

I am indebted to the following for regularly sending me relevant material from the internet: Gabriel Balayah, Mohamed Sudi and Abdi Musa God. I give special thanks to Said Samatar, Ahmed Samatar, Bereket Habte Sellassie and Kassahun Checole for intellectual stimulation and encouragement.

I have always benefited from the experience and wisdom of my colleagues, Judith Chubb and Charles Weiss. Our Department Secretary, Ms. Jean Evanowski, cheerfully helped in numerous ways including preparing this manuscript for publication. She received some assistance from Vanessa Tsetsos.

INTRODUCTION

B ritish Somaliland obtained independence on June 26, 1960. Italian Somaliland regained independence on July 1st, 1960; the date which the two formed the Somali Republic, even though there are debates concerning the proper legalization of the act of union. The Somali Republic practiced multi-party democracy for about 9 years. It soon became apparent that corruption, nepotism and clanism were wreaking havoc on the new fragile Republic. Governmental paralysis is symbolized by the inability to implement a script for the Somali language. Elections were marred with corruption, rigging, violence and chaos. During the 1969 elections, 60 political parties frantically scrambled for 123 parliamentary seats! Electoral violence led to the assassination of President Abdirashid Shermarke, bringing the Republic to the border of anarchy.

Into this void stepped General Mohamed Siyad Barre who pulled off a military coup on the 21st of October 1969. This was a backlash against the semi-anarchy of the multiparty era. The expanded Somali army, now Soviet trained and equipped, was a product of Somalia's irredentist policy—the need to reclaim and reunite with French Somaliland (Djibouti), Ethiopian Somaliland and the Northern Frontier District (NFD), in Kenya. At first, the military regime exhibited certain positive features. Siyad, more or less, practiced relatively proportional clan arithmetic: the inclusion of diverse clan representatives in the Supreme Revolutionary Council (SRC), the cabinet and various official bodies. The regime carried out environmental and agricultural campaigns; expanded the military, the state bureaucracy and the growth of parastatals under the banner of "scientific socialism". The major achievement of the dictatorship was the decree to provide the Latin script for the Somali language, followed by energetic urban and rural literacy campaigns.

In 1977-1978, the dictatorship went to war with Ethiopia over the question of Ethiopian Somaliland. The Soviets dumped his regime and backed Mengistu's Ethiopia with thousands of Cuban troops that drove the Somali army out of, what is journalistically termed, "the Ogaden". This crushing defeat led Siyad to practice destructive behaviour. Clan arithmetic proportionality was flagrantly distorted and turned into a proto-Soviet practice of "clanklatura" (instead of nomenklatura). The army, police and party organs, were expanded into a multi-layered coercive apparatus. Siyad transcended the now highly expanded military, and concentrated state power through the creation of personal rulership and personal rule networks based on his clan and those of affiliated clans. Ironically, personal rule, at first served as a grid to his regime; overtime it came to destroy his military dictatorship. The backlash led to the mobilization of clan-based armed opposition group such as the Somali Salvation Democratic Font (SSDF), the Somali National Movement (SNM) and the United Somali Congress (USC), (to name but a few, during the1980s). All this time there was also a deepening economic crisis. Armed opposition parties reflected clan groups' disappointments, frustration and anger. This represented a transformation from clan-in-itself to clan-for-itself. The tyrannical aspects of the regime were adopted to repress and destroy the resulting dissatisfaction.

The time came when the Syad military state collapsed (1991), because it could not perform the functions of state. State collapse is not a rebellion, nor a coup. Essentially the collapse was the consequences of the policies and practices of dictator Barre and his ruling elite. This provides another example of the fact that military led dictatorship is an important ingredient in the decay and disintegration of the military institution itself. The post-Siyad epoch reflects two contradictory movements. The negative side is represented by the rise and chaos of the warlords; the positive side is essentially reflected in the de facto Republic of Somaliland, and to some extent in Puntland and Bay regions. In the relatively peaceful areas, we encounter the spirit of decentralization and autonomy. People seek broad-based power sharing both as an echo of the past and as a key to a more participatory future. Women are playing an increasingly prominent role in Somali civil society. Civil society is used here to indicate the social, economic and political groupings that structure society, relatively independent of the state.

An Islamic revival is evident everywhere. For the most part it reflects core values, based on Somali Sunni traditions. Initially on the margins there were fundamentalist political groups; later represented by the Union of Islamic Courts (UIC). These grew and became popular as a backlash to the chaos, brutality and violence of the warlords found mostly in southern Somalia. There is a vigorous, free and unregulated market economy. There is also a relatively free press; represented by several informal newspapers, mostly in Mogadishu and Hargeisa, presenting various perspectives on current events. The revival of traditional institutions and blending these with elements of modernity is most marked in Somaliland.

Structures that are created and events that occur prior to and during the civil war can shape the way in which peace and governance is rebuilt after the fighting has stopped. Accordingly, the SNM in Somaliland has linked with traditional elders; and has rotated its leaders several times leading to the post-independence evolution of a consociational democracy including a Council of Elders (the Guurti) in its parliamentary system. This is an example of a democratic and relatively spontaneous liberation movement able to fill the vacuum brought about by years of neglect, corruption und repression. At first, Somaliland established a power sharing system marked by balanced clan arithmetic proportionality, indirect caucus based elections and consociational practices (1991-2001). It matured enough to implement a constitution local, presidential and parliamentary elections. Yet, it failed to win international recognition. Third World countries often have to choose between democracy and stability: Somaliland has shown that it is possible to promote democracy without causing havoc and anarchy. It has also shown that a trusting civic culture of tolerance and compromise—based on local grassroots negotiations and reconciliations—facilitates democratic institutions. This has led to a nascent citizenship individualism and citizenship equality in public decision making. In contrast, Eritrea waged its liberation struggles guided by a rigid ideology, semi-bureaucratic institutions and lack of leadership rotations; it has evolved into a repressive one-party dictatorship. Instead of a rotation of leaders, the ideological dynamics of the Eritrean struggle have produced a charismatic leader who does not intend to give up power. Hopefully, Somalia and the other countries of the Horn of Africa, may find useful lessons in the Somaliland experience.

The interaction between Islam and Somali politics went on for centuries. In the period around the 17th century, Somali Islam reflected expansionism; campaigns to convert Non-Muslim Somalis and Oromos. Islamic expansionism implies unity for the believers. Radical Islamism came with the revival movement of Muhamed Abdulah Hassan during the turn of the twentieth century. He waged a jihad (holy war), against the British, the Italians, and the Ethiopians. During the 1930's we witness tendencies toward moderate Islamic reformism. Islamic reformers believe that Islamic law (sharia) is historically conditioned and needs to be reinterpreted in the light of changing needs of society. They want sharia to be implemented flexibly, taking into account the specificity of Somali society. They are against the use of violence. Islamism also played a, mostly negative, role in the politics surrounding the choice of a script for the Somali language. Under the tyranny of Siyad Barre, Islamism retreated into a defensive position, emerging as a potent force in the post-Siyad era. The recent surge of political Islam, however, is essentially a backlash against the anarchy of warlordism and a yearning for law and order. Financed by rich Somalis wishing to promote the rule of law, this pragmatic response led to the establishment of sub-clan sharia courts, the mobilization of court militia and eventually a federation or the Union of Islamic Courts (UIC).

The UIC was able to vanquish the warlords by June 2006. It then went on to declare a Pax-Islamica from Beled Weyn, through Mogadishu, to as far south as the port of Kismayu. The UIC opened Mogadishu port and airport for the first time in a decade. It then began to negotiate with the UN sponsored and Ethiopian backed Transitional Federal Government (TFG).

There are at least three ways to put states back together after collapse: (1) democratization and the evolution of a democratic policy; usually through power sharing systems; (2) international intervention and (3) strongman solutions[1]. The first option was exercised by Somaliland as explained in Chapter 6. The de facto Republic has gone on to draft a constitution moving it from the clan-based system to a multiparty political system channeling the proposed parties not to be based on clan or religious lines, but drawing support from all regions. The system has survived even though the livestock economy has its ups and downs; the main source of finance has been remittances from Somalilanders living abroad in the Diaspora. The second option led to the large US/UN intervention between 1992 -1995. This was prompted by the media drawing world wide public attention to the plight of Somalis living in the Bay region devastated by the man-made famine caused by the civil wars. The humanitarian international intervention improved on the miserable condition of the starving masses. However, it failed to conduct disarmament, demobilization, a program to train and equip local police forces; and a program to equip and restore the courts and legal justice system. Moreover, it failed to put back the Somali state. The method it chose: the convening of factional (warlords) and other elites, conferences, mostly in Addis Ababa and Nairobi. This quick fix top down method of restoring the Southern Somali state failed 14 times.

Finally in September 2004, 275-members, appointed for the Parliament, convened in Nairobi under a new federal charter. The handpicked parliament appointed a transitional President, Abdillahi Yusuf, with massive Ethiopian support. The President went to appoint a pro-Ethiopian Prime Minister, Mohamed Ghedi. Thus a top-down Transitional Federal Government was formed and it went on to confront the UIC in December 2006. With massive military support from well-equipped and well trained Ethiopian troops, its victory was assured. This is a combination of the second option; international intervention—and a distorted version of the third option—a strongman solution.

This study is largely shaped by the author's career as a participant observer of Somali politics and society. From 1974 to 1987, I headed the Social Sciences Division of the Somali National University. During this period, I participated in several internal and external events as a delegate. In 1978, I became the founding President of the Somali Studies International Association (SSIA). I have co-edited 3 volumes of the proceedings of the SSIA Congresses. This year (2007), the SSIA is hosting its 10th Congress in Columbus, Ohio as well as in Djibouti. Involvement in the SSIA has exposed me to a wealth of academic literature and primary sources; it also gave me the opportunity to hear and consult with cutting edge Somali studies scholars. In 1981, I established, and directed a non-governmental organization (NGO): the Somali Unit for Research on Emergencies and Rural Development (SURERD). This gave me the opportunity to travel to most regions within Somalia. SURERD served as a bridge between local rural development projects—such as the Islamic cooperatives discussed in Chapter 7—and international NGO's like Oxfam, Action Aid and German Agro Action. The experience exposed me to primary sources and gave me insights as to the thinking of rural Somalis.

In 1985-1986, I was contracted as one of two UN experts to assist in the formation of the Intergovernmental Authority on Drought and Development (IGADD); based in Djibouti with Ethiopia, Sudan, Kenya, Uganda, and Somalia as members; Eritrea was added later. The "D" for Drought was also dropped later (IGAD). I prepared the draft Organization and Structure of this important subregional body. In preparing the original Plan of Action, I covered Kenya, Uganda, and Sudan; my Senegalise UN expert colleague covered Ethiopia, Somalia and Djibouti. IGAD, minus Eritrea's vote has called for international peace-keepers for Somalia, and is on the record endorsing the Ethiopian intervention, after the fact.

Given my participant observer perspective, I have adopted an eclectic approach with regards to theoretical considerations: modernization theory, democratization theory, class analysis, ethnic analysis, military studies, personal rule, Islamic Studies, civil wars, state collapse and on the state and civil society.

Earlier versions of these essays were researched and written over a long period; they were composed independently of each other; however within the framework of a predetermined and coherent future book.

Note

1. See William Zartman, *Collapsed States*, London: Lynne Rienner Publishers, 1995; p.267

CHAPTER 1

ANATOMY OF A TYRANNY

Sometimes when a candle is about to flicker out, it tends to shine more brightly for a while. For a decade or more the military regime headed by Mohamed Siyad Barre manifested a strong Somali military state that extended its influence into both urban and rural areas. Its legitimacy and functioning receded during the 1980s, ending in violent collapse in January 1991. The Siyad regime's concentrated power fell into a vacuum created by years of violent oppression of Somali civil society.

Postcolonial Somali history dates from 1960, when the former Italian colony of Somalia and British Somaliland, in the north, united to form the Somali Republic. Through the 1960s, irredentist attempts to unite Somalis in northern Kenya, eastern Ethiopia (Ogaden), and Djibouti failed (Laitin and Samatar 1987; Zurtman 1989). As a consequence of border and nationality tensions with the Ethiopian Empire under Emperor Haile Selassie, which had base and military agreements with the United States, Somali parliamentary regimes sought military aid and training from the USSR.

In these early years, Somalia's multiparty politics degenerated into greed and corruption. During elections, parties multiplied, as organizations and clans splintered; and following elections, there was a rush to join the leading party in order to obtain ministerial positions and other official perquisites. The parliamentary and ministerial edifice, built on sand, was bound to collapse. The military, headed by General Mohamed Siyad Barre, grabbed state power on October 21, 1969.

THE CLANS

The Somali population of 8 to 10 million is made up of five major clan-families (Hawiya, Darod, Isaq, Dir, Digil-Mirifle); each one is subdivided into six or more clans and each clan is subdivided into subclans and sub-subclans, all the way down to lineages and extended families. Within the series of concentric and interconnected circles, with kaleidoscopic and diffuse attachments, the most stable subunit is the lineage segment, consisting of close kinsmen who together pay and receive blood-compensation in cases involving homicide. In general, the Somali people, for the most part, share a common language (Somaale), religion (Islam), physical characteristics, and pastoral and agropastoral customs and traditions (Lewis 1969).

Clanism is the Somali version of the generic problem of ethnicity or tribalism: it represents primordial cleavages and cultural fragmentation within Somali society. After World War II, politicized clanism among Somalis favored nationalism and a Greater Somalia concept. At other times, clanism has assumed a negative aspect—the abandonment of objectivity when clan and local/parochial interests must prevail. Clan consciousness is partly a product of elite manipulation, the cooptation and corruption of politicians claiming clan leadership (Saul 1979: 391-423), but at times it is the elite themselves who are manipulated by politicized clanism.

On the other hand, aspects of clan consciousness, transcending false consciousness, reflect a plea for social justice and against exploitative relations among ethnic groups. Uneven class formation has led certain groups to utilize clan formation as embryonic trade unions. In such cases, affirmative action–type policies are the best way to overcome discrimination against clans and groups. Clan consciousness tends to rise during periods of extreme scarcities—drought, famine, wars. Clan conflicts are also instigated by memories of past wars for resources or for naked prestige. However, such disputes take place only between neighboring clans and intricate mechanisms have been evolved for conflict resolution, for clan territory is often extensive and sometimes even noncontiguous. By far the greatest damages brought about by clan conflicts spread over large geographic areas have resulted from elite manipulation and politicization of clan consciousness.

WHAT BROUGHT ABOUT SOMALI STATE COLLAPSE?

At first, the Siyad military regime seemed destined to strengthen the Somali state. Financial and administrative incapacity had limited the scope of Somali civilian governments: they ventured into rural areas only during elections. The military regime, unencumbered by the costs entailed in the parliamentary bargaining process, seemed to divert such energies to mobilizing resources for the expansion of the modern socioeconomic sector. The government conducted campaigns against urban and rural illiteracy (after scripting the Somali language), expanded health and education services, resettled drought victims, and encouraged self-help community projects.

Meanwhile, Siyad was consolidating his personal power and building an autocratic regime. He framed and executed those among his colleagues whom he considered to be key opponents. In 1975, he executed ten relatively unknown religious leaders for opposing his new family law on the grounds that it was contrary to Islamic teachings.

The era of creative sociocultural experiments lasted until 1977 – 1979, the year of the Ogaden War with Ethiopia, the abrogation of the USSR/Somali Treaty of Friendship, and the search for a Somali-American alliance (Samatar 1988). Thereafter, as the regime became more self-centered and vindictive, the opposition began to rise, first in the center and the north and then as widespread dissidence throughout the country. Why did the Somali state collapse? Below, under eight headings, I list the main factors. Seven of the eight are essentially internal. The eighth considers external factors.

Personal Rule

Like other African rulers, Siyad installed a personal rulership: his lasted from 1969 to 1991 (Jackson and Rosberg 1982). Over time, he was able to manipulate and modify his rulership style, from being a prophetic ruler advocating "scientific socialism" (1970–1977), to an autocrat (1978–1986), and finally a tyrant (1987 – 1991). During his earlier years, Siyad utilized mediatory mechanisms that postponed final confrontation, but his prolonged dictatorial rule damaged and distorted state-civil society relations. Later, as an outright tyrant, he applied absolute principles of governance, irrespective of human cost.

Military Rule

Siyad's dictatorial rule did not function in an institutional vacuum. The Somali military structure was considered to be one of the best in sub-Saharan Africa and Siyad also understood the importance of controlling other state sectors and civil society, through institutions and organizations such as the military, security, paramilitary, an elitist vanguard political party, and so-called mass organizations. As a personal ruler, he had the autonomy to operate above institutions.

Soon after independence, the Somali army numbered 3,000. The USSR agreed to train and equip an army of 12,000 and by 1977 an army 37,000 – strong entered the Ogaden War. By 1982 the Somali army had grown to a suffocating 120,000 (Adam 1993). The army of liberation had been converted to a huge army of repression.

From Nomenklatura to Clan-klatura

Essentially, nomenklatura involves appointing loyal political agents to guide and control civil and military institutions. The introduction of nomenklatura to Somalia by the Soviets involved politicization of institutions that were beginning to function reasonably well, relying on education and training, technical competence, specialization, and experience. As early as 1972, the military regime began to appoint political commissars for the armed forces, administrative institutions, social organizations for workers, youth and women, and cooperatives.

Siyad soon substituted clanism for ideology as criteria for such appointments. Foreign aid provided the glue that held the system together in spite of internal waste and corruption ("selective misallocation"). Clan-klatura involved placing trusted clansmen and other loyalists in positions of power, wealth, control/espionage. It also involved creating clan-klatura organizations. One such organization, Hangash, conducted military intelligence; the Dabarjebinta, literally, the backbone breakers, was military counterintelligence; then there were the military police, identified by their red berets. The majority of these forces were drawn from the President's clan, the Marehan of the Darod. In such a situation of divide and rule, state institutions were thrown into gridlock, jealousy, confusion, and anarchy.

From its inception, the Siyad regime rested on three clans from the Darod clan-family. Lewis (1988) describes how this background was "reflected in the clandestine code name 'M.O.D.' given to the regime. M (Marehan) stood for the patrilineage of the President, O (Ogaden) for that of his mother, and D (Dulbahante) for that of his principal son-in-law, head of the National Security Service.... [Although] no one could utter the secret symbol of General Siyad's power openly, the M.O.D. basis of his rule was public knowledge and discussed and criticized in private" (Lewis1988: 222).

From Class Rule to Clan Rule

Once he dropped "scientific socialism" as his guiding ideology, Siyad did not resort to Islam, as did Numeiri in the Sudan. Atavistically, he resorted to clanism. Hardly any members of his clan gained strong bourgeois roots during his long reign — neither educational qualifications, economic know-how, nor professional competence. Promising clan members were plucked out of educational institutions to fill clan-klatura posts. Siyad systematically sought to destroy the bourgeois elements of other clans—sending them to jail or to exile abroad. The damage done to the Somali elite class partly explains both the total state collapse and the delay in Somali state renewal. On this point, Frantz Fanon noted in 1968:

> We no longer see the rise of a bourgeois dictatorship, but a tribal dictatorship. The ministers, the members of the cabinet, the ambassadors and local commissioners are chosen from the same ethnological group as the leader, sometimes directly from his own family.... This tribalizing of the central authority, it is certain, encourages regionalist ideas and separatism. All the decentralizing tendencies spring up again and triumph, and the nation falls to pieces, broken in bits (Fanon 1968: 183-184). Virtually writing a script for Somalia, Fanon went on to observe that the actions of a tribal (clan)-minded dictator provoke the opposition to demand regional and ethnic distribution of national resources. However, the tribalist dictator, "irresponsible as ever, still unaware and still despicable, denounces their 'treason'" (Fanon 1968: 184). Siyad went beyond shouting about treason to bombing villages, towns,

and cities, destroying water reservoirs vital to nomads in what he called enemy territories, indiscriminate jailings, utilizing terror squads and assassination units, and intensifying interclan wars. He allowed no space for a nonviolent opposition movement. When one such group—the "Manifesto" opposition group—appeared, at the last moment in 1989, he jailed and harassed its leaders instead of negotiating with them in good faith.

Poisoning Clan Relations

The clan-klatura havoc within state institutions was exported into rural civil societies. After the Ogaden War (1977-1978), Siyad practiced brutal divide-and-rule, encouraging clan warfare. At first he used his army to conduct punitive raids, similar to those under early colonial rule. Later his troops armed so-called loyal clans and encouraged them to wage wars against "rebel" clans. The damage caused by elite manipulation of clan consciousness and clan conflicts contributed to the inability of civil society to rebound when Siyad fell from power. It will take years to heal these societal wounds.

Urban State Terror

Young people began to disappear in regional cities like Hargeisa in the north, considered to be rebel territory, during the early 1980s. This phenomenon, reminiscent of Argentina, continued in other towns, then spread to the capital city, Mogadishu. During 1989 and 1990, Siyad's clan-klatura forces massacred hundreds of religious protestors. Following killings in July 1989, one of Siyad's former ministers observed:

> What has shaken the Somali people has been the slaughtering of 47 young men in Jasiira Beach a couple of days after the prayer shootings. Taking a page from the book of Death Squads, an area of Mogadishu known to be inhabited by people from the North (Isaq) was selected. At least 47 individuals, taken out of their homes in the middle of the night, are confirmed to have been shot in cold blood and put in a mass grave. This is a crime not only against the grieving Somali people, but also against humanity (Galaydh 1990: 26).

A similar vendetta awaited Hawiye clans, raising a rebellion across the country. Siyad's vindictive terror-state laid the basis for wars of revenge that postponed civil society's ability to create a successor state.

Neofascist Campaign Against the North

Northern Somalia (formerly British Somaliland) came to resent the south for various reasons. At independence and unification in 1960, the south monopolized all key posts: president, prime minister, commander of the army, head of the national police, and so forth. The former prime minister of the north, Mohamed Ibrahim Egal, merely became minister of education in the union government. Popular resentment was manifested in an overwhelming negative vote among northerners during the constitutional referendum of 1961. Late in 1961, northern officers trained at Sandhurst, Britain's officer school, unsuccessfully attempted a secessionist coup. The judge sentenced them lightly, because a legal act of union had never been passed. In 1967, northern leader Egal had managed to emerge as prime minister by manipulating the multiparty system. The conflict between the north and the south generated low-intensity demands for distributional benefits within the political system, which, when unsatisfied, escalated into the current high-intensity demand for separate statehood and independence for Somaliland once the Siyad Bare state collapsed.

Once Siyad had taken over and armed opposition to his regime grew, he singled out the northern region, inhabited by the Isaq clan-family, for extraordinary punishment. Some say he hoped to unite the south by punishing the north and the (Isaq) Somali National Movement (SNM). Lewis (1990) observed:

> Male Ogadeni refugees [from the Ogaden War, who fled to Isaq territory] in Northern Somalia, who have long been subject to illegal recruitment into Somalia's armed forces, have been conscripted as a paramilitary militia to fight the SNM and man checkpoints on the roads. Ogadeni refugees have been encouraged to take over the remains of Isaq shops and houses in what are now ghost towns. Thus, those who were received as refugee guests have supplanted their Isaq hosts, many of whom —in

this bitterly ironic turn of fate—are now refugees in the Ogaden (Lewis 1990:59).

These Isaq refugees and displaced persons, almost a million of them, returned to their devastated village, towns, and cities in 1991. Thousands more awaited the removal of mines before they could return. Their bitter experiences and what they saw of their remnant towns led them to support the northern secession in May 1991.

External Factors

Military, technical, and financial foreign assistance played a key role in prolonging the life of Siyad's regime. Somalia's geographic position on the Red Sea and Indian Ocean has long attracted foreign interests. Early in Siyad's rule, the USSR provided substantial military and economic assistance, including fuel, supplying financing for project local costs that helped cushion the Somali economy from international economic conditions. After 1977, the United States replaced the Soviets in providing armaments—unlike the Russians, sending mostly defensive arms—and during the 1980s, about $100 million of economic aid per year (Foltz and Bienen 1985:100).

Italy provided the regime with bilateral aid, and was also a conduit for other European (EEC) assistance. During the mid-1980s Italy launched a 1 billion lira project in the Bari (northeast) region of Somalia. Italian parliamentary investigations later showed that Italian officials and the Siyad family siphoned off most of the funds (Galaydh 1990:23).

China invested in a series of remarkable projects, including the north-south tarmac road, a cigarettes and matches factory, a sports and theater complex, and rice and tobacco farms. China also provided light arms and spare parts.

The military regime also benefited from significant financial assistance from the United Nations system and the World Bank. Siyad maneuvered Somalia into the Arab League in 1974 and the regime received generous Arab petrodollar assistance. There was, for example, "an alleged unofficial transfer of substantial sums of money from Saudi Arabia to the Somali government in mid-1990 to ensure that [Siyad] Barre did not side with Iraq" (Drysdale 1992:4).

As long as resources did not dry up, Siyad was able to hold on to power. But U.S. congressional criticism of Siyad's human rights record, made dramatic and visible by the war in the north, led to the suspension of U.S. military aid in 1988. In 1989 economic aid, too, was blocked and other states and international organizations began to follow suit. The regime collapsed in January 1991.

In the world after the Cold War, internal protests and external donor pressures can facilitate nonviolent regime transitions, without engendering state collapse. In Somalia, an abrupt stoppage of all aid followed a history of too much aid. Modest assistance might have facilitated formation of flexible interim administrations. To cite examples, in providing pressure for multiparty elections in Kenya and Malawi in 1993 and 1994, the major donors backed up internal protests. Their unambiguous message in suspending economic aid could not be ignored. In Somalia, on the other hand, international intervention missed the window of opportunity that was framed by the rising rebellion in the north in the 1980s, the outbreak of urban opposition in 1988, and the immediate post-Siyad clan warfare in 1991.

THE CLAN-BASED ARMED OPPOSITIONS

Siyad's clan persecutions obliged the opposition to utilized their own clans as organizational bases for armed resistance, echoing the Swahili proverb: dawa ya moto ni moto (The medicine for fire is fire). The first clan-based armed opposition group seemed to have stumbled into existence. After failing in an anti-Siyad coup attempt in 1978, Col. Abdullahi Yusuf fled to Ethiopia where he established the Somali Salvation Democratic Front (SSDF). The front attracted support mostly from his subclan of the Majerteen clan (another part of the Darod clan-family that spawned Siyad). The SSDF, following a burst of cross-border activities, atrophied as a result of heavy reliance on foreign funding from Libya, Abdullahi Yusuf's dictatorial leadership, and Siyad's ability to appease most of the Majerteens as fellow cousins within the Darod clan-family. Eventually, with funds and clan appeals, he was able to entice the bulk of SSDF fighters to return from Ethiopia and participate in his genocidal wars against the Isaq in the north and later against the Hawiye in the south, including Mogadishu. More recently (following Siyad's fall) the

SSDF has claimed control of the Bari, Nugal, and parts of Mudug (northeast) regions of Somalia, under the new leadership of Gen. Mohammed Abshir; and later as Puntland under Abdullahi Yusuf.

The major opposition clan grouping was the Somali National Movements (SNM), which derived its main support from the Isaq clan-family of the north (see appendix at end of this chapter listing political factions). The SNM was established in London early in 1981 but soon decided to move its operations to the Ethiopian Somali towns and villages close to the border with former British Somaliland. It is alleged that Qadhafi disliked SNM leaders and so would not finance their movement; they were obliged to raise funds among the Somali Isaq communities in Saudi Arabia and the Gulf, in other Arab states, in East Africa, and in Western countries. This decentralized method of fundraising gave the movement relative independence: it also enhanced accountability to its numerous supporters. The SNM evolved democratic procedures. Between 1981 and 1991 it held about six congresses, during which it periodically elected leaders and evolved policies. In 1988, the SNM conducted several raids and a major military operation in northern Somalia following a peace accord between Ethiopia and Somalia that removed Ethiopian restraints on SNM operations. They were able to block Siyad's huge army barricaded in towns and bases for the next two years. The SNM played an indirect role in the formation of the United Somali Congress (USC), an armed movement based on the Hawiye clan-family that inhabits the central regions of the country, including Mogadishu.

Enter Aidid and Ali Mahdi

The USC was founded in 1989 at a contested congress held partly in Ethiopia, partly in Rome. A third faction of the USC continued to exist in Mogadishu—a nonviolent opposition called the Manifesto Group. The weakening military power of the Siyad regime had allowed a narrow space for a so-called loyal opposition that issued a manifesto during his last year. However, the rapid success of the Mogadishu USC facilitated by this political opening left them without a developed, politically mature, party program and organization.

The charismatic journalist founder of the group, Jiumale, died in mid-1990, leaving a bitter conflict between the USC's military wing leader, General Aidid, and its Manifesto representative, Ali Mahdi. In a typical example of elite manipulation, once Siyad was expelled from Mogadishu, conflict between the two for USC and national leadership led to internecine wars, in June and September 1991 and March 1992, between their sister clans. Large parts of the capital city were destroyed and the way was paved for creeping warlordism in southern Somalia; these conflicts have persisted to the present time.

Proliferation of Factions

A group of Ogaden clan soldiers and officers defected from Siyad's army in 1989 and formed the Somali Patriotic Movement (SPM). A splinter SPM faction, headed by Umar Jess and based in the Kismayu area, became allied to the Aidid faction of the USC.

After Siyad fell, a number of other protopolitical clan organizations were formed, much less well-armed than those that formed during the struggles to overthrow Siyad. The Rahanwiin (main branch of the Digil-Mirifle) and related clans around Baidoa formed the Somali Democratic Movement (SDM), which divided into two factions, one allied to Aidid's USC branch. The Somali National Alliance (SNA) provides a general title for the USC-SPM-SDM-SSNM alliance (see appendix). The Southern Somali National Movement (SSNM) represents Dir clans. Somali farmers of Bantu origins, normally outside the clan system, have formed the Somali African Muki Organization (SAMO). Another group outside the clan system, dwellers in the ancient coastal cities, have established the Somali National Union (SNU).

More needs to be said about the Somali National Movement (SNM), mentioned earlier, which attended the January and March 1993 Addis Ababa reconciliation conferences with observer status (the fifteen protopolitical groups that signed the agreement are listed in the appendix). Under conditions of peaceful political transitions, opposition parties are able to uphold state structure, authority, law, and political order so as to ensure state continuity; and mature and united armed political movements are able to develop experienced cadres and parallel structures facilitating their eventual control of state power. In Somalia, the SNM decided to concentrate on the northern region—more or less as did the EPLF in Eritrea. Ethiopia is agrarian: pastoral Somali society is much more deeply divided along clan lines and a protopolitical clan movements is little able to project its power beyond its natural clan territory. On the whole, the Somali opposition movement was weak, inexperienced, decentralized, clan-based, and unable to provide capable national leadership and vision. As Nietzsche said: "Those who set out to destroy monsters must beware they do not become monsters themselves" (Nietzsche 1966 edition: 89). This seems to be what happened in southern Somalia. Chaos, anarchy, and famine engulfed the country.

STATE COLLAPSE AND BEYOND

The visible collapse of the original Somali state has lasted almost two decades. In some respects the country appears to have reverted to its status of the nineteenth century: no internationally recognized polity; no national administration exercising real authority; no formal legal system; no banking and insurance services; no telephone and postal system; no public service; no educational and reliable health system; no police and public security services; no electricity or piped water systems; weak officials serving on a voluntary basis surrounded by disruptive, violent bands of armed youths.

Unlike in Liberia, where the capital at no point fell into rebel hands, chaos and anarchy engulfed Mogadishu. In most of Africa, countries with weak but nominal authorities in the capital city endured civil wars that caused state retraction—but not total collapse.

As in Chad, factional war erupted among the victors over the previous regime, in this case, the USC. Fought mostly in Mogadishu, the war brought the capital city to the centre of the civil wars, destroying all institutions and records of central government. Dictator Siyad fled Mogadishu in January 1991; unlike Mengistu in Ethiopia, he did not leave the country but established himself with loyal followers in his clan homeland near the Ethiopian and Kenyan borders. Less than a month after he left, his followers launched an attack on Mogadishu, but they were soundly defeated, returning to their homeland.

Siyad continued to pursue ReNaMo-type tactics (Mozambique) for most of 1991 and 1992. His military raids devastated the clan-family situated around Baidoa, between his home base and Mogadishu. The agropastoral Rahanwiin had to flee into the bush, abandoning farms and livestock, an exodus that led to the manmade famine so intensively covered by the media. Operation Restore Hope followed. This amounted to a Bosnia-type of situation, posing a choice between military intervention or arming the Rahanwiin to protect themselves: Operation Restore Hope launched by the US/UN had a positive humanitarian impact in south-central Somalia (Oakley, 1994).

Many Somalis, especially unarmed farmers and coastal city inhabitants, made desperate escape attempts, creating a "boat people" problem. Refugees sought asylum in Yemen or Kenya; many perished at sea. The punishment meted out in the north led the Somali National Movement (SNM) in May 1992 to opt for defacto independence as the Somaliland Republic, adding another complicated layer to the Somali crisis: an Eritrean-type situation. Putting the Somali state back together involves the possibility of renewing two states, rather than one. Somalis in the self-declared Somaliland Republic argue that their economic and social ties are closer to Somalis in nearby Ethiopia and Djibouti than those in Mogadishu and southern Somalia. Whether a new Somalia should be made up of one or two independent states, or perhaps a confederation of two autonomous states, is left to the Somali people to decide, hopefully with guarantees from the United States, the United Nations, and other external actors that the process be based on peaceful, political means, involving referendum and negotiation.

One urgent task involves disarmament. Somalia was armed in the Cold War in quantities not witnessed in other African crisis areas, and these arms are still available, often at prices cheaper than food. The political factions must be induced to give up their arms—especially heavy arms. This must be done fairly and simultaneously. Factions should not be permitted to import arms, as is done especially across the Kenya border. International force is required to disarm bandits and criminal gangs (peaceful rural nomads have traditionally reserved the right to carry a gun to protect their livestock).

PROSPECTS FOR RECONSTITUTION

There is a growing strength in Somali civil society—essentially because the state has collapsed so absolutely (Rothchild and Chazan 1988). In the north, and practically in areas of the country that did not require the intervention of foreign troops, the role of "traditional elders" (both secular and religious) has been both visible and positive. Women leaders have also been active, and women and children constituted a majority in demonstrations for disarmament and peace. Throughout the crisis, professionals, especially doctors and nurses who stayed in the country, have served as positive role models. Teachers have begun to revive rudimentary forms of schooling in urban areas; proto-Universities have been established in Somaliland.

As an aspect of civil society strength, the private sector has become revitalized. Gone were the so-called socialistic restrictions imposed by the dictatorship. The thriving small-scale private sector (in both the north and Mogadishu) has moved far ahead of embryonic regulatory authorities. In most parts of Africa, the state hampers or constrains civil society; in Somalialand the state is challenged to keep up with a dynamic small private sector. In 1988 there were eighteen Somali voluntary development organizations (VDOs); now the number of such organizations has grown and they need help from international VDOs to enhance the nonprofit private sector.

There is a palpable spirit of anticentralism, an atmosphere favoring local autonomy, regionalism, and federalism—and in the north, self-determination and secession. As corollary, there is a preference for locally controlled police forces over a large standing central army. In Somaliland, and to some extent in Puntland (northeast Somalia), there are embryonic manifestations of consociational democratic mechanisms involving consensus, proportionality, and avoidance of winner-take-all situations. Somali irredentism has collapsed with Siyad and in its place one finds broad cooperation and relative harmony between Somalia and Ethiopia. There is also a vibrant emerging free press—about six papers in Hargeisa and over sixteen in Mogadishu. Printed in Somali, they are produced by computers and mimeograph machines.

Operation Restore Hope and the UN have played very modest roles in rebuilding Somalia's infrastructure, including ports, airports, roads, and bridges. Operation Restore Hope undertook a number of transitional measures, such as providing food for famine-stricken zones. The United Nations is to continue food aid for Somalis, but it must ensure that this policy does not damage the agricultural private sector. Food aid needs to be carefully targeted: as food-for-work to strengthen the voluntary sector, the purchase of locally produced food can help monetize the economy and strengthen local markets; however, vulnerable groups should receive food through NGO/VDO-supported local health and maternity services. Somalis need assistance to evolve a public sector that is accountable to local tax-payers. Foreign aid helped facilitate corruption in the previous regime: the country needs to be assisted to get back on its own feet, without being put on the dole.

Attempts to reconstruct the state in Somalia have taken various forms.

Top-Down Negotiations

In May and July 1991, the Italian and Egyptian governments backed the USC faction of Ali Mahdi and the Manifesto Group in organizing two conferences in Djibouti with the objective of forming a national government. The Aidid USC group and the SNM refused to attend. This top-down approach was intended to confirm Ali Mahdi as interim president and reject Somaliland's independence. The July conference advocated reviving the 1960 constitution and its 123-member parliament for an interim period of two years. The parliament would elect a president nominated by the USC.

This attempt at parachuting state power from Djibouti to Mogadishu proved unworkable. Ali Mahdi was too impatient to await the parliamentary nomination process—he had himself sworn in soon upon his return. The method of filling parliament seats was never spelled out. Ali Mahdi renominated the northerner (Isaq) politician Omar Arteh as prime minister, but his eighty-three ministerial appointments could not obtain parliamentary and USC approval. The two leaders hoped to obtain quick injections of foreign aid to be able to function. They ignored the realities of post-Siyad Somalia: open warfare and banditry had made Mogadishu ungovernable; and foreign aid shrunk to a mere trickle.

The Islamic Temptation

Post-Siyad Somalia manifests a tangible Islamic revivalism for the most part involving traditional Somali Sunni Islam. The chaos has, however, encouraged groups of youthful Islamic fundamentalists, who offer politicized and distorted Islam as a solution to Somalia's problems. All the protopolitical, clan-based groupings-—SNM, SSDF, USC, SDM—have pockets of Islamic fundamentalists among their members and fighters. Some of them feel that their chances of capturing state power are in the long term, while others want to take immediate risks. They have not yet evolved significant leaders and the clan factor tends to check the fanatic Islamic element. The movement has been relatively strong in the northeast (Bari, Nugal, and Mudug regions). In July 1992, a fundamentalist faction took over the port town of Bosaso for over a month, but the SSDF and clan supporters fought back with the assistance of Ethiopian troops. The fundamentalists retreated to the port of Las Khore on the Somaliland border, and later on to Gedo region. Some of them received help from Saudi Arabia; others have links with Iran and Sudan. Islam will play a significant role in the post-Siyad era—the question is, how much and what kind of Islam? Between June and December 2006, radical Islamists captured Magadishu and large parts of the South but were defeated by Ethiopian troops. An Islamic state (or states) is not likely to arise out of the present turmoil and chaos.

Northern Grassroots

In the north, Somaliland is groping toward a grassroots approach to state formation. In 1988, following SNM attacks, Siyad's army pushed northern populations across the border into refugee camps in Ethiopia where they were organized by the SNM. Clan and religious elders played crucial roles, distributing food aid and other relief, adjudicating disputes, and even recruiting fighters for the SNM. A Council of Elders (guurti) was incorporated under the new constitution as a second chamber of the National Assembly.

The SNM called a congress of Isaq and other elders in Berbera in February 1991. A second, larger, popular assembly was convened in Burao in May the same year and it was there that the self-determination decision was taken, renouncing the union with southern Somalia. So far no state recognized the Somaliland Republic and this has posed problems for relief, reconstruction, and development assistance. Somaliland experienced clan and factional-related warfare between December 1991 and April 1992, and again in 1994-1996. Although the situation did not degenerate to the war-lordism of the south, it paralyzed the evolution of public institutions. The elders and other elements of civil society launched a peace and national reconciliation conference in Sheikh in November 1992, and Hargeisa in 1996, followed by local peace conferences throughout the north. Non-Isaq clans inhabiting Sanag, Sool, and Awdal regions have emerged as participants in what was previously mostly SNM territory. Many northerners believe that Siyad's wars brought conflicts to civil society that, unless healed, will inhibit the trust necessary to reestablish state organs. The northern grassroots peace and reconciliation movement culminated in a "grand conference" in Borama (a non-Isaq town) from late February to May 1993. The conference brought together elders from all clans and subclans, SNM leaders, professionals, diaspora representatives, young people, women, and veteran politicians from the parliamentary and Siyad era (including Omar Arteh, former Prime Minister Egal, and former Interior Minister Jama Mohamed Ghalib, who were originally opposed to the independence declaration). Omar Arteh ran for president in the May 1993 Borama elections but lost to the former northern independence prime minister, Mohamed Ibrahim Egal. An intellectual non-Isaq participant assessed the Borama conference as follows:

> Responsible traditional elders, drawing upon the salutary mediums and wisdoms of clan conflict resolution are continuously attending to alleviate the suffering of their nation. Increasingly the traditional elders are emerging as the spiritual government of Northern Somalia, and supplanting the legally installed government which is fast losing credibility and legitimacy.... The politics of consensus and compromises seems to be foreign to the existing ethical standards, with unabashed confrontation and total success over the opponent being the motto of the existing leadership, whether in power or in opposition. Though my optimism of success in Borama outweighs my hunches of its failure, the reverse could happen (Ali 1993: 4-5).

The Addis Ababa Compromise

Prior to 1993, the United Nations had lost prestige among many Somalis with its clumsy evacuation and abandonment of Somalia in 1991 and its slow, bureaucratic methods and lack of financial muscle. The UN had also been criticized for the unceremonious firing of UN representative Mohamed Sahnoun, who had begun to win Somali cooperation by advocating a gradual approach, in harmony with traditional mechanisms of conflict resolution. Sahnoun became convinced that establishing a national government from the bottom up was the best approach, even though that might take two or more years. He attended local peace and reconciliation gatherings, believing that Somali civil society needed strengthening before the pressures of state structures were imposed on it.

In January and March 1993, the UN called meetings of Somalia's clan-based protopolitical organizations in Addis Ababa. Those within the UN who expected to see the immediate formation of a juridical Somali state were disappointed. The fifteen protopolitical organizations that attended (listed in the appendix to this chapter), plus a large number of civil society representatives (secular and religious elders, women delegates, professional, business, and VDO representatives) called for a fair, simultaneous ceasefire and disarmament, and the establishment of regional police forces. The Addis Ababa conference agreed on a two-year transition period during which "emphasis will be put on the rehabilitation and reconstruction of basic infrastructures and the building of democratic institutions" (Addis Ababa 1993: 3). The conference adopted a regional autonomy approach based on Somalia's previous eighteen regions, each with a regional administrative council, police force, and judiciary, as well as district councils, leading Somali observers to comment that the conference decided to turn Somalia into eighteen Somalilands!

Avoiding the issue of forming a central government, the conference recommended the formation of a transitional national council (TNC), to be made up of three representatives from each region (including one woman), with five additional seats for Mogadishu, and one representative from each of the fifteen political factions. The TNC is to serve as a legislative body that appoints administrative heads to resurrect ministries. It will also appoint a transitional charter drafting committee and a national committee to bring about reconciliation with the SNM and Somaliland. Its main tasks is to prepare for democratic elections and a constitutional government by March 1995. The participants pledged "to abandon the logic of force for the ethic of dialogue" (Addis Ababa 1993: 3).

In order to deepen the process of peace and reconciliation, the Addis Ababa group needs to learn from the northern experience. At the meeting in Sheikh, for example, reconciling the Habar Yunis and Issa Musse clans, religious ceremonies were accompanied by "peace marriages": fifty women from each clan married fifty warriors of the opposite clan, a traditional trust-enhancing mechanism. Nothing similar has taken place between Hawiye and Darod clans in the south and Mogadishu has ceased to exist as a multiclan Somali capital. Warfare, banditry, and looting have chased clan members to their homelands. Obviously, multiclan, statewide institutions must be based in a neutral, federal-type capital. It will take time, in wartorn Mogadishu, to revive multual trust between clans.

The United Nations mobilized $142 million at a donors' conference organized just before the Addis Ababa political conference, to be spent for relief and rehabilitation, mostly in the Triangle of Death (Mogadishu, Baidoa, Kismayu) and similar war zones in southern Somalia. Somaliland, and the nearby northeast zone, excluded from UN efforts because unrecognized, also deserve their share, lest their stable situation unravel. Resources alone will not bring peace: steps have to be taken to heal civil society and build mutual trust.

THE UNITED NATIONS VS. GENERAL AIDID

The UN was mobilized to provide humanitarian assistance under UN Operation in Somalia (UNOSOM 1). For the United States, former Ambassador Robert Oakley negotiated UN approval for Operation Restore Hope (ORH). Oakley favored Sahnoun's style and encouraged grassroots and regional approaches. Restore Hope supported local peace efforts and the establishment of local police forces approved by and accountable to local administrative committees led by prominent members of civil society. Oakley encouraged Somali factions to disarm themselves, beginning with heavy armaments. He worked hard to reconcile General Aidid and Ali

Mahdi in an effort to reunite the capital city, avoiding overt political actions aimed at choosing sides among Somali political factions. ORH lasted from December 1992 until May 1993. At that point the United States ceased to play a leading role, although it continued to give significant support under UNOSOM 2.

The policies and practices of the United States and the UN changed radically with the appointment of Admiral Jonathan Howe to head UNOSOM 2, with a former U.S. ambassador to Iraq, April Glaspie, as his special political adviser. The new UN strategy was to isolate and confront Aidid while supporting General Abshir of the SSDF, who controlled the northeast regions (renamed Puntland).

In late May and early June 1993 Aidid's faction held surprising reconciliation meetings with SSDF leaders. A reconciliation of the two hostile organizations and clans would facilitate early departure of UNOSOM 2 from Somalia. Aidid felt that UN Secretary-General Boutros Boutros-Ghali was "tainted" by his previous experiences with the Siyad Barre regime. He was unhappy with the Egyptian government for having joined the Italian government in holding the Djibouti conferences that favored Ali Mahdi as the new interim president. During Boutros-Ghali's March 1993 visit to Mogadishu, Aidid organized demonstrations that humiliated the Secretary-General, preventing him from even visiting UNOSOM headquarters in Mogadishu. Then in June 1993 a confrontation between a UNOSOM unit and Aidid's militia left twenty-four Pakistani soldiers dead. Aidid was declared guilty, airpower was brought in to destroy his positions, and Admiral Howe placed a $20,000 reward on his head—a ridiculous (as well as humiliating) gesture in clan society! The Italians recommended isolating Aidid but recognized (and dealt with) his clan and his protopolitical organization—the Somali National Association (SNA) —as bona fide Somali political actors. Boutros-Ghali and Howe rejected the Italian suggestions, rebuked them for their initiatives, and deployed them out of Mogadishu.

Elders and prominent personalities from Aidid's Habar Gedir clan met on July 12, 1993, to explore their options: without warning U.S./UNOSOM helicopters strafed the building and over fifty respected leaders and supporters died. The clan decided to solidify behind Aidid, taking heavy casualties but also inflicting serious damage, paralyzing the UNOSOM operation. They began to shoot down U.S. helicopters and in one battle in August, eighteen U.S. elite soldiers were killed and one was taken hostage. President Clinton immediately reversed Boutros-Ghali's policy of militarily hunting Aidid. Not, he said, at the expense of U.S. troops. Ambassador Oakley was sent back to Somalia to pursue a policy of diplomacy involving regional actors such as Ethiopia and Eritrea.

It is early to draw comprehensive lessons from these events, but two points stand out. First, in assisting a country devastated by primordial conflicts and state collapse, it is important for international intervention to avoid overt political activities that favor one side at the expense of others. The murder of U.S. troops attests to the fact that Aidid's hunted clan came to see the U.S. and UN troops as simply another rival clan. Second, Aidid's example shows that, should even one segment of society decide to reject foreign interventionism, recolonization, or absorption into a larger state, and is willing to pay the heavy price demanded in waging a determined guerrilla war, they can cause radical policy reversals. There is, after all, an empirical reality in the resistance of African societies. Somalis love to tell how the United States and the United Nations were "defeated" by only one Somali clan. In a society imbued with warrior traditions, Somalis point out that Somalia has at least fifty clans and if even half of them had risen in armed rebellion simultaneously, the U.S. and UNOSOM forces would have been forced to evacuate the country or suffer unacceptable losses!

THE WAY TO RESTORATION

How to revive the Somali state/states? Following the U.S. intervention in December 1992, many Somalis felt that staying the U.S. course and deeping Operation Restore Hope, facilitating the empowerment of civil society and pursuing vigorous, creative diplomatic efforts would have put the United States in the best position to play midwife in the process of state renewal. Once the United States declared a halt to the Aidid hunt, Aidid supporters flew U.S. flags, to the applause of crowds. Mistrustful of the UN, Aidid insisted on using a U.S plane to fly to the third Addis Ababa conference in late November 1993. Practically all the Somali factions that waged war against the Siyad regime reflected pro-American attitudes, even though, paradoxically, the United States supported the Siyad regime from 1978 to its overthrow. Aidid has called upon the United States to replace the UN as Somalia's main patron. Aidid was later killed as a result of the Somali civil wars.

It is extremely important for the United States to remain committed to Somali development even after its troop withdrawal in April 1994. The United States can continue to play a pivotal external role, supporting the renewal process through diplomacy and resources, including assistance to U.S. NGOs in Somalia. President Clinton has appealed to Ethiopia, Eritrea, and other regional nations to mediate the Somali conflicts; these states can be effective only if they receive adequate U.S. encouragement and the provision of logistics and related services.

The United Nations had an excellent second chance in mid-1993. It could have built on the solid base created by Operation Restore Hope, initiated within a few months before UNOSOM 2 taking over. But the political outlook for the UN is full of question marks. Three options were under consideration: (a) to ask member states to maintain UNOSOM levels of troops (28,000) with some capability to undertake disarmament; (b) to maintain a force of 18,500, including logistics forces; and (c) to deploy only 5,000 troops with emphasis in assisting UN agencies and NGOs in the delivery of humanitarian aid and in undertaking development projects (Horn of Africa Bulletin, November/December 1993: 13). Disarmament would be entirely voluntary, under options (b) and (c), but Security Council support for option (a) is unlikely. Other industrial countries (France, Belgium, Italy, and Germany) have left with the United States. The future role of UN troops in Somalia presupposes that the local authorities would be prepared to cooperate with UNOSOM operating under UN peacekeeping rules (Article VI) rather than the enforcement provisions (Article VII). Somali state renewal still needs UN humanitarian and development assistance, including support for local and international NGOs.

There are numerous precedents for strongmen establishing and renewing states; but the basic structures of Somali society preclude Aidid's and others being able to play the role of such a strongman in

Somalia. He was not able even to exercise hegemony within his own clan-family, the Hawiye, let alone over all five Somali clan-families. The 1991 – 1992 intra-Hawiye civil war between his Habar-Gedir and Ali Mahdi's Abgal clan led to a stalemate and the Beirut-like division of Mogadishu into north (Ali Mahdi) and south (Aidid) zones. What emerged in southern Somalia was an era of warlords or strong regional leaders, especially if such leaders would be willing to assure minimum cooperation with each other to avoid famine and related catastrophes as occurred in 1991 and 1992. Such a scenario could evolve positively into power-sharing mechanisms or degenerate into embattled rulers and internal border wars. The UN war against Aidid served only to strengthen him, especially psychologically, but it was not sufficient to assure him overall prominence. Somali decentralized clan structures do not facilitate the role of a strongman; however foreign troops can be manipulated to impose a Somali strongman. This is currently taking place with Ethiopian troops attempting to impose Abdullahi Yusuf.

There is a democratic option for Somalia, where democracy can find indigenous roots. Historically, Somalis have lived in societies with rules but without rulers, as portrayed in I. M. Lewis's classic study, A Pastoral Democracy (1969). The democratic state renewal option has several advantages for Somalia/Somaliland: it is compatible with traditional consociational structures and mechanisms; it offers a real antithesis to the detested Siyad military dictatorship; and it situates Somali struggles within the global democratization movement, making the country more amenable to the international assistance necessary for rapid renewal, reconstruction, and long-term development. Other traditional African democratic or semidemocratic polities (e.g., the Kikuyu in Kenya and the Ibo in Nigeria), juxta-posed with centralized, hierarchical traditional polities (Nigeria's Hausa-Fulanis), cannot easily rely on traditional structures to construct a modern polity. Somalia, however, like Botswana, is relatively homogeneous and can hope to evolve a modern consociational democracy from its traditional consociational practices, moving from local, district, and regional finally to national levels. The UN tried to encourage the empowerment of district and regional councils in southern Somalia. UNOSOM personnel helped to set up forty representative district councils in Somalia's seventy seven districts (Somaliland not included) by September 1993. Three regional councils were formed in Garowe, Bakool, and Baidoa by mid-October. This kind of activity will probably mark the most significant attempted UN contribution to Somali renewal (Horn of Africa Bulletin, September/October 1993: 16).

Consociational democracy (modern versions of which are practiced in Switzerland, South Africa and other smaller European societies) recognizes and acknowledges ethnic, clan, or religious cleavages in constituting membership of governments, parliaments, and national commissions. In such societies, army, police, and civil service recruitment are based on the combined principles of merit and proportionality. Somaliland appears to be evolving along these lines and whether it rejoins the south or not, offers an excellent blueprint for Somalia. Somaliland cabinets since 1991 have striven to include modern elites and yet reflect clan diversity and representativeness. The interim National Assembly consists of a house of secular and religious elders (guurti) and a second house made up of modern elites. Somaliland had sketched out the stages in this activity: peace and reconciliation; formation of local and regional bodies; and then national representative institutions. Former Somaliland President Egal, in proposing a peace mission of seven elders each from Somaliland, Ogaden, and Djibouti, spelled out the alternatives.

> This would be a formulation of peaceful settlement originating from the grassroots and projected in a native indigenous framework recognizable and familiar to every member of the society.... The role of the United Nations in my proposed process would be one of support, encouragement and the provisions of logistics and services.... With all due respect to the conveners of the Reconciliation Conferences in Addis Ababa, men of whose sincerity and good-will there is no shadow of doubt, these conferences become forums where faction leaders tried to score points against each other. The rest of the participants were only confused by the alien surroundings and the foreign chairmen and other organizers of the conference whose speeches and languages they could not even understand (Horn of Africa Bulletin, November/December 1993).

APPENDIX: SOMALI POLITICAL FACTIONS

Somali African Muki Organization (SAMO)
Somali Democratic Alliance (SDA)
Somali Democratic Movement (SDM)
SDM (SNA*)
Somali National Democratic Union (SNDU)
Somali National Front (SNF)
Somali National Union (SNU)
Somali Patriotic Movement (SPM)
SPM (SNA*)
Somali Salvation Democratic Front (SSDF)
Southern Somali National Movement (SSNM)
United Somalic Congress (USC)
USC (SNA*)
United Somali Front (USF)
United Somali Party (USP)

(SNA* denotes affiliation with the Somali National Alliance, described in
the text of this chapter).

Some of the most acrimonious debates arose around the question
of representation. General Aidid (USC/SNA) and his allies felt
that too many Darod clan political factions were registered by the
UN: SSDF, SNDU, SNF, SPM, and USP. They claimed that some
of these, for example, did not represent Somalis who were substantially within the borders of the Somali Republic. The groups that
waged war against Siyad wanted more influence than those that had
formed recently in order to appear at the peace table. The leaders
of some of the groups were accused of being puppets of some of
the other groups. As of mid-1994, the farming communities were
represented by SAMO and the ancient coastal cities populations by
SNU. Factions of non-Isaq clans participating in Somaliland were
partly represented by SDA, USF, and USP.

The northern group, the Somali National Movement (SNM),
adopted observer status during the first two Addis Ababa confer-

ences but boycotted the third, held in late November and early December 1993; as well as the others that followed.

Note

1. About five months after Siyad was chased out of Mogadishu in 1991, I spent three weeks in northern Somaliland and three weeks in Mogadishu; I revisited the areas in 1994, 1997, 1999, 2000 and 2001.

References

Adam, Hussein M. (1993), "Somalia: The Military, Military Rule and Militarism." Mimeographed paper, April 1933.

Addis Ababa Agreement on National Reconciliation in Somalia (1993). Mimeographed document, March 27.

Ali, Mohamoud Abdi (1993), "The Grand Peace and National Reconciliation Conference in Borama: Background, Significance and Perspectives." Mimeographed paper, February 14, 1993.

Boutros-Ghali, Boutros (1992), *An Agenda for Peace: Preventive Diplomacy, Peacemaking and Peacekeeping*. New York: United Nations.

Drysdale, John (1992), "Somalia: The Only Way Forward." *Journal of the Anglo-Somali Society*. Winter 1992/93.

Fanon, Frantz (1968), *The Wretched of the Earth*. New York: Grove.

Foltz, William J. and Henry Bienen (1985), *Arms and the African*. New Haven: Yale University Press

Galaydh, Ali Khalif (1990), "Notes on the State of the Somali State," *Horn of Africa* 13, Nos. 1 and 2, January- March and April-June.

Laitin, David and Said Samatar (1987), *Somalia: Nation in Search of a State*. Boulder: Westview.

Lewis, I.M. (1969), *A Pastoral Democracy*. Oxford, England: Oxford University Press.

Lewis, I.M.(1988) *A Modern History of Somalia*. Boulder, CO: Westview Press.

Lewis, I.M. (1990), "The Ogaden and the Fragility of Somali Segmentary Nationalism," Horn of Africa, 13.

Nietzsche, Friedrich (1966 edition), *Beyond Good and Evil*. New York: Vintage.

Oakley, Robert and John Hirsch (1995), *Somalia and Operation Restore Hope: Reflections on Peacekeeping and Peacemaking*. Washington, DC: United States Institute of Peace.

Rothchild, Donald and Naomi Chazan (1988), eds., *The Precarious Balance: State and Society in Africa*. Boulder: Westview.

Samatar, Ahmed (1988), *Socialist Somalia: Rhetoric and Reality*. London: Zed.

Saul, John (1979), *The State and Revolution in Eastern Africa*. New York: Monthly Review Press.

Zartman, I. William (1989, 2nd edition), *Ripe for Resolution*. New York: Oxford University Press.

CHAPTER 2

PERSONAL RULE, MILITARY RULE AND MILITARISM

INTRODUCTION

Somalia from 1969 to 1991 offers an interesting and complex case of military rule. Following the 1969 military coup, the regime utilized the military for socio-economic project literacy programs, drought relief, and resettlement of drought victims. By the mid-1970s, military rule began to adopt a blatantly autocratic form, increasing to the point where the political system was transformed into one of the most tyrannical regimes witnessed on the African continent. This study will show the role that personal rule played in the transformations of the regime.

This chapter focuses on 'modes of military governance' (Hutchful 1989). As Hutchful has argued, even though 'radical' military regimes 'retain certain formal resemblances' their subsequent paths have tended to diverge significantly, making generalizations as to their social and political character difficult' (*ibid.*: 11). This study analyses and explains the evolutions of one such regime. It complements Hutchful's comparative argument by demonstrating as well the complex shifts of course within this regime like many of the progressive military regimes that Hutchful and others discuss during its 22 years in power (Hutchful 1986). While seeking to understand the trajectory of the Siyad regime, the analysis also examines the nature and role of the Somali army: its origins, size, equipment, training and foreign connections.

THEORETICAL CONSIDERATIONS

Three paradigmatic approaches have governed recent Somali studies. The first consists of descriptive, formalistic studies: legal, formal-institutional, historical monographs and biographical publications. A second category includes ethnic analysis: those who utilize clan, lineage and the kinship factor as the independent variable in understanding politics; works by I. M. Lewis, David Laitin and Said S. Samatar fit into this category (see Laitin and Samatar 1987; Laitin 1979; Laitin 1976; Lewis 1979; Lewis 1980). Recently, Ahmed Ismail Samatar, Abdi Samatar, Dan Aronson, Jeremy Swift and others introduced the third category, the theory of underdevelopment and dependency, into Somali historiography (Samatar 1988; see also Samatar 1989; Aronson 1980: 14-23). As corrective and complementary approaches, these contributions have helped to enrich Somali studies. The emphasis on class in these studies has helped to balance the excessive reliance on clan factors in previous studies. External constraints imposed on Somali society and the emergent class conflicts needed to receive some analytical attention. However, dependency and underdevelopment theorists have created other difficulties through an overemphasis on class relations and their tendency to consider national politics as a simple reflection of global and economic relations (Chazan *et al.* 1988).

From a dependency school perspective, the nature of the Somali ruling class fits the label 'petty bourgeoisie'. However, this is not a united class, given that some of its members are middle-and senior-level bureaucrats, military police officers, teachers and intellectuals and other professionals, while others are involved in transport, commerce and small-scale livestock exporting. The commercial stratum consists of merchants and petty traders, owners of service enterprises such as hotels, taxis, buses, trucks, construction and motor repairs, and so forth.

Within these factions of the petty bourgeoisie, there are secondary contradictions. The 1969 Siyad coup could be viewed as a victory for the 'military –bureaucratic' faction over the 'civilian-politician-commercial' faction. While the leaders of the parliamentary parties were drawn mostly from the civilian elite involved in business and commerce, the cream of the new military dispensation were bureaucrats and military officers who, in the case of the latter, had risen from previous obscurity. The former stratum took steps to promote private Somali capital through state action, while the latter opted for state-directed economic activity and the creation of public property.

Lacking direct economic means of extracting surplus on a significant scale, a segment of the petty bourgeoisie prefers state intervention for the accumulation of property. Control of the state apparatus facilitates the ex-colonial petty bourgeois tendency for consumption rather than production.

> This is what has been called 'rent-seeking' ... [which] pulverizes state institutions, compounding economic, political, and cultural vulnerabilities ... neglect or near abandonment of production, which rent-seeking leads to, further weakens the state class vis-á-vis metropolitan capital (Samatar 1988:5).

The dependency approach puts Somali politics within a historically long-range and continentally comparative framework. However, it lacks grounding in the specifics of domestic politics, thereby imposing a sterile uniformity. Ahmed Samatar argued that the Somali state was suspended over civil society. As an extension of his argument regarding foreign aid versus internal extraction, this makes sense. However, while profiting from foreign arms and funds, Siyad's regime at first tried to seduce, control and transform civil society, and later moved on to wage war against it.

My analysis and experience of Somali society suggests that neither the petty bourgeoisie as a class or a faction of it, served as a ruling class. One can say it reigned, exercised a weak hegemony perhaps, but it did not rule. From 1969 to early 1991, Somalia was, for all practical purposes, under the personal rule of Siyad Barre. A personal rule approach added to dependency and class approaches (the latter traditionally have had difficulty accommodating personalistic analysis) should provide us with a more comprehensive picture of Somali political realities. A single-minded emphasis on class structures tends to view political actors not as relatively free agents but as products of their class position. Class analysis in particular does not satisfactorily explain the marked variations and twists and turns of the Siyad regime. Why is it that the Siyad regime advocated 'socialism' and 'anti-imperialism' between 1969 and 1977, but dropped 'socialism' and allied itself with 'imperialism' between 1977 and 1991? The regime was favorably compared with Nyerere's Tanzania during its early period; it was considered worse than Idi Amin's Uganda during its declining years. Presumably the same faction of the Somali petty bourgeoisie exercised domination during the whole period. Personal rule theory can be brought in to shed light on the specifically political realm, which is relatively autonomous. Siyad's Machiavellian gifts in political manipulation and control, and the personal system of rulership he set up, are crucial for understanding both the unpredictability and the sustainability of his regime.

The personal rule approach used to complement and illuminate military rule in our case study relies on the theory developed by Robert Jackson and Carl Rosberg in *Personal Rule in Black Africa* (1982). Our research experience has allowed us to modify the theory to fit our case study. For example, the authors delineate a typology of four rulership types: princely, autocratic, prophetic and tyrannical (*ibid.*:77-80). Their book, moreover, fits each African ruler studied within a single type of rulership. This static approach lacks a sense of the fluid and dynamic basis of personal rule and the possible progression from one mode of personal rule to another. Our study, on the other hand, shows that military dictator Siyad Barre was able to transform his rulership mode from prophetic to autocratic to tyrannical.

Jackson and Rosberg theorize that personal rule arises out of a vacuum brought about by lack of institutions. Somalia in 1969 did represent a typical underdeveloped country with weak institutions. However, its civil service had been reorganized and strengthened by 1967; the Somali police force was well trained, equipped and commanded, and the army was soon to emerge as the best organized, trained and equipped force in Sub-Saharan Africa (Nelson 1982, especially chapter 5). This is a case where, whatever the idiosyncratic reasons for the emergence of personal rule, it proceeded to use and finally destroy Somali institutions. Siyad's, then, was not a case of personal ruleship entirely within the boundaries of the definition set by Rosberg and Jackson. It was personal rule rooted in and manipulating the façade of military rule to the point where it succeeded in destroying both military rule and the Somali state itself.

FROM CIVIL TO MILITARY RULE

Situated in eastern Africa, Somalia forms the cap of the Horn of Africa, with an area of about 638,000 square kilometers. Kenya lies to its south and west, the Gulf of Aden to the north, Djibouti to the north-west, Ethiopia to the west and the Indian Ocean to the east. Colonial powers in the past, and Cold War superpowers until recently, have always considered this a part of global strategic geography. Thus Somalia has attracted international attention out of proportion to its natural resources. Somalia has the longest coastline in Africa about 3,300 kilometers. Its strategic location is provided by the 'chokehold' that it commands at the entry to the Read Sea and the Suez Canal. Prior to the civil war, the population was estimated at between eight to ten million; in a land of sparse rainfall, more than half the population are pastoralists and agropastoralists, raising camels, cattle, sheep and goats. A small number relies on fishing, while the rest are urban dwellers. Livestock exports to neighboring Arab countries and to Italy have provided the mainstay to the modern Somali economy. Banana plantations established around the two main southern rivers the Shabelle and the Juba have provided the second important export to Italy and Arab states. In 1990, agriculture contributed about 65 per cent of GDP, of which livestock was responsible for just over 50 per cent, crops 38 per cent, and forestry and fisheries about 1 per cent each.

Somali historical and political developments may be summarized in terms of two broad trends. The first consisted of hinterland pastoral and agropastoral movements characterized by the lack of a single political entity, in which the people survived as a loose cultural grouping of various distinct and often opposed political units; and the second was the establishment, with the assistance of Arab and Persian settlers, of a number of coastal trading towns dating from at least the tenth century and probably earlier. Mogadishu, Marka, Brava and Bulhar, Zeila (both near Berbera in the north), constituted ancient Islamic city-states with centralized administrations utilizing Islamic law and involved in the Red Sea and Indian Ocean trade. Outside of these trading towns, however, the unity of the Somali community was maintained on a voluntary basis through relative cultural homogeneity rather than centralized structures.

Three aspects of Somali history and social structure have particularly influenced modern Somali politics. The first (alluded to above) was the highly decentralized (or 'stateless') character of pre-colonial Somali society. Historically, most of the Somalis have lived under clans in societies of rules without rulers termed 'pastoral democracies' by the British social anthropologist I. M. Lewis (see Lewis 1961). Somali society is segmented along lineages, the highest segment represented by the clan-family (about five), followed by clans, sub-clans, sub-sub-clans and so forth until one arrives at the primary lineage level. This provides fluid forms of identity; perhaps a more stable form of identity is represented by the *diya*-paying group. Diya is compensation paid by a person who has injured or killed another person. Diya-paying groups number anywhere between a few hundred to a few thousand men contractually linked to support one another, especially in the event of injury and death involving fellow members. The main clan-families are the Dir, Isaq, Hawiye, Darod, Digil and Mirifle (Rahanwin). The Digil and Rahanwin, located between the southern rivers around the town of Baidoa, are agro-pastoralists speaking a dialect different from that of the majority of Somali-language speakers. The Isaq are located mostly in the north, in what used to be British Somaliland. The Hawiye are situated in the central regions including the capital city of Mogadishu. Somalia, from an African perspective, is relatively homogeneous ethnically and culturally with a common language and religion, Sunni Islam. The people of Bantu descent living in farming villages in the south and the urban dwellers of the ancient Islamic coastal cities mentioned above constitute Somali minorities. The clan-based civil wars have imposed tragic and crushing burdens on Somali minorities and on the Digil and Rahanwin agropastoralists (Bongartz 1991).

Second, Somali was subjected to a particularly pernicious form of imperialism: strategic (as opposed to economic) imperialism. As a colony Somalia was not an end in itself, an economy to be exploited for its own resources but a means to an end: for the British a source of meat and water for the garrison in Aden and a key base on the route to and from India; for France a base and coaling station along the route to Madagascar and Indochina; while for the Italians the occupation of Somalia's southern territory was a byproduct of Italy's struggle for unification, which included a voracious appetite for overseas colonies. In other words, colonialism in Somalia was, in the main, a byproduct of colonial activities elsewhere. European interests and contacts with the Somali coast and the Horn of Africa were stimulated by the opening of the Suez Canal in 1869. The strategic rather than economic considerations that underlay imperialism in Somalia (and in general the Horn) determined the militaristic face assumed by imperialism in the region, with subsequent weaponisation of Somalia and neighboring societies.

Third, Somalia was subjected to not one but multiple imperialisms. By the end of the nineteenth century, Somalia had been partitioned between Britain, France, Italy and Ethiopia under Emperor Menelik. The Britsh carved out British Somaliland next to the Red Sea/Gulf of Aden, and also occupied another Somali portion to the south of the Italian colony which became the Northern Frontier District of British Kenya. France formally established the colony of French Somaliland in 1885 (now the Republic of Djibouti). Emperor Menelik sent troops to claim what is currently termed Region Five of Ethiopia, journalistically referred to as the Ogaden, and Italy colonized Eritrea and southern Italian Somaliland, with Mogadishu as its capital. The Somalis, under religious leader Sheikh Muhamad Abdulle Hassan, offered stiff military resistance to imperialist occupation and partitioning. His followers utilized guerrilla warfare against British, Italian and Ethiopian forces from 1899 to 1920. This colonial partitioning was to intensify the incidence of 'segmentary nationalism' in Somalia in much the same way as the existence of 'pastoral democracies' was to complicate the process of state formation. Although there was some uniformity in the colonial agendas, in that they all tried to impose modern state structures, they varied very much in the content of their structures and policies. In no case, however (and this becomes apparent in the account of Siyad's regime) did modern state structures succeed in displacing the underlying clan structures of Somali society; indeed in the case of the British these structures were to complement the superstructures of the state rather than compete with them.

Hence the Somali experience is riddled with seeming historical contradictions: while uniformity of language and social structures (the clan) on the one hand provided Somalia with a homogeneity rarely known elsewhere in Africa, on the other hand the absence of centralized pre-colonial political systems, the lack of unitary colonial experience and structures, and weak class structures springing in the main from the rudimentary nature of the colonial economy, imposed on Somalia a level of fragmentation that was also unusual even by African standards. It was within the interstices of these centrifugal and centripetal forces that the Siyad personalistic dictatorship was to emerge and attempt to sustain itself. Utilising the vehicle of irredentism and the material support of global powers and other external patrons, this dictatorship attempted to bring the Somali nation into congruence with the Somali state, using the modern state and army, superimposed over the society but lacking roots in it, both to accomplish this and to suppress Somali civil society. Clanism was then deployed to erode and capture the state and its institutions from within. In this inchoate and poorly articulated social formation, Siyad was able to rise above both state and clan structures, using the one to subdue and counteract the other in order to secure his personal rule. The collapse of the Somali state that followed from the failure of this enterprise led, ironically, to the reassertion of clan units as the fundamental reality of Somali society. The weakening of the state destroyed its monopolization of the means of violence honed to its logical extreme by Siyad's militarism producing once again a democratization of the instruments of violence within Somali society (much as was the case in the pre-colonial era) as clans successfully took up arms against the Siyad state and then against each other. In more ways than one Somalia has returned to its pre-colonial starting point, a 'stateless' society of autonomous clans, organized democratically for peace and war but today militarized in a manner alien even to the unusually warlike historical traditions of the country.

COLONIALISM, INDEPENDENCE AND THE CIVILIAN REGIMES

Somalia, like the rest of Africa, fostered modern nationalist politics during and after World War II. This led to the emergence of nationalist party organizations, then to elections and eventually fledgling states. The Somali Youth League (SYL) dominated politics in the Italian colony, which was transformed into a UN Trusteeship under Italian tutelage for the period 1950-1960. Other anticolonial parties included the Hizb al-Dastuur Mustagil al-Somal (HDMS), the party of the Digil and Rahanwin agropastoralists. Its leaders differed from the centralist vision of the SYL and other parties and energetically advocated that 'the only method of unifying the Somalis is through a federal constitution which accords full regional autonomy' (cited in Touval 1963:96). About four parties pursued independence in British Somaliland. The dominant party, the Somali National League, agreed to campaign for independence and unification with the Italian-administered south. Together they adopted a centralized unitary state against the wishes of the main opposition party, the HDMS. This debate between centralism and federalism in Somalia has proved a durable one.

British Somaliland obtained independence on 26 June, southern Somalia on 1 July, 1960. Somalis in the north pressured the northern premier, Ibrahim Mohamed Egal, to go to Mogadishu and consummate a union with the south. The *de facto* union constituting the Somali Republic on 1 July got off to an unpromising start. First, the union treaty was never legally ratified. Northerners became disillusioned at a very early stage, in part because all key ministries were monopolized by southerners including such posts as commander of the army, commander of the police forces, president and of course prime minister. When a Republic Constitution (prepared by southerners) was put to a referendum in June 1961 they voted overwhelmingly against it. In December 1961 a group of Sandhurst-trained northern military officers attempted one of the first-ever military coups in black Africa. But they lacked popular support and were opposed by fellow northerners who were at the time not yet ready for secession. Ironically, the absence of a legally valid Act of Union assisted the defence of the rebellious northern officers; at their trial the judge decided to acquit them on the basis that in the absence of an Act of Union, the Court had no jurisdiction over Somaliland (Rajagopal and Carroll 1992:15) Through skilful parliamentary politics, former northern premier Egal was able to capture the post of union prime minister in 1967.

In another of those ironies: Even as Somalia struggled to establish internal political unity, and a single national identity, Somali irredentism (Pan-Somalism), the belief that the Somali Republic should be united with all Somali-occupied territories, came to dominate the post-independence era. This led to fighting in northern Kenya (1963-67), a war with Ethiopia in 1964 and the build-up of the Somali military, especially when the Soviets indicated willingness to serve as military patrons. In the meantime, Somalis continued to experience difficulty in consummating the national union: national parties degenerated into clan, lineage and even one-man parties during electoral competition. The various governments were perceived as inefficient and corrupt. Prime Minister Egal's policies of better relations with Ethiopia and Kenya led to bitter criticisms by Somalis devoted to Pan-Somalism. While visiting drought-stricken areas in northern Somalia, President Sharmarke was assassinated by a policeman on 15 October 1969. The National Assembly, gathered on the evening of the 20th to choose his successor. During the early hours of 21 October 1969 the commander of the Somali National Army, Mohamed Siyad Barre, engineered a successful coup and Somalia came under military rule.

MILITARY RULE AND THE MILITARY

The Somali National Army (SNA) was created in 1960 through a merger of the former British Somaliland Scouts stationed in the north and the former Italian-trained paramilitary police of the Trust Territory in the south. The new army, 5,000 strong, chose 2 April, the date of the definitive cease-fire following the 1964 Ethiopian Somali war, as official SNA Day. Before becoming a potent instrument of Siyad Barre's personal rulership, the SNA enjoyed tremendous prestige. It served as a shield against external threats and as a symbol and potential instrument to achieve the objectives of irredentist nationalism. Before the coup the primary mission of Somalia's armed forces had been to protect Somalia's territorial integrity from foreign invasion. A secondary mission involved assisting the national police force in maintaining internal security. Civilian governments (1960-69) assigned various roles in nation-building to the national army. This was encouraged by Western donors, who feared the irredentist potential of the Somali Army. The governments relied on the military establishment for civic action in times of natural disasters such as floods (those of 1961 for example) and famine (1965). Military and police aircraft and vehicles transported food and medical supplies to people and livestock in the stricken areas. In 1964, the embryonic Somali military, backed by a highly professional, well-trained police force, seemed able to withstand Emperor Haile Selassie's larger, better-equipped forces. In 1969 and for some years after, the SNA was seen by Somalis and external observers as well in idealized terms: organized and disciplined, more rational than the political system and civil society, technically oriented and skilled.[1] The attribute of asceticism was also applied to its senior officers, partly due to the outstanding example of the founding SNA head, General Daud Abdulle Hersi (from the Hawiye, Abgal clan). When it came to breakdown of law and order during 1968/9, as a consequence of electoral anarchy, the SNA was able to present itself idealistically as a disciplined, and coherent military organization positioned outside the anarchy of society, and restoring order to it.

Following the 1969 coup, power was assumed by the Supreme Revolutionary Council (SRC), consisting of twenty-five military and a few police officers with Siyad as its president. The national constitution, all political parties, courts, trade unions and voluntary associations were abolished. The army, assisted by the police, ruled the country; military officers served as regional governors and district commissioners. The SRC ruled with the help of a largely civilian Council of Secretaries of State (CSS) to administer ministries.

The ruling military officers approached national development in a militaristic fashion, in a series of relatively uncoordinated campaigns. For this militarization of the development process, they utilized an appropriate Somali word, *olol*, which literally translates as 'battle-formation', and which was here used to represent the notion of a campaign. Civilian administrators and diplomats were required to undergo a three-month military course. A similar, somewhat longer course was instituted for school graduates. Military participation in state affairs increased even when the SRC was disbanded and a socialist vanguard organ, the Somali Revolutionary Socialist Party (SRSP), was established in 1976. In 1980, the SRC was reconstituted as an element of the ruling power structure, and military officers were appointed to administer most of Somalia's districts and regions. Siyad preferred subordinates who would take orders rather than convey popular wishes. Thus military officers were easier to manage than civilian officials.

After the coup, Siyad increased the visibility of the army in civilian service. At first the army built new barracks, dormitories, mess facilities, theatres, playgrounds, stores and offices for itself.[2] Later on it used its self-help experience for the benefit of national construction. A number of effigy-burning campaigns were waged against tribalism. The army took a leading role in the creative programmes of the early 1970s: for example, the agricultural 'crash programmes' to mobilize resources for labour-intensive projects destined to reduce unemployment and to increase national self-sufficiency; digging and maintaining, wells and irrigation canals and stabilizing sand dunes. The army also helped construct the Somali National University, hospitals, prisons, orphanages and factories. Perhaps its most significant civilian role lay in its evacuating 120,000 nomads from regions stricken by the 1974/5 drought to southern fishing and agricultural settlements. Unlike Emperor Haile Selassie, who lost his throne hiding the calamity, the SRC proclaimed an immediate state of emergency and effectively mobilized domestic and international assistance for the destitute and starving nomads. The crisis also provided an opportunity for schemes to resettle and transform nomadic society. About 100,000 nomads were transported to hastily prepared agricultural settlements next to the Shabelle and Juba rivers while an additional 20,000 were settled along Somalia's long coastline to begin a new life as fishermen. Other nomads had their herds restocked so they could return to the traditional nomadic life. Unlike what happened in Ethiopia later, this was essentially a voluntary, not a compulsory, resettlement programme.

Benefiting from the relative popularity the military enjoyed as a result of the 1964 Ethiopian-Somali war, Siyad proceeded to militarise the Somali state and society. Some of the military officers were transferred to the domestic and diplomatic civil service, some because Siyad wanted them out of the army, others because he had confidence in them and the posts were meant as a reward. Apart from the lowest levels, the militarized court system consisted of the National Security Court with its regional and district branches staffed with officers with virtually no legal preparation or experience. Among other things, militarization of the state administration consisted of compulsory military/political orientation courses at the Halane military training camp near Mogadishu. Apart from courses for central and regional civil servants, there were others for diplomats, graduates of educational institutions and returnees from foreign training institutions. In due course a compulsory two-year national service programme was instituted for secondary school graduates. Military training constituted a substantial part of this.

On the first anniversary of the coup (21 October 1970), Siyad declared 'socialism' as the ideology of the military regime. The regime nationalized most of Somalia's small commercial sector, including the utilities, while gaining a major interest in the Jowhar sugar facilities, up till then the largest agro- industrial complex. Later on, with Arab funding, the regime came to build a larger sugar project in Marere, near Kismayu (south of Mogadishu). The unemployed urban youth were given military orders to march back to the countryside or march in tune with agricultural crash programmes that have expanded the acreage under cultivation. The goal of reaching food self-sufficiency by 1980 was never achieved nor attempted after that date. Military commandism achieved impressive short-range goals but, in the long run, the militarist approach, together with unrealistically controlled prices, produced agricultural disasters.

On the other hand, the regime refrained from nationalizations within the livestock and transport sectors. Nor did nationalization extend to the large Italian- and Somali-owned banana plantations. Certain radical observers criticized the regime for this and for 'pampering' large livestock merchants despite its socialist rhetorics (Samatar 1988; Samatar 1989; Aronson 1980; see also Swift 1979). The emphasis on agriculture in the 1974/1978 plan budgetary allocation hid the fact that relatively insignificant sums were spent on the largest rural sector: livestock. On the other hand, a great deal of the agriculture investment went into agricultural crash programmes, other forms of large-scale state farms and large irrigation projects. Not much attention was paid to the needs of poor and small-scale farmers. In time, nationalization came to imply nothing more than an expansion of the state sector and an enlarged spoils system for the president and his cronies.

Perhaps the regime's greatest achievement lay in the 21 October 1972 decision to prepare an alphabet for the Somali language, utilizing a modified version of the Latin script (Adam 1980). In the past, a faction supporting the Arabic script, another for Latin and yet a third, vocal faction propagating Osmaniya (invented by a Somali elder) competed vigorously, ending up paralyzing the civilian governments on this issue. This decision was followed by an urban literacy campaign and a Rural Development Campaign (launched in 1974 and involving about 20,000 students and teachers) that achieved significant results. Written Somali allowed the country to attain a tangible measure of cultural autonomy. It also gave a major boost to the expansion of education, which, like health, was provided free of charge by the state.

In the area of foreign affairs also, the Somali Democratic Republic exercised much more influence than its civilian predecessors. This was partly due to toning down Somali irredentist nationalism, partly due to USSR support in placing Somalia among the group of nations considered 'anti-imperialist and progressive'. The signing in July 1974, of the 'Treaty of Friendship and Cooperation' between Somalia and the Soviet Union was a culmination of all previous economic and military agreements and was the first of its kind in Black Africa. Umar Arteh Ghalib, as the foreign minister until 1977, contributed to Somalia's impact. In February 1974, he and Siyad engineered Somalia's entry into the Arab League following a long-standing invitation. This was a popular move at the mass level especially in the northern region, where a number of the people work as migrant laborers in Saudi Arabia and the Gulf.[3] Joining the Arab League was intended to diversify Siyad's diplomatic and foreign aid options, particularly in the light of the shift in global power and resources brought about by the 'oil shock' in 1973. Joining the Arab League, however, did not seem to have blunted the apparently progressive thrust of the regime. In 1975, Siyad went on to proclaim a radical marriage and family law banning polygamy and equalizing the inheritance portions for brothers and sisters. When religious leaders complained that this amounted to undermining the basic structures of Islamic society, twenty-three were arrested and ten of them were publicly executed by firing squad (Nelson 1928:16). Hosting the Organization of African Unity (OAU) in 1974 allowed Siyad the honor of serving as its chairman and strengthened the regime's claim to Pan-Africanism.

It is not easy to provide fully reliable socio-economic statistics indicating improvements during those years. However, the atmosphere that was created differed from the relatively chaotic era that preceded military rule. Among those of us who lived in Mogadishu during those years, there was an atmosphere of bustling purposefulness and movement toward tangible goals. Soviet military and economic support kept the shilling stable; rent control, food price supports and reliable public transportation made Mogadishu an affordable city, despite relatively low wages and salaries. It was these projects and this atmosphere that Julius Nyerere saw or sensed during the 1974 meeting in Mogadishu of the OAU heads of state and government. For someone who disliked military rulers on principle, Nyerere did indeed pay Somalia's experiments a great compliment: 'The Somalis are practicing what we in Tanzania preach' (Farer 1976:95).

Why did this apparently 'progressive' and 'Pan-Africanist' government degenerate into a repressive and militaristic regime? The reasons are complex and of internal and external origins, but I find the most persuasive framework of interpretation to be that of personal rule. At the same time, however, the concept of personal rule as elaborated by Rosberg and Jackson is unsatisfactory and simplistic at a number of levels. First, even within the assumptions of the model it is rather static, precluding the possibility of progression from one form of personal rule to another. Second, it assumes that personal rule necessarily operates outside of institutions and is opposed to institutionalization. I argue that Siyad's personal rule had a complex interaction with institutions and appreciation for their utility in extending the reach of personal power. Siyad situated himself above Somali institutions while using these same institutions to constrain and regulate social groups within the country. In the same vein Rosberg and Jackson's approach, in highlighting the personal character of African post-colonial regimes, has sometimes focused much more on the traits and characteristics of the personal ruler than on an analysis of state organization and interactions, in particular tending to overlook 'the relationship between public institutions and specific social groups' (Chazan *et al* 1988:20). To remedy this defect, I have included the military institution as a major factor complementing our personal rule analysis. Thus, in my analysis of personal rule in Somalia, I focus also on the mechanisms that glued specific social groups to the operations of public institutions, allowing the personal ruler to govern in a systematic grid-like manner rather than purely through ad-hoc personal relationships.

THE SIYAD MILITARY AND PERSONAL RULERSHIP

The durability of Siyad's military dictatorship is explained by the number of political resources he utilized to sustain his regime. The first political resource was his solid base within the country's armed forces. Foreign aid provided a second major pillar. Even though our analysis focuses on internal developments, this external factor, a byproduct of the Cold War is extremely significant. Without a reliable military dependency and without the economic resources necessary to maintain patron client relationships, the regime would have collapsed much earlier. Thus the importance of the external factor cannot be overestimated. Politicization and manipulation of traditional clan divisions provide a third factor, especially when Siyad was able to transform Russian *nomenklatura* practices into a Somali 'clanklatura' control system. Somali irredentist nationalism constituted a fourth political resource. The Machiavellian personal system of rulership allowed his regime to arise and survive; it was also mostly responsible for the ultimate destruction of his dictatorship.

The armed forces provided Siyad's major political resource as a power base and will be considered first. The fact was that the process of militarization by which the Somali military came to dominate the Somali state and civil society at the same time consolidated Siyad's personal power. Among Siyad's colleagues in the military and the regime this process was accomplished relatively early. Most of the officers on the SRC were captains and majors. before Siyad's coup there were rumors of a colonel's coup and Siyad wasted no time in jailing some officers, including the future factional leaders,

Mohamed Farah Aydid and Abdulahi Yusuf. In the first few years of the regime he also neutralized or physically eliminated several of his key military rivals.[4] But the process went further than this. An important aspect of Siyad's militarization of the Somali state and civil society was the creation of the national militia as a paramilitary institution. These Victory Pioneers (*Guulwaddeyaal*) were considered a 'revolutionary group' consisting of unemployed youth from urban areas. As a wing of the army, they were organized directly by the presidency and were headed by one of Siyad's sons-in-law. For a while they received Cuban training in their main camp in Afgoi. In rural areas they served as vigilance corps and in urban areas, this green-uniformed militia was highly visible as policemen on the streets especially during public gatherings. Numbering about 10,000 during the 1980s, they had powers of arrest independent of the police, and prior to 1978 their duties included spying on contacts between Somalis and foreigners. Control of state and society was heightened by the various security organs created by the regime the most visible being the National Security Service, headed by another son-in-law, who was a member of the SRC. In time, other overlapping institutions were created, for example the presidential guard, or recreated by manipulating existing units such as the military police. Siyad came to establish an elaborate security network with personnel spying on other state organs, on society and on each other while the dictator manipulated them all. This security system, involving clan loyalties as well as material incentives, partly explains the regime's durability, from 1969 to 1991.

All along (1969-75), Siyad insisted that the SNA represented the revolutionary vanguard. 'The Army today constitutes the revolutionary vanguard, because all its components come from the masses, who in their turn are the vanguard of the Revolution' (cited in Pestalozza 1974:129). The First Charter of the 1969 coup stated that the SRC would guide the country towards elections at an appropriate time. Siyad had no intention of doing so. The Russians pressured him to create a civilian vanguard party and social organizations to help demilitarize his regime. After years of stonewalling, the pressure for political competition with Ethiopia made him change his mind.[5] A congress of about 3,000 participants was called to form the Somali

Revolutionary Socialist Party (SRSP) on 1 July 1976. During the following year, congresses were also held to form the Somali Women's Democratic Organization (SWDO), the Somali Revolutionary Youth Union (SRYU), the Confederation of Somali Trade Unions (CSTU) and the Movement for Somali Cooperatives Organization (MSCO). Another Soviet institution was copied in the formation of a children's Organization, Flowers of the Revolution.

At the formation of the SRSP, the military Supreme Revolutionary Council (SRC) was declared dissolved, only to be officially resurrected in 1980! All members of the SRC and all (1976) cabinet members were included in the first seventy-three-member Central Committee of the SRSP, consisting of both civilians and military officers. The tiny SRSP Politburo consisted entirely of military figures: General Siyad as the general secretary of the SRSP, Vice-President Mohamed Samatar, Vice-President Hussein Kulmiye, Vice-President Ismail Ali Abokor and Colonel Ahmed Suleyman Dafle, the president's son-in-law and director of the National Security Service (NSS).

THE DYNAMICS OF DEPENDENCY

Foreign aid and external dependency, especially on military arms and equipment, provided the regime with a second significant resource with which to legitimize itself and prolong its rule (Campagnon 1991:209-10). Regional and superpower rivalry to influence the direction of Somalia's political and military development, and through it the balance of power in the Horn, preceded Siyad's regime. Under the civilian government, Nasser's Egypt furnished the SNA with its first military aid. Somalia's fears of retaliation for supporting the struggles of Somalis in neighboring countries for self-determination was reinforced by the Ethiopian-Kenyan defense pact signed in 1963. Elected Somali governments appealed for international military aid and began to make overtures towards Western as well as Eastern states. In 1962 they appeared favourable to a US$ 4 million joint military assistance offer from Britain and Italy. News about a pending USSR offer obliged even the most reluctant power, the USA (Ethiopia's ally), to join Italy and West Germany in proffering approximately US$ 10 million to train a 5,000-soldier army. The aid had clear political strings: in accepting, it, Somalia would agree not to seek military assistance from other sources. The civilian government decided to look elsewhere. During the epoch of multi-party politics, the United States was the largest non-military aid donor to Somalia, after Italy. Upon Siyad's assumption of power and declaration of 'scientific socialism', however, the United States suspended its aid programme. West Germany suspended its aid programme when the newly renamed Somali Democratic Republic (SDR) recognized the East German Democratic Republic. This did not prevent the new regime from obtaining substitutes and vastly increasing the amount of foreign aid to the SDR. Military aid, training and equipment were increased substantially following the 1972 visit by Soviet Defense Minister, Andrey Grechko, who signed an agreement on access to military facilities to be constructed in the northern port of Berbera by the USSR air force and navy. In 1963, the USSR agreed to lend Somalia US\$ 32 million for equipping and expanding an army of 10,000, a modest navy and an air force equipped with MIGs. About three-quarters of the assistance took the form of grants.

By 1969, more than 800 Somali officers were reported to have been trained in the USSR. By the time Somalia and Ethiopia went to war in 1978 over the so-called Ogaden region, the SNA constituted a well-equipped force of 37,000. The USSR provided fuel for the army as well as for the nationalized petroleum agency to help it recover local costs for Soviet projects. Less significant than Soviet military aid, economic aid amounted to about US\$ 154 million over a fifteen-year period ending in 1977. Nevertheless, while Soviet fuel supplies secured military preparedness, they also helped to cushion the Somali economy from inflation. The foreign exchange rate, for example, was stable at 6.35 Somali shillings to one US dollar for most of the 1960s and 1970s. About three and a half years after the break with the USSR, the Somali currency was devaluated to 12.46 shillings to one US dollar, the first of a series of devaluations that by the late 1980s had greatly reduced the value of the Somali shilling.

Foreign patronage and dependency became the main avenue to military expansion. Following the 1969 coup, the SNA grew to roughly 20,000 soldiers. On the eve of the so-called Ogaden War in 1977, the SNA had been expanded to 37,000 strong. By then, the

SNA consisted of six tank battalions, nine mechanized infantry battalions, two commando battalions, five field artillery battalions, and five anti-aircraft artillery battalions. This was probably the largest armored force in Black Africa at the time, about three times the size of that of Ethiopia, which had by far the largest army in Africa (about 49,000 in the 1960s, rising to 225,000 and finally over 300,000 by 1990). The USSR provided the SNA with its large tank force: about 250 Soviet medium tanks, including at least 100 newer T-54s and T-55s by 1975. The SNA also possessed about 25 MIG-15s, MIG-17s and MIG-19s, a squadron of 24 MIG-21s, a six-plane transport squadron, as well as a helicopter squadron. The Soviets also helped Somalia establish a navy which, by 1976-77, included combat ships: two SO1-class submarine chasers, each with four machine guns and anti-submarine rockets, two OSA-II guided missile boats, about six Poluchat-class patrol boats, and a number of Soviet P-4 and P-6 torpedo patrol boats. They also provided Somalia with fuel to alleviate military fuel costs, as well as raising local funds for all Soviet projects.

Ironically, once this fighting force had tried and failed in its realization of greater Somalia aspirations, its logic of expansion remained intact. Compulsory mobilization and training involving 70,000 people was undertaken during the post-war years. Following the cease-fire in 1978, the army had expanded to 96,000 in 1980 (out of which combat forces constituted 60,000). Even though internal conflicts were relatively marginal, Siyad increased the size of the army to 115,000 and eventually to 123,000 by 1984/1985[6]. A vastly expanded SNA had been converted from an army for 'liberation' to an army of 'repression' practicing forms of 'internal colonialism'.

While facilitating the creation of a vast military machine, this external dependency had its problems. Even before the break with the Soviets the army, navy and air force all suffered from insufficient spare parts and a poor rate of serviceability of Soviet equipment. It has been argued that some of these difficulties were engineered by the Soviets both as a way of checking Somali military ambitions and retaining some control over the military machine that they had helped to create; hence supplies of spare parts, uniforms and fuel were deliberately kept tight.

RECYCLING PATRONS

Following the expulsion of the USSR in 1977, the Achilles heel of the Siyad regime rested in the failure to find a foreign donor to replace Soviet military aid. Siyad claimed that the United States promised to replace Soviet aid before the rupture with the USSR. In 1980 he requested US$ 2 billion in exchange for US use of naval installations at Berbera and the adjacent airfield. The United States rejected this inflated request and offered $53 million in economic aid and $40 million in military credits for defensive equipment and training: long-range air defense radar, twelve Vulcan defense guns and associated communications equipment, support gear and spare parts. While the USSR was very generous in military aid and less so in economic assistance, the United States provided less military aid and relatively generous amounts of economic assistance.

After 1978, Italy became the major Western supplier of arms. It provided, for example, the vast majority of service vehicles used by the armed forces. Many of the armored personnel carriers were of Italian origin. Fiat sought to expand its commerce in Somalia by selling light tanks and armored cars. By the late 1970s, Somalia was receiving 20 per cent of total Italian aid; Italy also facilitated Somalia's associate status within the European Economic Community (EEC). Following the 1977 independence of Djibouti, France also felt comfortable enough to sell Somalia arms, provided it was able to pay in cash.[7] Arab aid also became increasingly important: Somalia received assistance totaling some $310 million from a group of Arab countries led by Saudi Arabia, Kuwait and Abu Dhabi. China delivered bilateral aid totaling $162m. There was also considerable financial assistance from multilateral sources: the EEC, the World Bank, OPEC, the Islamic Development Bank and the African Development Bank.

While external patrons may have been relatively easily recycled, reorienting military sources proved more difficult. The SNA continued for some years to depend on left-over Soviet weaponry. However, most of this could not be put into operation. This included the original Soviet tanks, armored personnel carriers and SAM-25 and SAM-3 missiles, as well as Soviet models delivered to Somalia from Egypt. About 50 percent of the 25 MIG-17s and MIG-21s were kept operational by third-party technical assistance. In 1981, the Chinese supplied 30 MIG-19 type Shenyang fighter-bombers. The air element also had a transport squadron composed of a variety of aircraft delivered over the years mostly Italian, as well as the four Boeing 707s and 720Bs that could be commandeered from the parastatal Somali Airlines. The Siyad regime had to enter the international arms bazaar, creating profitable clanklatura networks for individuals and cliques.

Given its perceived strategic position, Somalia received considerable aid after 1960 at an average figure of US$ 90 per capita, the highest ratio in sub-Saharan Africa (Mehmet 1971: 34). However, by 1990 the Siyad regime, waging wars on its civil society, lost practically all foreign aid. Unpaid soldiers began to rob and loot the population, especially in Mogadishu. Siyad's military and personal rulership fell in January 1991.

THE MILITARY AND THE ECONOMIC COSTS OF ARMAMENTISM

In spite of statistical deficiencies, figures on Somalia's total military costs are among the highest in Africa. In 1961, military expenditures amounted to 14 per cent of the national budget, rising to 21 per cent in 1968. By 1973, public expenditure on the military on a per capita basis was double the combined expenditure for education and health; while the military expenditures rose about 10 per cent per year between 1963 and 1973, the gross national product (GNP) grew at an annual rate of a little less than 3 per cent. Funding for the armed forces amounted annually to about 27 per cent of total government expenditures between 1972 and 1977, 37.1 per cent in 1978 and 39 per cent in 1979 (Nelson 1982). These figures do not include expenditures on the police, the militia, national security service and other paramilitary forces; Somali defense budgets allocated funds only for current expenditures (wages, simple maintenance and so forth) and not for capital (hardware) expenditures. Nor did they include supplies of weaponry, spare parts and fuel, which the Somali Ministry of Defense did not even bother to record. This habit was continued even after the Soviets departed in 1977.[8] The ratio of military personnel to both the general Somali population and those of military age was higher than that of any other African nation south of the Sahara. The consistently high levels of the defense burden on the national economy also ranked the Somali military among the most costly in Africa.

Personnel payments of the Ministry of Defense constituted on average 80 per cent of the defense budget. This part of the budget averaged 1.5 million Somali shillings during the early 1960s. It remained relatively stagnant until the end of the 1970s, thereafter rising to 3.2 billion shillings in 1982/3 and 5.1 billion in 1986/7. Generally speaking, army pay included subsidized health benefits, housing, subsidized stores for basic services. A recruit from the nomadic society found army life relatively comfortable and predictable. Officers had, obviously, great privileges and allowances – for some this included the use of an army vehicle. Otherwise, around 1962, starting salaries of up to 650 Somali shillings for a non-commissioned soldier and 2,000 for a colonel shows that the cash salary differential was not excessive. Between 1978 and 1982, inflation rates of about 400 per cent or higher began to wreak havoc with this stable and relatively flat pyramid of incentives. The drastic inflation provided an enabling environment for corruption, extortion and loot for what was fast becoming a repressive 'semi-colonial' army.

IRREDENTISM AND WAR

Both the process of militarization and foreign dependency were linked crucially to the irredentist project of Pan-Somalism, which was in turn to constitute the third political resource of the Siyad regime. The last civilian government of Premier Egal began a process of peace and détente with Ethiopia, Kenya and the French in Djibouti. Egal defended his initiative through a strict, legal interpretation of the Somali constitution which recommended only peaceful, legal means for the attainment of Somali unification. When Siyad came to power, he more or less continued this policy until 1977, hiding the militant, irredentist face of Somali nationalism. In retrospect, this was not as paradoxical as it seemed: it merely reflected Siyad's deliberate manner of consolidating international support and domestic control before launching major initiatives. Mogadishu hosted the OAU in 1974 and Siyad was elected OAU chairman for a year as is the diplomatic custom. He diverted internal pressures by claiming that he could not go to war as OAU Chairman. As late as March 1977, speaking to a group of Somali artists who had participated in the World Black Arts Festival (FESTAC 77) in Nigeria, Siyad claimed that he would not let Blacks shed other Blacks' blood to the satisfaction of imperialist forces. Barely a few months later, however, he went into full-scale war, claiming much more than the traditional Somali territories within Ethiopia. He had also armed a faction of the large Oromo nationality and baptized them the Somali Abbo Liberation Front (SALF). The façade of both Pan-Africanism and socialist internationalism collapsed, in part due to the pressure of domestic irredentism. In mid-1977, he rejected Fidel Castro's mission to establish a loose socialist confederation of Ethiopia, Somalia and South Yemen. The break with the USSR and the risking of war for a Somali cause gave the regime a new measure of legitimacy and popularity.

CLANISM AND CLANKLATURA

Manipulation of the clan divisions within Somali society provided the regime with a fourth major political resource. Paradoxically, the regime obtained early popularity for being symbolically anticlanism. The rural practice of paying blood-money (*diya*) for murder or homicide was abolished. The adoption of scientific socialism on 21 October 1970 was expected to foster the complete eradication of 'tribalism' (even though the sociological reality involves clan-families and clans, Somali politicians speak of 'tribalism' as do all African politicians). Symbolic burials and burnings of effigies representing these enemies took place throughout Siyad's rule. Prior to 1977/8, he utilized clanism to strengthen his regime in a relatively 'invisible' manner. During later years, the regime's clan basis became more open and blatant. In the public perception the so-called revolutionary regime depended on a clan pyramid headed by the Marehan (Siyad's clan), followed by the Ogaden, his mother's clan, and then the Dulbahante, the clan of his son-in-law, Ahmed Suleyman Dafle, head of the dreaded National Security Service (NSS). Irrepressible Somali commentators came up with an acronym based on the first letter of each clan MOD all three of which belong to the Darod clan-family.

However, the descent of the Siyad regime into clanism was not as crude or direct as this account might suggest. Rather, it was routed, elaborately, through the Soviet concept of *nomenklatura*, initially adopted as a means of controlling the party and the mass organizations established by the regime as well as the military and state structures. Over time, the principle (or rather practice) of *nomenklatura* was 'indigenised' and metamorphosed by Siyad and his clique into what, for want of a better term, I have decided to label 'clanklatura'. Within the Soviet system, all important posts, ranging from ministerial offices and media/ newspaper editorships to factory manager ships and headships of institutes and schools, could be filled only with the confirmation of a specific party organ. *Nomenklatura* essentially involves a list of people who are regarded as competent and politically reliable and suitable, therefore, for appointment to one of a number of such listed posts. The Soviets exported the concept and practice of *nomenklatura* into the SNA as early as 1971.

In my talk with General Samatar... the commander-in-chief of the army laid particular stress on the work of 'politicizing' the soldiers... In this framework the creation of commissars or political officers is in keeping with a specific guideline, and the importance of their role is borne out by the fact that in very section, independent of their rank (even if they are lieutenants), they are automatically deputy commanders of the unit. They are in direct contact with the political headquarters, set up in the High Command (Pastalozza 1974:315-16).

At first some of those so appointed included ideologically trained officers and cadres regardless of clan affiliation. By the mid-1970s, this imported control mechanism had been 'indigenised' and corrupted to reflect clan-based appointments. A junior officer who happened to belong to Siyad's Marehan clan could therefore serve as deputy commander and control a superior, professionally trained officer from the so-called 'non-revolutionary clans'. Through such appointments Siyad was able to cast his control network far and wide with loyal eyes and ears penetrating military, paramilitary, police, security, civilian bureaucratic and socio-political institutions. The creation of the vanguard party, the SRSP, and the social organizations in 1976/7 vastly expanded this clanklatura system. Selected members of the three Darod clans, constituting the Siyad-created MOD alliance, formed the inner core of the clanklatura system. Siyad's own Marehan clan sat at the top of the hierarchy.

Clanklatura involved the politicization of institutions that function best when they rely on professional standards, training and education, technical competence, specialization and experience. It created a major crisis of confidence among the Somali elite, the intelligentsia, lawyers and other professional and dedicated, experienced civil servants. Frustration, bitterness and diminishing material incentives led to a rapidly accelerating brain drain.

Siyad's adoption of *nomenklatura* and its transformation into clanklatura was facilitated by several factors: Siyad's own police espionage background, clan cleavages and consciousness, economic resources, manipulation of written Somali and the creation of clanklatura organizations. Observers have spoken of Siyad's prodigious memory and appetite for detail; according to a former minister in his government: 'Personal relations, face-to-face contact and an insatiable demand for-raw-intelligence data have been his preferred ways for domination and control' (Ali Khalif Galaydh 1990:24-5). In addition Siyad was blessed with robust health, giving him virtually round-the-clock energy to devote to the pursuit of political control and domination. He would sit into the wee hours of the morning, though advanced in age, chain-smoking, talking, absorbing huge amounts of tedious raw data on people that interested him for benign or malicious reasons.

The second factor involves clan differences and clan consciousness in Somali society. Siyad's ability to manipulate the clans was facilitated by the fact that many elements within the Somali petty bourgeoisie take clanism quite seriously themselves. Clan identities do not transform themselves into clan politics or conflict (clanism). On the contrary, the primary stimulus of clanism is provided by the petty bourgeoisie, as could be seen during the competitive party politics of the 1960s. Richard Sklar (cited in Saul 1979:394) made this point forcefully several years ago: 'Tribalism then becomes a mask for class privilege... An analysis along these lines does not underestimate the intensity of tribal conflict. It does suggest that tribalism should be viewed as a dependent variable than a primordial political variable in the new nations'. 'By the end of the 1980s, however, clanism seemed to many observers to reflect an 'independent' variable, so entrenched did it appear. While it is critical not to ignore or neglect the social class factor, it is just as distorting to fetishise it or to stereotype all aspects of clan consciousness as 'false consciousness' without a deeper analysis. Negative clan consciousness can be provoked as a result of memories of past clan conflicts due to competition for resources or for prestige. Famines and other natural disasters sometimes trigger such conflicts. In a positive vein, clan conflicts sometimes reflect the struggles of oppressed clans for justice and equality. However, this negative modern form of clanism was incubated in the cities and later exported to the countryside. The average Marehan, Ogaden or Dulbahante (MOD) nomad in rural areas had little to gain from this urban elite system; in some ways he was as much a victim as the other Somali rural masses. He is often blamed and condemned for the sins of his elite.

The third factor facilitating Siyad's clanklatura system is economic resources. Young (1966:38) explains:

> Beyond and often in addition to affinity, personal interest is the most reliable collateral for loyalty. Accordingly, rulers must reward generously and impose severe sanctions for any weakening or zeal. Thus, pubic resources become a pool of benefits and prebends, while dismissal from office, confiscation of goods, and prosecution face those who show slackness in their personal fidelity. Holders of high office individually tend to become clients of the ruler and collectively a service class.

During the epoch of dependency on the Soviets, the regime's military needs were more than met. However, apart from fuel and the local currency it generated, most Soviet aid was aid in kind. Apart from local costs, the budgets for all other Soviet economic projects were also mostly controlled by the Soviets, who provided not only the designs but all imported materials and machines. Soviet (and Chinese) aid therefore did not create enough 'surplus' financial resources to grease the clanklatura system. During those years, these came from local resources and other sources of aid. This partly explains why there was much less visible corruption during those early years.

As we have seen, once the Soviet linkage was abrogated in 1977, Somalia had to search for various donors to cover significant military purchases. While the United States refused to substitute fully for Soviet largesse, Gulf states, for example, provided about US$ 400 million as their contribution to Somalia's 1977 war effort. While the Somali society suffered severe economic scarcities, the regime benefited from cash flows from regimes that did not and could not ensure fiscal responsibility and accountability (Nelson 1982:242).

Perhaps the best example of someone who profited most from Siyad's clanklatura was his Marehan relative Abdi Hoosh. He used to be a simple driver, but by the early 1980s he emerged as a multi-millionaire owning, among other properties and businesses, a huge complex in Mogadishu, including garages and offices for importing and repairing land-rovers, tractors and other vehicles, as well as a luxury hotel. Whenever his fleet of imported land-rovers arrived, a memo would go to ministries and parastatals signed by a very high official, urging them to buy the vehicles for their organizations. The president told Ministry of Defense officials that his plans were to assist Hoosh enterprises to establish defense-related industries for the country.

Another example of 'clan-rent' and the process of creating a business-cum political dynasty was provided by Siyad's elder son, Maslah, who at one point headed the military construction wing of the army. His father would order public projects to be contracted to his construction unit so the family-regime cold earn 'rent': the Ministry of Higher Education, for example, awarded him bids for the National Museum and the National Library;[10] the Ministry of Sports allowed him to build the National Stadium extensions funded by Arab states.

CLANKLATURA AND THE MILITARY

Applied to the military, clanklatura provided the key mechanism by which military rule proper was transmuted into personal rule. Even as the Somali state was narrowed down to its military form, so the military as an institution was eroded and captured from within by clanklatura, a complex of 'specialized' organizations formally military in character and function but staffed by the president's clan and owing loyalty to the clan and through it to him. This included the *Hangash,* military intelligence. In 1980, military intelligence was removed from the jurisdiction of former NSS boss Ahmed Suleyman and placed under the president's cousin, Colonel Mohamed Samatar. The military counter-intelligence provided another one of these state terror institutions. Its name in Somali, *Dabarjebinta,* literarlly means' the back-breakers'. The military police was made up of soldiers wearing red berets, the *Koofiyad'asta* in Somali. The majority of the members of these forces were Marehan. Presidential security came under the 5,000-man presidential guard, stationed in Mogadishu around army headquarters and the presidential palace compound. This was virtually a full-scale Marehan monopoly. One may also recall the National Security Service (NSS) and the party-associated militia, the *Guulwadayaal.*

Somalis have always been sensitive to matters involving the relative strengths and representation of their clans and clan-families. Within the army and elsewhere, balanced clan representation remained a sensitive issue. For many years, the SNA made it a regular practice that any recruitment notice, whether for officers or for all ranks, specified the proportional number of men to be recruited from each district, establishing a *de facto* clan balance.[11] Whenever serious clan imbalance occurred, transfers and efforts to correct the imbalance through localized recruiting efforts were undertaken.

General Daud Abdulle Hersi, First Commander of the SNA, is generally credited with laying down such policies. General Daud was from the Hawiye clan-family, Abgal clan. He was religious and reflected an ascetic lifestyle. This increased his popularity among nomadic soldiers and ordinary Somalis everywhere. He is reported to have manifested no political ambitions and therefore helped enhance the army's earlier reputation as a professional, non-political corporate entity. When Hasan Keid and other young northern officers attempted a coup, he welcomed a lenient approach and used the incident to reduce imbalances within the armed forces. He appointed the most senior northerner, General Ainashe, head of the army in the north. Later on Siyad would appoint Ainashe as vice-president and then have him executed for-so-called treason.

General Daud died in 1965 and his deputy Mohamed Siyad Barre assumed command. At first, he pursued the policies laid down by General Daud as far as army recruitment and promotions were concerned. In the composition of the SRC, there was a tilt though not a pronounced one in favor of his clan-family, the Darod (10 members); other clans included were the Hawiye (6), Isaq (4), Dir (2), Rahanweyn (1), and non-clan/settled Somalis (2). Out of the ten Darod SRC members, his own Marehan clan held three seats. From a Somali point to view, this was not seen as an equitable or effective method of representation. However, under the circumstances, it was deemed fair enough, since most people decided to give Siyad the benefit of the doubt and a chance to prove himself and his military regime.

Over time, however, clanism in the military became more blatant. In 1969, apart from Siyad himself, there had not been a single other Marehan general in the army. In 1990, the number of Marehan generals totaled 16, most of them promoted during the period 1986/90: Ogaden generals numbered 7, Dulbahante 6, Warsangeli 2, and Majerteyn 10, making a total of 41 for the Darod clan-family. The whole Hawiye clan-family, with a long tradition of army officers, ended up with fourteen generals, two less than the share of the Marehan clan alone. The Isaq clan-family ended up with five and the Dir had only one officer promoted to the level of general.[12] As early as 1976, when Colonel Omar Mohamed Farah was asked to train and command a tank brigade stationed in Mogadishu, he found that out of about 540 soldiers, at least 500 were from the Marehan clan.[13] The whole tank division was headed by a Marehan officer, Umar haji Masala.

THE SOMALI LANGUAGE POLICY

This discussion would not be complete without a brief reference to language policy in Somalia. The manipulation of written Somali to distort and corrupt educational and administrative standards constituted the fourth facilitating factor in Siyad's power base. In implementing written Somali, Siyad saw the opportunity to banish English, which he believed favored northerners. Borrowing distorted slogans from the Chinese Cultural Revolution, he proclaimed that 'red' (in actuality, politically loyal or of the right clan origin) was far better than 'expert'. Through learning to read and write their own language, the Somali masses were told that they could now finally replace 'neocolonial-minded, foreign-educated Somalis' in running their country. This was an essential prop for putting his own clan into administration: instead of educating and training Marehan relatives to national and international professional standards, he decided to pull down Somali professional levels to those of an average Marehan who had only recently acquired literacy in the Somali language.

PROPHET, AUTOCRAT, TYRANT

Jackson and Rosberg (1982:8) claim to have developed a view of personal rule as a 'distinctive kind of institutionless polity'. They go on to generalized about such rulers operating largely without the aid of strong institutions. Obviously such generalizations apply to many of Africa's personal rulers. However, Siyad's personal rule system was imposed both within and outside institutions, the Somali military system, from the perspective of both those inside and those outside Somalia, began as an effective institution. Besides, Siyad himself understood the importance of controlling the rest of the state organs and civil society sectors through institutions and organizations: military, security, police and paramilitary organizations, as well as the party and the so-called mass or social organizations for women, youth, workers and cooperatives. As a personal ruler, he had the autonomy to operate above institutions while others were constrained by the same institutions. Ultimately, however, his manipulations caused the institutions to lose effectiveness, degenerate and finally collapse, leading to statelessness and anarchy.

Somalia under Siyad reflected all the features analyzed under personal rule: clientelism and patronage, factionalism, attempted coups, purges, plots and succession crises (Jackson and Rosberg 1982:6). Siyad's control was so effective that the country experienced only one visible coup attempt in twenty-one years. Siyad and those on top of the pyramid provided resources in exchange for loyalty and political support; those in the middle tiers were expected to share some of their resources with those below them. Like other personal rulers, Siyad fabricated a cult of personality which did not go well with traditionally egalitarian notions of power among Somalis. The system was, therefore, inextricably linked to material incentives and rewards. At its core was the clan element, centred on the MOD during the early years, but expanding to include elements from the broader Darod clan-family as the clanist practices of the regime deepened.

Siyad proclaimed himself a Prophetic Ruler when, on the first anniversary of the coup, 21 October 1970, he issued the 'Second Charter of the Revolution'with the announcement (cited in Pestalozza 1974:29), 'We solemnly and resolutely proclaim ourselves a socialist state', thus becoming the second African state after the Congo (Brazzaville) to declare Marxism-Leninism as its official ideology. Journalists and Africanists began to compare Siyad to President Nasser of Egypt, Kwame Nkrumah of Ghana, Ahmed Sekou Toure of Guinea and Julius Nyerere of Tanzania. To distinguish himself even further, Siyad criticized their 'African socialism' as fake, claiming his brand of Marxism-Leninism as closer to the world socialist movement. Nevertheless, Siyad had to undertake a series of radio talks, public lectures and seminars to minimize the apparent conflicts between Marxism-Leninism and the religion of Islam.

According to Jackson and Rosberg (1982:79), the proclamation of scientific socialism brought Siyad into a minority of Africa's rulers who may be described as 'visionaries, wanting to reshape society in ways consistent with their ideology, which in Africa has been primarily socialist... To pursue an ideological vision of a better world is the only valid justification of rule for the Prophet.' Such claims are made on risky and idealist terrain. We now know that Siyad did not believe in ideology with the sincerity of a Nyerere, for example, although in his early years he did appear to be a true believer in socialism. He adopted' socialism' to consolidate his regime, to distance it from the previous civilian regimes and, more important, to obtain greater military, diplomatic and economic aid from the USSR. It may not be entirely coincidental that during this period Siyad also began to play the Pan-Somali and irredentist card. He allowed Western Somali Liberation Front (WSLF) fighters to infiltrate into Ethiopia and wage guerrilla warfare. Somali soldiers and military officers dressed as WSLF guerrillas were also sent to the front in increasing, numbers. Obviously neither 'socialism' nor pressures from socialist benefactors restrained him from attacking a fraternal 'socialist' neighbor, Ethiopia.

Siyad's prophetic rule facilitated the development of a cult of personality. It has been suggested that this personality cult was inspired by visits to North Korea and to a lesser extent Sekou Toure's Guinea, Romania, Syria and Iraq. In all these instances he liked what he saw: socialist rhetorics, cults of personality and, underneath, tight, dictatorial control guaranteed by family rule at the top of the pyramid. Praise-singing in all schools and workplaces formed one of the cornerstones of this personality cult; one of the composers of such praise-songs, Mohamed Nur Hassan (Shareo), a relative of the president in the military, received rapid promotions until he became a general of the SNA. This 'prophetic' mantle did not completely disguise the hard core of repression, underpinned by arrests and executions (exercised against both civil society and rivals of the regime), that characterized Siyad's rule even at this stage.

The 1977/8 war, and the resolute switch by the Soviet Union and Cuba to the Ethiopian side, ended the phase of Prophetic Ruler for Siyad. Having dropped the ideological or prophetic mantle, Siyad revealed his essential self: that of an autocrat who tends to dominate the oligarchy, the government, and the state without having to share power with other leaders... the party and government officials his servants and agents' (Jackson and Rosberg 1982:78). However, this was not before Somalia had undergone a brief liberalizing trend. The return of USAID, the World Bank, the IMF and other Western institutions and donors rekindled hopes that Somalia might return to a free market and a competitive democracy. In 1979, Siyad unfolded his first-ever constitution. He held cosmetic elections for the National Assembly in 1979, to persuade his new masters, the Americans, to increase their military and economic aid. He had the rubber-stamp parliament elect him president to legitimize his power. On 12 October 1980, however, Siyad reversed his direction. He declared a national state of emergency, suspended the constitution, which was still less than one year old, and revived the militarist Supreme Revolutionary Council (SRC). Following a 1984 constitutional amendment, the president was to be elected by universal direct elections. The first such elections took place on 2 December 1986, with Siyad standing as the sole candidate and receiving 99.9 per cent of the votes cast! The tempo of repression increased sharply thereafter. When the SSDF opposition movement began to make anti-Siyad broadcasts from Ethiopia, he detained most of the elites who happened to belong to that clan (the Majerteyn). This move, though distasteful, was partly expected; what was not expected was that he would order the army to attack the nomadic relatives of the attempted coup-makers who formed the opposition. He began to take the first steps down the slippery slope from autocracy to tyranny. The repression was exported to the rural areas, which are usually treated with benign neglect by most African regimes. In Mudug region, around the town of Galkayo, the army destroyed *berkeds* (cement water tanks for livestock,), burned villages and confiscated livestock. The urban elites were confused through clanism and punished through various humiliations, denials of contracts, purges and jailings. Thousands were hounded into exile.

Northern exiles from the Isaq clan-family formed the Somali National Movement (SNM) in London in April 1981. Later, they moved to eastern Ethiopia to establish armed bases in areas near their homeland. Outraged by this challenge, Siyad embarked on a wholesale persecution of the Isaq, thereby transforming the SNM from a few dissidents to a mass movement. Having declared the Isaq an enemy clan-family, he instigated clan wars against them. In the east he ignited warfare between the Dulbahante (Darod) and the Habar Jeclo (Isaq). In the centre and across the border with Ethiopia, he launched conflicts between the Ogaden (Darod) and the Habar Yunis (Isaq) and later between the Ogaden and the Eidagale (Isaq). Siyad had reduced the north to a 'colony' of his regime, as Lewis (1990:58) observed:

From the early 1980s, the north was administered by increasingly harsh military rule with savage reprisals meted out to the assuredly pro-SNM local population who were subject to severe economic, as well as political harassment. The north as I saw when I last visited it in 1985, began to look and feel like a colony under a foreign military tyranny.

Siyad was also able to extend his MOD clanklatura base by locating the 1977/8 refugees in those parts of the country inhabited by non-Darod clans. Many were settled in the north among the Isaq, others in the Hiran region among the Hawiye, with sometimes unpleasant results for their hosts:

> Male Ogadeni refugees in Northern Somalia... have been conscripted as a paramilitary militia to fight the SNM and to man check-points on the roads. Ogadeni refugees have been encouraged to take over the remains of Isaq shops and houses in what are now ghost-towns. Thus, those who were received as refugee guests have supplanted their Isaq hosts, many of whom in this bitterly ironic turn of fate are now refugees in the Ogaden (Lewis 1990:59).

The bulk of the army in the north consisted of Ogaden, Majerteyn, other Darod clans, soldiers from the Hawiye and other southern clans and non-clan groups. Marehans figured mostly as officers or members of special paramilitary and security units. The tactic of 'divide and rule' through rural clan warfare was practiced in the south as well. During the early 1980s Siyad instigated several clan wars including those between his Marehan (Darod) clan and the Habar Gedir (Hawiye) clan of General Mohamed Farah Aydid (whom he had relased from prison and appointed ambassador to India). He also incited wars between the Majerteyn (Darod) clan and the Habar Gedir.[14] Thus were sown the seeds for the Darod Hawiye civil wars which erupted at Siyad's overthrow in 1991 and have, more or less, continued ever since.

On 23 may 1986, Siyad was involved in a serious road accident and, while still in a coma, was rushed to Saudi Arabia for emergency treatment. By the time Siyad recovered and began to function once again, to the disappointment of most of his citizens, he had deteriorated to the status of a 'tyrant... In a tyranny not only legal, but also all moral constraints on the exercise of power are absent, with the consequences that power is exercised in a completely arbitrary fashion according to the impulses of the ruler and his agents' (Jackson and Rosberg 1982:80). By the mid-1980s, Siyad had transformed his regime once again. Terror was elevated to the cardinal principle of his rule; in 1989 alone there were the massacre at the Mogadishu National Stadium and the assassination of Catholic Archbishop Colombo, and soon afterward the arrests and massacre of Islamic believers following Friday prayers (Ali Khalif Galydh 1990:26). The army was increased to the staggering size of 123,000, backed by a plethora of paramilitary forces to intimidate the population.

The manipulation of clan differences and the repression of 'dissident' clans backfired with the rise of clan-based opposition movements. Taking advantage of the weaponisation of the Somali environment by Siyad, these opposition movements became, in turn, increasingly armed and militarized. Clan resistance fused with the popular warrior traditions of the Somali people. In May 1988, the SNM re-entered northern Somalia and attacked the main military garrisons in Hargeisa, Burao and elsewhere. Siyad ordered total war: the air force, tanks and heavy artillery were all ordered to bombard civilians and property indiscriminately. Over 500,000 Isaqs from Hargeisa, Burao and other towns and villages fled to refugee camps across the border with Ethiopia, settling in the area (the Haud) traditionally occupied by Isaq clans. The occupying troops destroyed most of the houses in Hargeisa, Burao, Gebile and other settlements (see Greenfield 1987a:14-16; Greenfield 1987b: 1; Africa watch 1990; *Horn of Africa Bulletin* 5 (1):44). By 1989 the large Hawiye clan-family, situated in the centre of the country and including the capital city Mogadishu, began to forge their own armed opposition movement, the United Somali Congress (USC). When its leader, the famous journalist Jiumale, died in 1990 the USC fragmented into at least three factions a military faction headed by General Aydid and based in Ethiopia, a clandestine wing headed by Ali Mahdi in Mogadishu and an external wing based in Rome. Earlier on, Hawiye dissidents worked as a group affiliated to the northern SNM. Aydid's armed USC supporters entered central Somalia and captured town after town in the Hawiye areas as they advanced towards Mogadishu during most of 1990. Earlier on, some of the Ogadeni troops in the north, led by Colonel Omar Jess, defected and the SNM facilitated their movement to the south, the Kismayu area, to join other rebellious Ogadeni troops under the banner of the Somali Patriotic Movement (SPM).

The regime finally fell as a result of the combined blows of the decentralized, armed clan-based opposition movements together with the cutting of the umbilical cord of external dependency. During the 1980s, the United States provided Somalia with about US$ 100 million of aid per year. After 1985, Congressional criticisms of Siyad's human rights record led to the suspension of military aid in 1988 and by 1989 blocked both military and economic aid for Somalia. The consequences for the Somali economy were devastating. Remittances from abroad and the informal economy kept many from leaving the country. Civil servants could no longer rely on their salaries to support themselves and their families: most earned less than 10,000 shillings a month, the cost of two cans of beer in 1990. Traders had to pay anywhere between 30 and 50 percent of the value of their goods as 'taxes' on commercial transactions. In 1990, the official exchange rate of the Somali shilling was 2,380 to the dollar and 3,250 on the 'black market' (Drysdale 1991:16-17).

Sensing the mortal danger for his rentier regime, Siyad offered a new constitution on 12 October 1990 allowing for a multi-party system. On 25 December 1990, he got his new prime minister to announce that the government had scheduled 'free' elections for February 1991. The armed opposition movements rejected 'cheap cosmetic reforms'.[17] By mid-1990, USC forces had captured most towns and villages surrounding Mogadishu, reducing the former dictator to the dubious title of 'Mayor of Mogadishu'. In December the war was carried into Mogadishu itself with an urban uprising led by the Hawiye. On 27 January 1991, Siyad fled Mogadishu in a tank, escorted by his son-in-law, General Mohamed Said Morgan.

The fall of Siyad in January 1991 did not end the war but signified a new round of inter-clan fighting. One of the USC factional leaders, Ali Mahdi Mohamed, declared himself interim president and was opposed by the USC military leader, General Aydid, and the SNM, SPM, SSDF and other opposition groupings. Skirmishes followed between Ali Mahdi's Abgal (Hawiye) supporters and General Aydid's Habar Gedir (Hawiye) clan. The fighting reduced Mogadishu to another Beirut, with a 'green line' dividing the two opposing forces – Mahdi in northern and Aydid in southern Mogadishu. An intense war broke out in September of 1991 and lasted still 1992, when the

United Nations arranged a cease-fire. The fighting in the capital city prevented Somalia from installing even a nominal government that could seek international recognition. It symbolized state collapse in the most radical sense. As if to make this collapse irrevocable, a popular assembly meeting in Burao in May 1991 formally endorsed an independence proclamation establishing the northern Somaliland Republic and abrogating the Somali union.[18] So far, the Somaliland Republic has not received international *de jure* recognition (although it does appear to enjoy some *de facto* recognition).

FROM MILITARISM TO ANARCHY AND RECONSTRUCTION?

The civil wars have produced massive dislocation in Somali society. It is estimated that about 400,000 people died of famine or disease or were killed during the civil wars, and nearly 45 per cent of the population was displaced inside Somalia or fled as refugees to neighboring countries, to the Middle East, or to the West.[19] Militarism as ethos and social practice has penetrated into most aspect of Somali civil societies. Somalis have fought clan wars before, but never with the quantity and quality of modern arms that have flooded the country as a result of Cold War rivalries. One must emphasize the disastrous effects of large masses of weaponry dumped in Somalia and the resulting, if unintended, 'democratization of violence', particularly severe given the underlying segmentation and fragmentation of Somali society. Two aspects of this militarization and the trends countering it require mention. The first is the militarization of children (as is so often the case in African civil wars), particularly significant given the depopulation and breakdown of normal structures of social reproduction. What the emergence of a generation of youth weaned on the gun, both as a norm of social relations and as an economic proposition, implies for the future of Somalia remains to be seen. Second is the gender distribution of this militarization. While the civil wars have been fought primarily by men, women are taking the lead in peace and reconciliation activities. At the March 1993 Addis Ababa Reconciliation Conference, the women delegates insisted that one of the three representatives from each region to the Transitional National Council (TNC) must be a woman, a position that was carried with UN support. While men have engaged in endless contestation for control over the state, an energetic, though also chaotic, petty private sector has mushroomed in all towns and cities, again with women exercising a leading role.

In spite of (or perhaps because of) the widespread militarism, public opinion in post-Siyad Somalia seems set against the establishment of a new 'National Army'. The mood is favorable to the establishment of local police forces, locally recruited and vetted and accountable to local authorities. The UN has been involved in supporting this process. The prevailing mood also favors regional or federal approaches to a new political system; the Somaliland secession is only an extreme manifestation of a widely shared sentiment. This is obviously a realistic recognition of the fact that Somalia today is a significantly fractured country. On the other hand, Somali irredentism seems to have vanished with Siyad and relations between all Somali factions and Ethiopia are extremely warm and cordial.

As Somalia continues to drift in a state of statelessness, at least two political cultures have begun to emerge. In the north, Somaliland, the SNM has had a long tradition of decentralized fundraising and the holding of regular, popular congresses. Through the principle of elections, it has rotated leaders peacefully on seven or eight occasions. Leaders are openly criticized by the public and the embryonic press. Northerners feel that the process of peace and reconciliation cannot be separated from the state-formation process. They have been engaged in establishing local, district and regional authority structures which are representative and better able to retain the confidence of the people. Thus the collapse of the Somali state has regenerated traditional structures in this region, giving rise to alternative forms of socio-political organization. Traditional elders have played key roles in building these 'grassroots' structures. They have held peace and reconciliation congresses in Burao, Sheikh, Erigavo and Borama. The large gathering in Borama lasted from January to May 1993: it resolved outstanding clan conflicts, adopted guidelines for a new constitution and elected Mohamed Ibrahim Egal as the new president.

On the other hand, the south has developed a culture of warlordism. In some respects, it looked as if the military dictator Siyad has been replaced by a number of local Siyads! Ex-Italian Somaliland continues to suffer from the political culture of personal rulership in general and the militarist legacy of Siyad in particular.[21] Traditional elders have not been able to play the critical peace and reconciliation roles that they have exercised in the north. In the north, the consensus that is emerging is genuinely transforming and indigenous, not an external imposition. In the south, however, the United Nations has taken an active (and not always appropriate) role. With too many global conflicts on its agenda, the UN has applied pressure while hoping to move quickly to supervised elections (even the revised date of March 1995 seemed unrealistic), and from there to a new, elected central government.

CONCLUSION

In a sense, personal rulership collapsed from its own internal contradictions, which were already apparent by the mid-1970s. Even then, it was difficult to avoid the impression that the Somali Democratic Republic was being strangulated by a series of contradictions: the complete lack of meaningful mass participation in spite of socialist rhetorics and a past of excessive political participation; the failures in top-down commandist development programmes; the humiliating failure of a top-down militarist effort to 'liberate' the Ogaden in Ethiopia; the gap between an expansive, parasitic state sector and a vibrant though suffocated private sector; contradictions between the ritualistic burning and burying of clanism ('tribalism') and the regime's rigorous reliance on and manipulation of clanism; contradictions between inherited principles of merit understood by the modern trained elites and the wholesale use of political and clan criteria for appointments and promotions. A key reason for the collapse of personal rule was the incoherence in the various elements of Siyad's power grid. Militarization, clanklatura, irredentism and external dependency collided fatally. An expansionist military machine was controlled through clan manipulation, thus eroding the potential advantage of military modernization and armamentism. This relates closely to second tension between military professionalism and national security on the one hand and the security of the regime and the personal ruler on the other. Clan manipulation backfired as it disrupted the age-old balance between the clans and prompted defensive clan mobilization and resistance, which was fed in turn by the weaponisation of the Somali environment initiated by the regime; the inability of the state to defend its monopolization of weaponry contributed in turn to the democratization of the means of violence, eventually bringing down both the state and regime. Irredentism abroad and repression at home alienated first one and then the other set of foreign patrons. Nothing speaks more eloquently (or ironically) to the failure of Siyad than the progression from Somali irredentism itself articulated to a poorly cemented nationalism and clan-dominated social structure to the breakup of the Somali nation, from the dream of 'Greater Somalia' to the reality today of 'micro-Somalias'. Siyad's difficulties in rationalizing the various sources from which he extracted his power (and this is perhaps typical of the manipulativeness of personal rule) contributed to the incoherence and eventually the collapse of his regime.

Notes

1. See Nelson 1982; Kaplan et al. 1977:187; also interviews with several former Somali military officers

2. Interviews with ex-soldiers Mohamed Abokor and Hassan Sabriye in Mogadishu, 27 July 1991.

3. Nevertheless, with regard to the timing, Somali cynics circulated an underground joke saying that it took the 1973 world oil crisis to shake Siyad into discovering his identity as an Arab!

4. This included the arrest in April 1970 of the vice-president of the SRC and the commander of the police forces, General Jama Ali Korshell, and the executions in 1971 of another vice-president of the SRC, General Mohamed Ainashe, as well as SRC member and minister of public works Salad Gobayre and Abdilkadr Deel, a former army colonel.

5. In late 1975 or early 1976, as result of this sudden policy shift, I was sent, with a colleague, to Cuba and the USSR to study methods for forming vanguard parties.

6. Interview with Colonel Abdillahi Kahin, Toronto, 1 and 3 August 1992. Colonel Kahin served as director of finance and administration for the Ministry of Defense for the period 1977-87.

7. Interview with General Abokor, Washington DC, 15 October 1992. Abokor had served military attaché to both Washington and Paris.

8. Interview with Colonel Kahin, *op.cit.*

9. For this and the following information on army weaponry and equipment, see Nelson 1982: 231175.

10. Interview with Mahamed Nero, former official of the Ministry of Higher Education and Culture, Mogadishu, 6 August 1991.

11. This view was expressed during interviews with several military person at home and abroad.

12. Colonel Abdillahi Kahin recalled this date for me; later on it was reconfirmed in conversations with Colonel Omar Farah, Colonel Omar Nur and General Abokor, *op. cit.*

13. Interview with Colonel Farah, *op.cit.*

14. Interview with General Abokor, *op. cit.*

15. This massacre was confirmed in interview with several eyewitnesses in Mogadishu, 25 July 1991.

16. Historically, these traditions have been quite prominent in the cultures of the Horn. The Afar of Djibouti and Ethiopia, for example, have women performing cultural dances bearing sharp swords and knives. For the Somalis of Afgoi near Mogadishu, the seasonal new year (*dabshid*) is celebrated in a festival consisting of a mock battle between groups of men from both sides of the river, which would become quite bloody. Traditionally, Somalis have divided society into a majority of warriors (warranle) and men of religion (wadad). Military prowess was rewarded, for among nomads force or the potential for exerting force usually decided whether equality and justice would prevail. In essence war was democratic: because the entire group was responsible for paying blood money or diya to compensate for its losses, war began only with the unanimous approval of its participants. Under the Imam Ahmed Gurey and others, Somalis evolved traditions of waging wars or jihads against Christian highland rulers of Abyssina and later against the forces of colonialism. The most important anti-colonial jihad was led by the Dervish forces of Sayyid Mohamed Abdullah Hassan against British, Italian and Ethiopian colonial expansion from 1899 until his death in 1920. In the rapid deterioration of his initially inspiring and creative leadership, the construction of a destructive personality cult and fanatical dictatorship, and his exacerbation of clan and religious conflicts among the Somali people, some have seen suggestive historical parallels between the Sayyid and Siyad.

17. Interview with former chairman of SNM Central Committee, Ibrahim Meygag Samatar, Washington DC, 23 February 1991.

18. Talk given by Burao conference participant Ali Khalif Galied, ASA Annual Meeting, St. Louis, Missouri, November 1991.
19. Putnam and Nour 1993:4. Recent surveys by the International Committee of the Red Cross estimate that 500,000 Somali refugees have entered Ethiopia, while 250,000 have entered Kenya and a further 90,000 and 65,000 have taken refuge in Djibouti and Yemen respectively.
20. Interview with Ismail Hureh, SNM, in Hargeisa, 2 July `99`, and Colonel Khalif Sheikh Yusuf in Mogadishu, 3 August 1991.
21. It must be noted, however, that there arc parts of the south that enjoy relative stability and security. There is a respected leadership presiding over the activities of the SSDF-controlled north-eastern regions.
22. Interview with Colonel Khalif Sheikh Yusuf, op. cit.
23. Interview with Dr. L. Kapungu of UNOSOM, Toronto, 26 February 1994. See also Horn of Africa Bulletin (HAB) 6(1), January- February 1994:16.

References

Adam, Hussein M., 1980, *The Revolutionary Development of the Somali Language*, Los Angeles, Occasional Paper no. 20 for the African Studies Center, University of California.

Africa Watch, 1990, "Somalia: A Government at War with Its Own People: Testimony about the Killings and the Conflict in the North", London, *Africa Watch* Committee, January.

Aronson, Dan R., 1980, "Kinsmen and comrades: towards a class analysis of the Somali pastoral sector", *Nomadic Peoples* 7, November.

Bongartz, Maria, 1991, *The Civil War in Somalia*, Uppsala: Nordiska Afrikainstitute.

Campagnon, Daniel, 1991, "Somalie," in Jean-Fancois Bayart (ed.), *Etats d'Afrique Npore*, Paris, Editions Karthala.

Chazan, Naomi, *et al.*, 1988, *Politics and Society in Contemporary Africa*, Boulder, Lynne Rienner.

Drysdale, John, 1991, *Somaliland: The Anatomy of a Secession*.

Farer, Tom, 1976, *War Clouds on the Horn of Africa: A Crisis for Détente*, New York, Carnegie Endowment for International Peace.

Galaydh, Ali Khalif, 1990, "Notes on the state of the Somali state", *Horn of Africa* XIII (1 and 2), January-March and April-June.

Greenfield, Richard, 1987a, "Somalia's letter of death," *New African*, July.

Greenfield, Richard, 1987b, "Somalia: an anti Issaq plan", *Indian Ocean Newsletter* 283,2 May.

Hutchful, Eboe, 1986, "New elements in militarism: Ethiopia, Ghana and Burkina", *International Journal* XLI, Autumn.

Hutchful, Eboe, 1989, "Military and Militarism in Africa: A Research Agenda," Dakar, CODESRIA Working Paper 3/89.

Jackson, Robert, and Roseberg, Carl, 1982, *Personal Rule in Black Africa*, Berkeley: University of California Press.

Kaplan, I., 1977, *Area Handbook for Somalia*, Washington DC, GPO for Foreign Area Studies, The American University.

Laitin, David, 1976, "The political economy of military rule in Somalia", *Journal of Modern African Studies* 14(3).

Laitin, David, 1979, "Somalia's military government and scientific socialism", in Carl Roseberg and Thomas Callaghy, Socialism *in Sub-Saharan Africa: A New Assessment*, Berkeley, University of California Press.

Laitin, David, and Samatar, Said S., 1987, *Somalia: Nation in Search of a State*, Boulder, Westview Press.

Lewis, I.M., 1961, *A Pastoral Democracy*, London, Oxford University Press.

Lewis, I.M., 1979, "The politics of the 1969 Somali coup," *Journal of Modern African Studies* 10(3).

Lewis, I.M., 1980, *A Modern History of Somalia: Nation and State in the Horn of Africa*, London: Longman.

Lewis, I.M., 1990, :The Ogaden and the fragility of Somali segmentary nationalism", *Horn of Africa* XIII (1 and 2), January-March and April-June.

Mehmet, O., 1971, "Effectiveness of foreign aid: the case of Somalia", *Journal of Modern African Studies* IX(1).

Nelson, Harold D.(ed.), 1982, *Somalia: A Country Study*, Washington DC, Foreign Area Studies, American University.

Pestalozza, Luigi, 1974, *The Somalian Revolution*, Paris, Societe d' editions Afrique, Asie, Amerique Latine.

Putnam, Diana B., and Nour, Mohamood, 1993, *The Somalis. Their History and Culture*, Washington DC, Refugee Service Center, October.

Rajagopal, B., and Carroll, Anthony J., 1992, "The case for the independent statehood of Somaliland", Washington DC, unpublished manuscript.

Samatar, Abdi, 1989, *The State and Rural Transformation in Northern Somalia*, 1884-1986, Madison, University of Wisconsin Press.

Saul, John, 1979, *The State and Revolution in Eastern Africa*, New York, Monthly Review Press.

Swift, Jeremy, 1979, "The development of livestock trading in a nomad pastoral economy: the Somali case," in *Pastoral Production and Society*, Cambridge, Cambridge University Press.

Touval, Saadia, 1963, *Somali Nationalism*, Cambridge, MA: Harvard University Press.

Young, Crawford, 1986, "Africa's colonial legacy", in Robert Berg and Jennifer Whitaker (eds.), *Strategies for African Development*, Los Angeles, University of California Press.

CHAPTER 3

SOMALI CIVIL WARS

In January 1991, Somalia experienced a cataclysmic event, virtually unheard of since the Second World War. For most of Asia, Latin America, and Africa in particular, this period was one of nation- and state-building. By contrast, Somalia witnessed complete state collapse. It saw not simply a military coup, a revolutionary replacement of a decayed and ineffective dictatorship, or a new, radical regime coming to power through a partisan uprising. Somalia's collapsed state represented the literal implosion of state structures and of residual forms of authority and legitimacy.[1] Liberia experienced partial state collapse, and in Rwanda, the rebellious Tutsis replaced by the decayed, genocidal Hutu dictatorship. In the former Yugoslavia, a relatively "hard" state – Serbia – preys on neighboring "soft" states such as Bosnia, Croatia, and Slovenia.

Not many years ago, the Horn of Africa was considered to have a high risk of interstate war, notably between Somalia and Ethiopia.[2] During recent years, an explosion of intra-state wars has led to a radical ethnic restructuring of the Ethiopian state and the total collapse of the Somali state. Somalia has experienced civil strife before – in limited clan wars described in Somali poetry, in the interstate and intra-state wars of the sixteenth century briefly discussed below, and in the Islamic anti-colonial *jihad* led by Sayyid Muhamed Abdallah Hassan, 1899-1920. Sayyid's Dervish movement began as a pan-clan crusade against British, Italian, and Ethiopian forces, but it soon degenerated into intra-clan warfare as well as intra-elite theological differences. The resulting man-made famine exacerbated environmental problems and weakened Somali societies, especially in the northwest and northeast. Unlike the American Civil War, fought by two relatively conventional armies, the current Somali civil violence has taken the form of a series of civil wars, beginning around 1980 in armed opposition to the clan-based military dictatorship under Major-General Mohamed Siyad Barre. The state collapsed as the decentralized, clan-based opposition groups failed to form governing coalitions. Since conflict among the victors of 1991 unleashed a series of civil wars, "Somali civil wars" is a more appropriate description of the current catastrophe. What has distinguished them from earlier ones has been the abundance of destructive modern armaments. "Weapons were sometimes cheaper than ammunition."[4]

The Somali population of eight to ten million is made up of five major clan-families (Darod, Dir, Hawiye, Isaq, Digil and Mirifle), each subdivided into six or more clans, and each clan, into subclans and sub-subclans, and the way down to lineages and extended families. Given concentric and interconnected circles, with kaleidoscopic and diffuse attachments, the most stable subunit is the lineage, consisting of close kin who together pay and receive blood compensation in cases involving homicide. In general, the Somali people share a common language (Somali), religion (Islam), physical characteristics, and pastoral and agropastoral customs and traditions.[5] There is, however, a difference between the Somali dialect spoken by the Digil/Mirifle agropastoralists and the other four, predominantly pastoral clan-families.

Clanism is the Somali version of ethnicity or tribalism: it represents primordial cleavages and cultural fragmentation within Somali society. After the Second World War, clanism among Somalis favored nationalism and a Greater Somalia. At times, however, it has assumed a negative aspect – the abandonment of objectivity when clan and local/parochial interests have prevailed. Clan consciousness is partly a product of elite manipulation – the cooptation and corruption of politicians claiming clan leadership[6] – but at times it is the elite itself, that is manipulated by politicized clanism.

Aspects of clan consciousness, transcending false consciousness, reflect a plea for social justice and against exploitative relations among ethnic groups. Uneven class formation has led certain groups to use clan formations as embryonic trade unions. In such cases, affirmative action-type policies are the best way to overcome discrimination against clans and groups. Clan consciousness tends to rise during periods of extreme scarcities – drought, famine, wars. Clan conflicts are also instigated by memories of past wars for resources or for prestige. However, such disputes take place only between neighboring clans, and intricate mechanisms have evolved for conflict resolution, because clan territory is often extensive and sometimes even non-contiguous. By far the greatest damage brought about by clan conflicts spread over large geographical areas has resulted from cynical elite/class manipulation of clan consciousness.

The thesis of this chapter is that deep historical, structural factors – a mismatch between the state and the relatively non-hierarchical Somali civil society – are the underlying cause of the Somali catastrophe. While rooted in historical, socio-economic structures of society, including such factors as ethnic/clan cleavages, the Somali civil wars were the immediate result of the Siyad military regime's style of governance. Its cynical manipulation of these cleavages led bad governance to overwhelm historical, structural factors.

ROOT CAUSES: DOMESTIC FACTORS

For purposes of this study, "civil war" means "large-scale violence among geographically contiguous people concerned about possibly having to live with one another in the same political unit after the fight."[7] It has ended when "the level of violence had dropped below the Small-Singer threshold of 1,000 battle deaths per year for at least five years."[8]

As in most of Africa,[9] the tangible cause of Somalia's civil wars derives from a militarist state and its brutal repression of a vibrant social reality. In a deeper, historical sense, the state's collapse represents a classic mismatch between the post-colonial state and the nature and structure of civil society. In the real world, the conceptual separation between the state and civil society is blurred, though I keep it in this context for purposes of analysis. Imperialism began the commercialization of Somali pastoralism, its subordination to centralized states, and its integration into the global economy.[10] The post-independence parliamentary regime (1960-69) favored the emerging commercial and bureaucratic petty bourgeoisie as it facilitated political marginalization of the pastoralists and cultivators.

The Cold War sustained Siyad's military regime, which kidnapped the emerging state in 1969 and moved on to centralize power, as well as the means of coercion. Siyad used a narrow clan base while condemning and denying political space for other clan bases. In due course, decentralized, clan-based, armed opposition groups rose up to challenge his military dictatorship. The end of the Cold War reduced, even severely limited in some cases, the opportunities for states "suspended" over their civil societies from extracting adequate military, technical, and financial resources from external sources. Somalia became the perfect illustration of this basic contradiction and its collapse, precisely because the Cold War had imposed an exceedingly heavy military regime on decentralized, relatively democratic civil society, surviving on meager resources.

Unlike the rest of Africa during the 1960s, Somalia seemed to be a "nation" in search of a "state."[11] Colonial partitions had dismembered the Somali-speaking people into British, Italian, and French (Djibouti) and Ethiopian Somalilands. British Somaliland obtained independence on 26 June 1960 and voluntarily joined Italian Somaliland to form the Somali Republic on 1 July 1960. The young and fragile republic set out to unite with the three remaining Somali territories.[12]

Even though the potential for irredentism in Africa is relatively high, independent Somalia turned out to be the only consistently irredentist state. In 1963, it encouraged and supported an uprising in Kenya's NFD. In 1964, the Ethiopian army attacked several Somali border posts to dissuade Somalia from supporting a guerrilla uprising within the Ogaden. The relatively pro-Western Somali parliamentary regime turned to the USSR to increase its army from 3,000 to 10,000. On 21 October 1969, Somali military commander Mohamed Siyad Barre overthrew the "artificial democracy" (multi-party parliamentary regime) and instituted a military and personal dictatorship with Soviet support. He increased the army to 37,000 and sought in 1977 to reclaim the Ogaden in a major war with Ethiopia. Ironically, what began as the search to establish a state corresponding with the greater Somali nation ended up with the total collapse and fragmentation of the existing Somali state in January 1991.

Beyond noting the mismatch between the state and civil society, we need to analyze Siyad's military regime, its repressive mechanisms, and its errors of policy and conduct. By re-emphasizing the primacy of political factors over purely historical/structural ones, I am defending the possibility that Somalis can (partly) determine their future beyond the civil wars through careful political choices. Siyad's socialistic measures, including radical nationalizations, were a disincentive for rural producers, especially farmers. Somalia came to produce less and less of its basic food needs and to rely increasingly on imported foods. Constrained domestic economic opportunities intensified the sense of grievance among social groups, especially those suffering clan/regional discrimination.

Like many other African leaders, Siyad installed personal rule.[14] Over time, he was able to manipulate and modify his leadership style, from being a prophetic ruler advocating "scientific socialism" (1970-77), to an autocrat (1978-86), and finally a tyrant (1987-91). During his earlier years, he used mediatory mechanisms that postponed final confrontations, but his prolonged dictatorial rule damaged and distorted state-civil society relations. Later, as an outright tyrant, he applied absolute principles of governance, irrespective of human cost.

Siyad's dictatorial rule did not function in an institutional vacuum. The Somali military structure was considered one of the best in sub-Saharan Africa,[15] and Siyad also understood the importance of controlling other state sectors and civil society through institutions and organizations such as the military, security, paramilitary, an elitist vanguard political party, and so-called mass organizations. As a personal ruler, he had the autonomy to operate above institutions. Ultimately, however, arbitrary personal rule destroys supportive military and related institutions.

Nomenklatura involves appointing loyal political agents to guide and control civil and military institutions. The introduction of *nomenkalatura* to Somalia by the Soviets involved politicization of institutions that were beginning to function well, relying on education and training, technical competence, specialization, and experience. As early as 1972, the military regime began to appoint political commissars for the armed forces, administrative institutions, social organizations of workers, youth, and women, and cooperatives.

Siyad soon substituted clanism for socialist rhetorics as criteria for such appointments. Foreign aid provided the glue that held the system together in spite of internal waste and corruption ("selective misallocation"). "ClanKlatura" involved placing trusted clansmen and other loyalists in positions of power, wealth, and control/espionage. It also involved creating "clan-klatura" organizations. One such body, Hangash, conducted military intelligence; the Dabarjebinta, literally, the backbone breakers, were military counterintelligence; then there were the military police, identified by their red berets. The majority of these forces were drawn from the president's clan, the Marehan of the Darod clan-family. In such a situation of divide and rule, state institutions were thrown into gridlock, jealousy, confusion, and anarchy.

From its inception, the regime rested on three clans from the Darod clan-family. Lewis describes how this background was "reflected in the clandestine code name 'M.O.D.' given to the regime."[16] "M (Marehan) stood for the patrilineage of the President, O (Ogaden) for that of his mother, and D (Dulbahante) for that of his principal son-in-law, head of the National Security Service. ... [Though] no one could utter the secret symbol of General Siyad's power openly, the M.O.D. basis of his rule was public knowledge and discussed and criticized in private."[17]

After he dropped "scientific socialism" as his guiding ideology, Siyad did not resort to Islam, as did Numeiri in Sudan. Atavistically, he resorted to clanism. Hardly any members of his clan gained strong bourgeois roots during his long rule – not educational qualifications, economic know-how, or professional competence. Promising clan members were plucked out of educational institutions to fill "clan-klatura" posts. Siyad systematically sought to destroy the bourgeois elements of other clans – sending people to jail or to exile abroad. The damage done to the Somali elite class partly explains both the eventual state collapse and the delay in its renewal.

The "clan-klatura" havoc within state institutions was exported into rural civil societies. After the Ogaden War (1977-78), Siyad practiced brutal divide and rule, encouraging clan warfare. At first he used his army to conduct punitive raids, similar to those under early colonial rule. Later his troops armed so-called loyal clans and encouraged them to wage wars against "rebel" clans. The damage caused by negative and destructive elite manipulation of clan consciousness contributed to the inability of civil society to rebound when Siyad fell from power. It will take years to heal these socictal wounds.

Young people began to disappear during the early 1980s from regional cities such as Hargeisa in the north, considered rebel territory. This phenomenon, reminiscent of Argentina, continued in other towns, then spread to the capital city, Mogadishu. During 1989 and 1990, Siyad's "caln-klatura" forces massacred hundreds of religious protestors. In July 1989, Siyad's terror squads randomly rounded up and slaughtered on the isolated Jezira Beach (near Mogadishu) a group of forty-seven young northern (Isaq clan-family) youths. Once the armed opposition to the regime grew, Siyad singled out the northern region, inhabited by the Isaq clan-family, for extra-ordinary, some say neofascist punishment. Perhaps he hoped to unite the south by punishing the north and the Isaq-based Somali National Movement. Previously the conflict between the north and the south generated low-intensity demands for distributional benefits from within a unified political system; however, vindictive warfare led to the current high intensity demand for separate statehood and independence for Somaliland once Siyad's state collapsed. A similar vendetta awaited Hawiye clans, raising a 1989 rebellion across the country. Siyad's vindictive state terror laid the basis for civil wars of revenge that postponed civil society's ability to create a successor state.

Siyad's clan persecutions obliged the opposition to use its own clans as organizational bases for armed resistance. The first clan-based armed opposition group seems to have stumbled into existence. After failing in an anti-Siyad coup attempt in 1978, Colonel Abdullahi Yusuf fled to Ethiopia, where he established the Somali Salvation Democratic Front (SSDF). The front attracted support mostly from his subclan of the Majerteen clan (another part of the Darod clan-family that spawned Siyad). The SSDF, following a burst of cross border activities, atrophied as a result of heavy reliance on foreign funding from Libya, Abdullahi Yusuf's dictatorial leadership, and Siyad's ability to appease many of the Majerteens as fellow cousins within the Darod clan-family. Eventually, with funds and clan appeals, he was able to entice the bulk of SSDF fighters to return from Ethiopia and participate in his genocidal wars against the Isaq in the north and later against the Hawiye in the south, including Mogadishu. More recently (following Siyad's fall) the SSDF has claimed control of the Bari, Nugal, and parts of Mudug (northeast) regions, under the combined leadership of Mohamed Abshir and Abdullahi Yusuf.

The major opposition clan grouping was the Somali National Movement (SNM), which derived its main support from the Isaq clan-family of the north. The SNM was established in London early in 1981but soon decided to move its operations to Ethiopia's Somali towns and villages close to the border with former British Somaliland. Because Qadhafi disliked SNM leaders and would not finance their movement, they were obliged to raise funds among the Somali Isaq communities in Saudi Arabia and the Gulf, in other Arab states, in East Africa, and in Western countries. This decentralized method of fund-raising gave the movement relative independence: it also enhanced accountability to its numerous sup-porters. The SNM evolved democratic procedures. Between 1981 and 1991 it held about six congresses, during which it periodically elected leaders and established policies. In 1988, the SNM conducted several raids and a major military operation in northern Somalia, fol-lowing a peace accord between Ethiopia and Somalia that removed Ethiopian restraints on SNM operations. The SNM was able to bottle up Siyad's huge army, barricaded in towns and bases, for the next two years. The SNM played an indirect role in the formation of the United Somali Congress (USC), an armed movement based on the Hawiye clan-family that inhabits the central regions of the country, including Mogadishu. It also facilitated formation of the Somali Patriotic Movement (SPM) by Colonel Omar Jess and other disgruntled Ogadeni officers from Siyad's army.

The proliferation of proto-political groups or factions is related to the expansion and duration of Somali civil wars. The term "faction" may be useful when discussing the political groupings, leaving "clan" for a specific "ethnic" or "kinship" community. Some of the newer groups – the SDM, SNU and SAMO – represent Rahanwin, Benadir, and Bantu farmers, respectively, who have suffered dispro-portionately because of the civil wars. Somalia's shape and size – as big as Texas – ensured the existence of remote regions, strengthening armed resistance forces and worsening the problems of the regime in spite of its huge army. The armed opposition did not emerge for over a decade, as most Somalis hoped that the regime would allow room for peaceful protest. But once the government decided to respond through the use of military force, the factions were easily able to gain access to arms. The availability of arms enabled repressed groups demanding participation in the state to resort to war. To combat clan-based armed opposition groups, the regime created loyal clan militias, thereby heightening the carnage and disseminating modern armaments and the culture of violence.[18] The total collapse in 1991 of the over 300,000-strong Ethiopian army flooded the local markets with huge amounts of modern armaments and ammunition.

CONTRIBUTING CAUSES: INTERNATIONAL FACTORS

Military, technical, and financial foreign assistance played a key role in prolonging Siyad's regime. Somalia's position on the Red Sea and the Indian Ocean has long attracted foreign interests. Early in Siyad's rule, the USSR provided substantial military and economic assistance, including fuel and financing for project local costs that helped cushion the Somali economy against international economic conditions. After 1977, the United States replaced the Soviets in providing armaments – unlike the Russians, sending mostly defensive arms – and, during the 1980s, about $100 million of economic aid per year.[19] China invested in a series of remarkable projects, including the north-south tarmac road, a cigarette and match factory, a sports and theatre complex, and rice and tobacco farms. It also provided light arms and spare parts.

The military dictatorship also benefited from significant financial assistance from the United Nations system and the World Bank. Siyad manoeuvred Somalia into the Arab League in 1974, and the regime received generous Arab petrodollar assistance. There was, for example, "an alleged unofficial transfer of substantial sums of money from Saudi Arabia to the Somali government in mid-1990 to ensure that [Siyad] Barre did not side with Iraq."[20] As long as resources did not dry up, Siyad was able to hold on to power. But U.S. congressional criticism of Siyad's human rights record, made dramatic and visible by the war in the north, led to the suspension of American military aid in 1988. IN 1989 U.S. economic aid, too, was blocked, and other states and international organizations began to follow suit. The regime collapsed in January 1991.

In the world after the Cold War, internal protests and pressures from external donors can facilitate non-violent transitions in regimes, without engendering state collapse. An abrupt stoppage of all aid to Somalia after the regime collapsed followed a history of too much aid. Modest assistance might have facilitated the formation of a flexible interim administration. In Somalia, international intervention missed the window of opportunity framed by the rising rebellion in the north in the 1980s, the outbreak of urban opposition in 1988-89, and immediate post-Siyad clan warfare in 1991.[21]

International actors helped to worsen state-society relationship in Somalia; their military, technical, and economic aid encouraged the dictatorship to believe that, because of foreign backing, it was capable of imposing its will on society. In spite of losing Soviet military and economic aid in 1977, Somalia continued to receive military aid from the United States, Libya, France, Egypt, Italy, and China.[22] The regime had reason to believe that, with such foreign backing, it could proceed against the opposition with impunity. As in all of Africa's wars, foreign involvement unquestionably raised the level and scope of violence. The armed resistance found shelter in the vast Somali-speaking population of Ethiopia. Ethiopian President Mengistu was only too happy to receive it and provide it with initial armaments and broadcast facilities. He saw this as an opportunity to take revenge against Siyad's irredentist incursion into the Ogaden in 1977. Libya assisted the SSDF with arms and finances but later switched to the side of the dying Siyad regime. Facilitated by the disintegration of Somalia and by Ethiopia's backing, the armed opposition groups managed in time to obtain automatic weapons, ample supplies of ammunition, and anti-tank as well as anti-aircraft weapons from local markets.

COST OF SOMALI CIVIL WARS

In 1977, the ruling cliques in Somalia and Ethiopia plunged their impoverished countries into "the most ferocious [conflict] in Africa since World War II".[23] The Siyad regime failed to recognize both American reluctance and Soviet-Cuban readiness to get fully involved in the conflict. This misunderstanding led Siyad to terminate the Treaty of Friendship of 1974 with the Soviet Union and to break diplomatic relations with Cuba. Soon after the Ogaden debacle, Somalia witnessed the commencement of a series of civil wars. During the Somali-Ethiopian War, Somalia is estimated to have sustained a death toll of 25,000 and, following the war, to have received a crushing burden of 700,000 Ethiopian Somali and Oromo refugees.[24] A coup attempt by officers of a Majerteen (Darod) subclan was foiled on 9 April 1978.

In 1979-80, the SSDF made modest guerrilla forays into Somalia. Siyad retaliated by imprisoning some Majerteen military and civilian leaders and dismissing many others from their jobs. He declared open war on the Majerteen subclan of Abdullahi Yusuf; his army looted its camels, destroyed it's *berkeds* (water reservoirs), and confiscated its ordinary arms. In 1981, some members of the Isaq clanfamily formed the Somali National Movement (SNM) and began similar guerrilla forays into northern Somalia. In 1986 Mengistu and Siyad met in Djibouti and began to work out a deal to rein in armed opposition movements directed against each other's territories. Nevertheless, Mengistu looked the other way as the SNM launched a massive attack on government forces in Burao on 27 May 1988 and in Hargeisa on 31 May 1988. Frustrated by efforts to defeat the SNM in direct combat, Siyad's army turned its fire-power, including its air force and artillery, against the civilian population, causing predictably high casualties. Even in those towns spared of SNM attacks, the army engaged in looting on a massive scale; women were raped as hundreds of people were shot and their homes and businesses ransacked. Africa Watch estimates "the number of people killed by government forces in the vicinity of 50,000. The war has caused over 400,000 refugees to flee, principally to Ethiopia. Another 40,000 refugees were in Djibouti, and tens of thousands have gone to stay with relatives in Mogadishu, the capital, or escaped to the United Kingdom, Holland and Canada. In addition, close to 400,000 people ... are displaced within the Somali countryside, living without any international assistance."[25]

The policy of blanket punishment of innocent "potential" opposition supporters and bystanders continued during the next four years. These measures laid the basis for clan revenge practices as the raw armed youth – the so called *moryaan* – entered Mogadishu and other towns as the new victors of the anti-Siyad resistance movements. This attack on innocent civilians was but one aspect of the overall policy of poisoning clan relations. In the north, for example, following the 1988 crisis, the regime intensified its policy of recruiting and forcibly conscripting refugees from the Ogaden (Somalis and Oromos). It also financed and armed paramilitary groups among the refugees, using these as a fighting force against the Isaq. Prior to the fall of Mogadishu, Siyad ordered loyal Darod officers to persecute and even massacre Hawiye "sympathizers" of the opposition movement, the USC. In a primordial society, the anticipated reaction followed, as most of the Darod communities had to flee Mogadishu following Siyad's overthrow by the Hawiye-based USC.

At stated above, clan political identities in Somali society are in a state of constant flux. As soon as Mogadishu was "liberated," personal political ambition and personal differences between USC leaders Ali Mahdi (Abgal clan of the Hawiye) and General Mohamed Farah Aidid (Habar Gedir clan) began to surface. It is alleged that the Italian ambassador, Mario Sico (considered highly pro-Siyad), encouraged businessman Ali Mahdi to declare himself "interim president," as Aidid was busy pushing Siyad's remaining forces south of Mogadishu.[26] Aidid's faction of the USC rejected Mahdi's claim, as did the SNM, the SSDF, and other opposition groups. In June, a USC congress elected Aidid chairman in an attempt to get him to accept Mahdi's self-declared position as long as the interim president consulted with the USC's chairman in all major policy decisions and appointments.

The attempt at reconciliation did not receive solid international backing (the UN and diplomatic missions had all left Mogadishu by early 1991), and it failed. Intra-clan fighting resumed in Mogadishu, between Habar Gedir and Abgal rivals. This intra-USC conflict reduced Mogadishu to another Beirut, complete with a dangerous "green line."

The SNM supported northern Somalia's decision of May 1991 to establish its region as Somaliland, which added yet another complicated layer to the costs of Somali civil wars. Unfair measures experienced by the north since the 1960 unification, coupled with the savage punishment meted the north by Siyad's formidable military machine, led to the relatively popular decision to dissolve the union of 1960 and declare a Somaliland Republic in May 1991. Ali Mahdi's "grab for power" was seen as a most recent example of "southern arrogance."

Perhaps the most complicated and tragic aspect of Somali civil wars occurred in the southern, more fertile parts of the country. Siyad Barre, unlike Mengistu, did not leave Somalia following his retreat from Mogadishu. He barricaded himself in his clan homeland, on the Somali-Ethiopian frontier, southwest of Mogadishu. From this base, he waged a Renamo-type spoiler war in surrounding areas and launched at least two serious military campaigns to recapture Mogadishu. He failed, the second time in May 1992 disastrously, and had to flee into Kenya with Aidid's forces in hot pursuit. He went into political asylum in Nigeria, where he died on 2 January 1995.

Andrew Natsios sums up the impact of Somalia's civil wars on both farming/livestock activities and access for relief efforts: "Hardest hit by these two deadly circumstances was the area between the Juba River and the Shebeli River further north. This interriverine area contains the country's richest agriculture land and serves as its breadbasket. The area is inhabited by the Bantu and Benadir people who are outside the caln structure and by the Rahanwin clan; ... Rahanwin and Bantu farmers were caught in the clan feud between Darod and Hawiye ... Barre's retreating troops targeted the Rahanwin for massacre. These warring clans took, then lost, and took again this farming area from each other: each time the area changed hands the supplies of food dwindled."[28]

As of June 1995, the UN estimated that some 4.5 million people (in a country of about 8 – 10 million) were in urgent need of food.[29] By 1992, it was believed that about 400,000 people had died of famine or disease or been killed in the war.[30] That number steadily climbed towards one million. Relief organizations estimated that by early 1993 one-half of all Somali children under five had died.[31] In the 1991-92 civil war-induced famine, most fatalities resulted from malnutrition-related diseases. "Of the estimated seventy hospitals in Somalia in 1988, only fifteen remain partially operational today, and are totally dependent on external assistance."[32] A study by the U.S. Centers for Disease Control showed that in the city of Baidoa, the centre of Rahanwin communities, at least 40 per cent of the population had died between August and November 1992.[33]

Thus an anatomy of Somali civil wars reveals multiple problems that appear as a single problem in other countries. Since 1984, indiscriminate use of land-mines became a central feature of the army's counterinsurgency policy against the SNM. Somaliland is reported to have inherited at least a million mines, which have maimed and handicapped thousands, especially women and children.[34] It was also estimated that over fifty thousand modern weapons had been abandoned by the army as the civil war reached its peak in January 1991. Militias of stronger, better armed clans and subclans – and opportunistic criminal bands – preyed on weaker groups, causing large-scale transfers of assets as well as protracted insecurity, during which consecutive planting seasons were missed. Food became an instrument of war as thousands perished because of anarchy and the corresponding inability to contain epidemics. War is highly destructive of wildlife, and Siyad made matters worse by financing ivory-smuggling bandits who roamed as far as Kenya to raise funds to fuel his wars. Complete herds were eliminated with machine-guns and even anti-aircraft guns mounted on vehicles. Desperate escapes, especially by the unarmed farming and ancient coastal-city minorities (both outside the Somali clan structure), gave Somalia its own boat people. During 1991-92, frantic refugees in overcrowded, rickety boats sought asylum in Yemen or Kenya, and dozens perished in the sea.

AFTER SIYAD: PROBLEMS AND PROSPECTS

The long-term costs of Somali civil wars and delays in the restoration of the Somali cultures and societies are largely unresearched, but of great significance. In education, for example, Somalia is already losing generations. The visible collapse of the state has lasted over a decade: Somalia has no internationally recognized polity; no national administration exercising real authority; no formal legal system; no banking and insurance services; no telephone and postal system; no public service; no educational and reliable health system; no police and public security services; no electricity or piped water systems; and weak officials serving on a voluntary basis, surrounded by disruptive, violent bands of armed youths. Unlike in Liberia, where the capital at no point fell into rebel hands, chaos and anarchy engulfed Mogadishu. In most of Africa, countries with weak but nominal authorities in the capital city endured civil wars that caused state retraction, but not total collapse. Most states have begun to refuse Somali passports as valid documents. Thus Somalis today, as Eritreans yesterday (who used Somali passports), have to rely on Ethiopian, Kenyan, Yemeni, or Eritrean passports in order to travel abroad!

Writings on the Somali crisis have focused exclusively on the negative aspects of state collapse and militarism. There are, however, certain redeeming features, which, if handled creatively, would facilitate emergence in Somalia of a restored state (or states) that is (are) more indigenous and sustainable than the colonial and Cold War states of the past. There is growing strength in Somali civil society, essentially because the state has collapsed. In the north, and in areas of the country that did not require intervention of foreign troops, the role of "traditional elders" (both secular and religious) has been both visible and positive. Women leaders have also been active, and women and children constituted a majority in demonstrations for disarmament and peace. Throughout the crisis, professionals, especially doctors and nurses who stayed in the country, have served as positive role models. Teachers have begun to revive rudimentary forms of schooling in urban areas.

As an aspect of civil society's strength, the private sector has become revitalized. Gone were the so-called socialistic restrictions imposed by the dictatorship. The thriving, small-scale private sector (in both the north and Mogadishu) has moved far ahead of embryonic regulatory authorities. In most parts of Africa, the state pulls or constrains civil society; in Somalia the embryonic state is challenged to keep up with a dynamic, small private sector. In 1988 there were eighteen Somali voluntary development organizations (VDOS);

now the number has grown, and these bodies need help from international VDOS to enhance the non-profit private sector.

There is a palpable spirit of anti-centralism, an atmosphere favoring local autonomy, regionalism, and federalism – and in the north, self-determination and secession. As a corollary, there is a preference for locally controlled police forces rather than a large, standing central army. In Somaliland, and to some extent north-eastern Somalia, there are embryonic manifestations of consociational democratic mechanisms, involving consensus, proportionality, and avoidance of winner-take-all confrontations. Somali irredentism has collapsed with Siyad, and in its place one finds broad cooperation and relative harmony between Somalia and Ethiopia. There is also a vibrant, emerging free press – about six papers in Hargeisa and more than sixteen in Mogadishu. Printed in Somali, they are produced by computers and mimeograph machines. Somali minorities, farmers, and Benadir communities have become more self-conscious and willing to stand up for their rights as a result of bitter struggles. They have formed their own political organizations and militia for self protections, as indicated above.

Perhaps it is still too early to offer a meaningful analysis of the resolution of Somali's civil war. Employing Zartman's analysis, one might conclude that the conditions for "ripeness" and the readiness for conflict resolution have not yet emerged.[35] Based on other cases of civil war, resolutions to the conflicts can emerge under a remarkable variety of conditions.[36] In the following section we examine three attempts at resolution in Somalia since 1991: foreign intervention, strongman's hegemony, and consociational, democratic mechanisms.

With the departure of UNOSOM II troops in March 1995, it has become more obvious that Somali civil conflicts will have to be resolved internally by the parties themselves rather than through external intervention. At present, clan divisions and crude military balances seem to rule out resolution through conquest by a single armed strongman. However, if negotiated settlements continue to fail, the outcome, at least for a while longer, may be protracted, low-intensity conflicts, rather than resolution.

THE MIRAGE OF FOREIGN INTERVENTION

In 1992 and 1993, many people thought and hoped that massive foreign intervention would resolve Somalia's civil wars and help Somalis restore some semblance of state authority. In 1992, famine-related deaths in Baidoa (Bay region), peaked at 3,000 a week and declined to 1,700 and later to 500 or fewer when outgoing U.S. President George Bush ordered 36,000 troops, including 27,000 U.S. troops, to intervene under UN mandate as Operation Restore Hope (ORH) in December 1992.[37] Deaths reported by mid-1992 by the media and relief organizations galvanized pubic opinion around the world, causing Bush and the UN Security Council to act. By the summer of 1992, food prices had risen 800-1,200 per cent and relief food could not be adequately delivered on account of looting and banditry. ORH had a narrowly defined mission: to establish a secure environment in the so-called triangle of death (Mogadishu-Baidoa-Kismayu), which covers about 30 per cent of Somalia. The U.S. mission on behalf of the UN cost $2 billion by the time it ended in May 1993; it was followed by direct UN intervention (UNOSOM) from June 1993 till March 1995, at a cost of $4 billion.

What did the United States and UNOSOM achieve at such staggering financial costs? In the short run, perhaps one million people were saved from starvation. Thousands have resumed economic productivity, and Somalia has experienced bumper crops and lower food prices. In 1992, in contrast, "Somalia became the ICRC's largest relief effort since World War II, dwarfing all other NGO efforts combined in Somalia, consuming nearly fifty percent of the ICRC worldwide budget." To deliver food, the International Committee of the Red Cross (ICRC) reportedly hired over 20,000 Somali armed guards before ORH began. "While 465,000 Somali refugees remain in neighboring countries and another 300,000 remain internally displaced, this is down from the nearly two million people who were driven from their homes at the height of the crisis. Morbidity and mortality rates have returned to normal levels."[40] The reality is that the numbers of starving people and of deaths as a result of war have decreased dramatically following the U.S. and UN intervention, and besides relief being received, some progress has been made towards restoring local and regional administration.

However, a more compelling reality remains: despite tremendous cost in funds (and to some extent in lives), ORH and UNOSOM have failed to reduce the level of armaments to end the civil wars, to promote reconciliation, and facilitate restoration of a reconstructed Somali state (or states). In my view, part of the failure of foreign intervention transcends ORH and UNOSOM; it is failure in preventive diplomacy. The other cause is arrogance resulting from a residual Cold War, conventional-war mentality; lack of impartiality; and the lack of consistent, experienced diplomacy, equipped with local political, social, and cultural knowledge.

Former Algerian ambassador and OAU official Mohamed Sahnoun was appointed by UN Secretary-General Boutros Boutros-Ghali in April 1992 as head of UNOSOM I. Sahnoun argued that foreign intervention could have been more effective in preventing/resolving Somali civil wars in 1988, when the civil war violently erupted in northern Somalia; in 1990, when prominent civilians, risking jail terms, issued a democratic "Manifesto" against the Siyad regime; or in 1991, when the government in Djibouti called a peace conference following the fall of the Siyad regime.[41] ORH lasted from December 1992 till May 1993. Under the acronym UNOSOM II, the UN took charge of Somalia and very soon fell into a destructive war with General Mohamed Farah Aidid and his allies.[42] Aidid's militia was alleged to have killed twenty-four Pakistani UN troops on 5 June 1993, and Admiral Howe, head of UNOSOM, backed by Boutros-Ghali, declared war on Aidid and his supporters, as they sought to arrest him. From June to October 1993, this UN-sponsored and U.S.-backed manhunt put a hold on most of UNOSOM's work at reconciliation and reconstruction. In October, American helicopters were shot down, and, in one street fight alone, eighteen American soldiers were killed, one was captured, and over seventy-five were wounded. This event prompted U.S. President Bill Clinton to shift American policy back to diplomacy and politics, as he ordered an end to the manhunt. These events also caused the United States to ask the UN to reverse policies.[43] Among other things, these destructive engagements postponed the critical task of demobilizing Somalia's clan militias and promoting the political process. This conflict did show, however, that even when formal state sovereignty is lacking, civil society, or its parts, can exercise sovereignty. Following this conflict, the clamour for an "international trusteeship" to run Somalia evaporated.

The issue of disarmament also shows that UNOSOM lacked insight into the general situation. To have succeeded, ORH/UNOSOM disarmament strategy would have needed a demobilization program to provide job-training for the youthful militias; a serious program to train and equip local police forces; a program to equip and restore the legal justice system. On its own initiative, the northern Somaliland Republic has carried out demobilization programs, while UNOSOM failed to promote demobilization during its mandate in southern Somalia. U.S. forces in Somalia, unlike those in Haiti more recently, failed to include a civil affairs program to ensure the success of its military-oriented program. In addition to troops dealing with civil affairs, more than eight hundred police advisers were sent to Haiti.[44]

As early as January 1993, USOSOM wanted to push Somali elites to set up a juridical Somali state, oblivious of the fact that such pressures contributed to the prolongation of the civil wars. The Addis Ababa Conference of 15-27 March 1993 resisted pressure to form a centralized state and adopted a regional-autonomy approach, based on Somalia's eighteen regions (actually thirteen without the five northern regions). UNOSOM finally backed this plan and speeded up the process, especially after it freed its energies from the hunt for Aidid. As of 1994, UNOSOM had assisted in the formation of fifty-three district councils out of eighty-one (excluding Somaliland), and eight out of thirteen regional councils (again, excluding Somaliland).[45]

Obviously, circumstances did not allow massive foreign intervention a mediating role. Third-party intervention has been critical in providing relief but conspicuously ineffective in facilitating resolution on the conflicts – some Somalis argue even that outside forces exacerbated matters, thereby delaying, if not reducing the chances of, peaceful settlement. Current experience shows that the UN system is highly inept in resolving civil wars. Unfortunately, the harsh realities of the post-Cold War era have witnessed a mushrooming of such destructive struggles.

THE PROBLEMATIC OF A STRONGMAN POLITY

Throughout history, states have been established by a conquering strongman, while others have been revived by a winner in civil wars. The fragmented, politicized clan structures and relative military balances in Somalia make it highly unlikely that someone will conquer and pacify the country. Only Siyad, supported by the Cold War antagonists, could temporarily impose a military hegemony over all of Somalia. Even a top-down solution would have to emerge not through decisive armed force but via a negotiated settlement among the warring strongmen – a form of "consociational or power-sharing authoritarianism" or "decentralized Leviathan," if that is not a contradiction in terms. Some of the Somalis who refer to this scenario as "decentralized Siyadism" are willing to consider it not as the best but as the optimal antidote to the Hobbesian "war, where every man is enemy to every man ... and which is worst of all, continual fear, and danger of violent death; and the life of man, is solitary, poor, nasty, brutish and short."[46]

The press has popularized the term "warlords" in reference to Somalia's more notorious strongmen. Unlike the situation China of 1910-49, where the term received widespread use, Somalia is dominated by clans rather than by a class. The clan-recruited militias are youthful, lack military experience and training, are voluntary, and lack discipline, including the tendency to obey higher authority. Warlords preside over anarchy while attempting to manager chaos. Only in Somalia's clan-based society do we encounter an ex-dictator who re-emerged as a warlord in his own right. There are those who argue that during the years that witnessed the disintegration of the Somali National Army, Siyad became the first Somali warlord. Certainly, by mid-1980, barricading himself and his loyal troops in Mogadishu (the press dubbed him "Mayor of Mogadishu"), Siyad had fallen from the pinnacle of national power to the status of a regional warlord.

THE VISION OF A CONSOCIATIONAL POLITY

It is useful to provide at least a rough, working definition of democracy to offer suggestive comparisons with evolving Somali political developments. Larry Diamond et al., in *Democracy in Developing Countries: Africa,* provide a useful definition, containing three main conditions: competition among individuals and organized groups that is both meaningful and extensive; a high level of political participation in the selection of leaders and policies through regular and fair elections; and an adequate level of civil and political liberties.[47] As of 1994, the northern republic of Somaliland began to meet at least some of these conditions within its embryonic consociational or power-sharing political processes and institutions. Southern Somalia is still groping to achieve sufficient reconciliation among competing clans to ensure peaceful political cooperation.

Historically speaking, Somali clans have evolved their own specific forms of politics which "at bottom, means men's cultivation of forms for public power and authority that enable them to meet external challenges and internal needs. Ethnic groups are proving that nations do not have a monopoly on political development."[48] Reconciliation legitimizes and facilitates political cooperation. For the most part, leaders in Somaliland have taken a grass-roots approach to the process. Traditional secular and religious (local) elites, modern elites, representatives of non-governmental organizations, and ordinary citizens have participated in peace and reconciliation conferences held in virtually all the main towns: Berbera, Borama, Burao, Erigavo, Hargeisa, and Sheikh.

Siyad's wars brought conflicts to civil society, and unless these are healed, there awill be none of the mutual trust necessary to re-establish state organs.[49] Following the 1992 conflict between two Isaq clans – the Issa Muse and the Habar Yunis – the Sheikh reconciliation *shir* assisted the process of building trust through the use of traditional practices, including group marriages between the two ex-warring clans to demonstrate good faith. This approach has won the support of most non-Isaq clans, and the SNM was therefore able to transform Somaliland from a single-clan to a multi-clan or territorial project. Relying on the territorial basis of the British colonial borders, Somaliland therefore includes a heterogeneous grouping of at least four non-Isaq clans as well as numerous Isaq clans.

Until recently, SNM and Somaliland constitutional practices included leadership rotation and indirect electoral participation within a relatively grassroots approach; in the south, faction leaders hold power without electoral legitimacy. The SNM has proved the most democratic of the insurgency movements. At its 1981 founding in London, it elected Ahmed Jiumale from the Habar Awal clan as its first chair. It raised funds in a decentralized manner from local and expatriate members of Isaq clans and subclans. This saved it from coming under the control of Libya's Colonel Quaddafi, who funded the SSDF. It continued to hold elections regularly, according to its constitution. It enlarged its Central Committee early in 1991 to include, on a proportional basis, representatives of non-Isaq clans, in order that it could serve as the parliament or national assembly of the Somaliland Republic. Membership became pruned and refined enough to constitute a seventy-five-member House of Elders (Guurti) and a seventy-five-member House of Representatives.

It was Arthur Lewis, in his thought-provoking *politics in West Africa,*[50] who first recommended that Africans drop the winner-take-all electoral principle and form grand coalitions as a more realistic way to operate governments. From ideas such as those of Lewis, Lijiphart and other European political scientists have formulated a "consociational" theory of democracy that seeks to avoid the pitfalls of the majoritarian, winner-take-all model.[51] The South African transition from apartheid was achieved through consociational mechanisms. David Laitin has argued that Somalia is in an excellent position to evolve its own unique version.[52]

Somaliland has already taken several steps towards a consociational or power-sharing democracy. The facilitating conditions include the fact that no clan-family or clan can hope to dominate/impose a hegemony (Siyad tried, using the huge national army, which has since evaporated, and there are no plans to establish another one). The clans have recognized leaders who have, at least in the past, cooperated with one another. Traditional Somali society endorses the principle of proportionality, as discussed above. It is also tolerant of the use of a mutual veto for any group that considers a proposed measure vital to its survival and well-being. Segment autonomy, to allow each group sufficient resources, may be achieved through territorial or regional autonomy/federalism, which has already been formally endorsed. Many Somali clans are clustered in given territories, while multi-clan regions might adopt proportional power sharing. The civil service, commissions, committees, and other bureaucratic appointments could be implemented on the basis of merit criteria, combined with the spirit of proportionality. Consociational practices would facilitate clan organizations and clan competition, which might discourage violent clan conflicts. At least that is the hope implied in the vision of a consociational polity.

CONCLUSIONS

The challenge for Somali political development is to transform violent clan conflicts into peaceful competition. Clans cannot simply be wished away, and the current situation represents a basic reality-clans exits, and they need to be harnessed and gradually modified to promote positive political developments. Manipulation of elites by both government and opposition groups provides the major source of clan conflicts. Colonial elites first introduced this practice within a centralized state, leaving a divide-and-rule legacy to be exploited by the post-independence elite. Clanism operates in a defensive manner for those struggling for social justice and equality; the elite and masses are bound together by a consciouness of shared oppression, which is significantly different from forms of "false consciousness" artificially manufactured by a cynical elite.

In the south, the political situation continues to pose dangers of violent clan conflicts. More than half of the political factional leaders, including Mohamed Farah Aidid (USC-SNA), Abdullahi Yusuf (SSDF), Umar Jess (SPM-SNA), Abdi War-same (SSNM), and Umar Masala (SNF), were senior military officers in Siyad's army. Because of the clan factor, today none of them can conquer Somalia militarily. To create a government, they need to compromise and create a coalition of strongmen drawn from different clans along consociational lines.

Consociationalism facilitates a form of democracy based on a primordial group – it does not guarantee the substance of democracy. Unbridled petty capitalism since 1991 has unleashed significant productive forces in agriculture, livestock, fishery, and the commercial sector, including a reviving export/import sector (much stronger in the port of Berbera, Somaliland, which now serves larger parts of Ethiopia as well). However, authentic development is more than the sum of individual entrepreneurial action, which, devoid of social regulation, could have large net costs to future Somali society. Somalia's emerging non-profit sector (and, it is hoped, some of the anticipated political parties) will have to evolve social democratic policies to situate development as an activity in which coordination plays a part and that has broad social benefits. The politics of class, gender, profession/occupation, and to a certain extent religion needs to find political space in order to complement and attenuate the divisive politics of clans.

For serious, long-term socio-economic development, Somalia, like its neighbors, will have to rely on an emerging common market in the Horn of Africa, with the Inter-Governmental Authority on Development (IGAD) manifesting its promise and potential. Since 1994, IGAD, with Eritrea as its newest member, has provided the highest diplomatic forum for attempts to attain negotiated settlements for the Sudanese and Somali civil wars. Most probably the Somali civil wars will have to be resolved internally by the parties concerned, but sub-regional actors, motivated by a spirit of neighborliness, could be facilitators. The 2006 Ethiopian military intervention was undertaken with the blessings of IGAD.

Perhaps the most crucial lesson one can derive from the tragic and prolonged Somali civil wars is the pivotal role of good governance. After all, commonality of ethnic origins, language, religion, and culture has not ensured for Somalia political unity, peace, and stability, any more than ethnic, linguistic, racial, and cultural heterogeneity has prevented Tanzania from enjoying political unity, peace, and stability.

Notes

1. Martin van Crevel, *The Transformation of War* (New York: Free Press 1991).
2. John Drysdale, *The Somali Dispute* (New York: Praeger Publishers 1964).

3. Abdi Sheikh-Abdi, *Divine Madness: Mohamed Abdulle Hassan (1856–1920)* (London: Zed Books 1993).

4. Andrew Natsios, "Humanitarian Relief Interventions in Somalia: The Economics of Chaos," Paper presented to Princeton University Conference on Somalia, "Learning from Operation Restore Hope," April 1995.

5. I.M. Lewis, *A Pastoral Democracy* (London: Oxford University Press 1969).

6. John Saul, *The State and Revolution in Eastern Africa.* (New York: Monthly Review Press 1979), 391-423.

7. Roy Licklider, ed., *Stopping the Killing: How Civil Wars End* (New York: New York University Press 1993), 9.

8. Ibid., 11.

9. Raymond Copson, *Africa's Wars and Prospects for Peace* (New York: M.E. Sharpe 1994), 74-5.

10. Abdi Samatar, *The State and Rural Transformation in Northern Somalia, 1884-1986* (Madison: University of Wisconsin Press 1989).

11. D. Laitin and S. Samatar, *Somalia: Nation in Search of a State* (Boulder, Col.: Lynne Rienner 1987.)

12. Peter Woodward, "Conflict in the Horn," *Contemporary Review*, no. 231 (Dec. 1977), 281-5.

13. Donald L. Horowitz, *Ethnic Groups in Conflict.* (Berkeley: University of California Press 1985).

14. Robert Jackson and Carl Rosberg, *Personal Rule in Black Africa* (Berkley: University of California Press 1982).

15. Harold D. Nelson, *Area Handbook for Somalia* (Washington, DC: GPO for Foreign Area Studies, American University, 1982).

16. I.M. Lewis, *A Modern History of Somalia: Nation and State in the Horn of Africa* (Boulder, Col.: Westview Press 1988).

17. Ibid., 222.

18. John Prendergast, *The Gun Talks Louder Than the Voice: Somalia's Continuing Cycles of Violence* (Washington, DC: Center of Concern, July 1994).

19. William J. Foltz and Henry Bienen, *Arms and the African* (New Haven, CT: Yale University Press 1985), 100.

20. John Drysdale, *Whatever Happened to Somalia? A Tale of Tragic Blunders.* (London: HAAN Associates 1994), 4.

21. Mohamed Sahnoun, *Somalia: The Missed Opportunities* (Washington, DC: United States Institute of Peace 1994).

22. Copson, *Africa's Wars and Prospects for Peace*, 106.

23. Woodward, "Conflict in the Horn," 281.

24. Ahmed Samatar, *Socialist Somalia: Rhetorics and Reality* (London:Zed Books 1988), 137 and 139.

25. Africa Watch, *Somalia: A Government at War with Its Own People: Testimonies about the Killings and the Conflict in the North* (New York: Africa Watch Committee 1990), 10.

26. Drysdale, *Whatever Happened to Somalia?*

27. Sahnoun, *Somalia*, 11.

28. Natsios, "Humanitarian Relief,"2-3.

29. Sahnoun, *Somalia*, 18.

30. Dianna Putnam and Mohamood Nour, *The Somalis: Their History and Culture* (Washington, DC: Refugee Service Center, Oct. 1993), 1.

31. Prendergast, *Gun Talks Louder*, 16.

32. Ibid., 16.

33. Ibid., 15.

34. Africa Watch, *Somalia*, 94.

35. William Zartman, *Ripe for Resolution* (New York: Oxford University Press 1989).

36. Licklider, ed., *Stopping the Killings*, 17.

37. Natsios, "Humanitarian Relief".

38. Ibid., 3.

39. Ibid., 4.

40. Ibid., 14.

41. Sahnoun, *Somalia*, 5-11.

42. Drysdale, *Whatever Happened to Somalia?*

43. Shoumatoff, Alex, "The 'Warlord' Speaks," *Nation*, 4 April 1994.

44. Admiral Jonathan Howe, "Relations between the United States and the United Nations," Paper presented to the Princeton University Conference on Somalia, "Learning from Operation Restore Hope," (April 1995),18.

45. HAB, *Horn of Africa Bulletin*, 6(Jan.-Feb.1994),16.

46. Thomas Hobbes, *Leviathan* (New York: Collier Books 1969), 100.

47. Larry Diamond et al., *Democracy in Developing Countries*, vol. 2, Africa (Boulder, Col.: Lynned Rienner 1988), xvi.

48. Cynthia H. Enloe, *Ethnic Conflict and Political Development* (New York: University Press of America 1986), 14.

49. Ken Menkhaus, "The Reconciliation Process in Somalia: A Requiem," Paper presented to the Princeton University Conference on Somalia, "Learning from Operation Hope," April 1995.
50. Sir Arthur Lewis, *Politics in West Africa* (London: Allen and Unwin 1965).
51. Arend Lijphart, *Democracy in Plural Societies: A Comparative Exploration* (New Haven, CT: Yale University Press 1977.)
52. David Laitin, "A Consociational Democracy for Somalia," Horn of Africa, 13 nos. 1 and 2, Jan.-March and April- June 1990, 63-8.
53. Horowitz, *Ethnic Groups.*

CHAPTER 4

CLAN CONFLICTS: THE INVENTION OF ENMITY

Community of language and culture does not necessarily give rise to political unity any more than linguistic and cultural dissimilarity prevents political unity.
- Meyer fortes and E.E. Evans-Pritchard

Even in the most severely divided society, ties of blood do not lead ineluctably to rivers of blood.
- Donald L.Horowitz

INTRODUCTION

In Somali society, ethnic conflicts take the form of clan conflicts. The Somali people share a common language, religion (Sunni Islam), physical characteristics, oral literary traditions as well as pastoral and agropastoral customs. They constitute a widely spread "ethnic community" or "tribe" which is in turn subdivided into clan-families, clans and subclans, all the way down to lineages. At the top level of segmentation, Somalis are divided into five unranked clan-families: Hawiye, Darod, Isaq, Dir and Digil/Mirifle, under which comes the Rahanwin clans of agropastoralists occupying the inter-river areas around the town of Baidoa. During periods of clan conflicts, clans undergo rapid fusion and fission transformations due to a series of kaleidoscopic and diffuse attachments. Within these concentric and interconnected circles, the most stable sub-unit is at levels below sub-subclans, the *diya*-paying group which "consists of close kinsmen united by a specific contractual alliance whose terms stipulate that they should pay and receive blood-compensation (Arabic, *diya*), in concert" (Lewis 1988:11).[1]

Historically, most infighting among the Somalis has been at levels below the clan-family (Lewis 1961). Intra-clan and inter-clan conflicts have been recorded in Somali classical poetry and other forms of oral folklore. Perhaps on account of scale and geography, recorded history does not provide us with examples of warfare at the level of the five major clan-families. The civil wars, raging from the early 1980s until today, have escalated clan conflicts to the level of the clan-families transforming these, perhaps temporarily, to entities resembling "nationalities." Each one of them has created proto-political organization(s) as well as armed militias.

Somali traditional society has imposed a ranked dimension to a minority of Somali groups who are considered to exist beyond the clan system (Cassanelli 1982). One such group consists of those who have, paradoxically, managed to master rudimentary rural technologies – tool, weaponry, and utensil making, leather craftsmanship, and herbal medicines. A caste-like oppression has been imposed on them forbidding even marriage links. Apart from this rigid ranked system, the ranked relationships with the other two minority groups are more flexible and indirect, without any taboos placed on marriage relationships – among the Arabized ancient city dwellers of Mogadishu, Merca and Barawa, as well as the riverine farmers of Bantu origins (Luling 1984). The inhabitants of the historical city of Barawa as well as the Bantu Somali farmers speak varieties of Swahili dialects, though they also speak Somali as a second language. The Digil/Mirifle clans speak a distinct Somali dialect, but many of them also understand the standard (Radio Mogadishu) Somali dialect. The four pastoral clan-families tend to view the agropastoralists as somewhat "backward." In response, the agropastoralists consider the nomads as "anarchists," unable to "manage anything besides their herds" (Mukhtar 1988).

This chapter analyzes clan conflicts from the perspective of conflict management and institutional innovations within the evolving Somali context. Currently, policies of state decentralization to contain violent clan conflicts in the Somali context must take into account the *de facto* partition between southern Somalia and the northern, self-declared Republic of Somaliland. It analyzes sources of the clan conflicts especially through an analysis of the Siyad military regime (Bongartz 1991). The major challenge is to promote reconciliations in order to tame savage clan conflicts and channel them into peaceful competition.

Drawing on concrete recent experiences rather than speculations, this study discusses selected examples. Autonomist, federal and neofederal arrangements need to be taken into consideration; there is also an urgent need for constitutional and electoral system innovations that would reduce and eliminate violence in politics, while promoting inter-clan coalitions. By delving into Somali proverbs and poetry, this study also offers glimpses of clan consciousness experienced at mass levels, an aspect that remains invisible to those who ignore expression in the Somali language. With regard to democratization possibilities, the de facto Republic of Somalia seems to be evolving towards its own brand of consociational democracy as will be analyzed below. If southern Somalia is to succeed in forming a government, it will most probably have to be based on a power-sharing formula: power-sharing among "strongmen" rather than a genuine consociational system (Ronen 1986).

A PSYCHOCULATURAL DIMENSION

Clan conflict in Somalia, like ethnic conflict elsewhere, has an "instrumentalist" orientation (Glickman 1994). It is fueled by struggles for concrete interests – water and grazing rights, for example. Beyond material, economic interests there are non-material, psychic factors that serve to complement such interests. Somali poetry records numerous wars for "prestige" – broadly defined to include material and psychic interests and incentives. Proverbs can also be analyzed in terms of clan consciousness.

In Somali, the word for clan/kinship, *tol*, also represents the verb "to sew, to stitch together;" thus the proverb *tol wa tolane* implies that clansmen are stitched or knitted together (Bulhan 1989:2). It is a powerful image contradicted at the same time by the realities of segmentation. In the fission and fusion of clan politics, groups share unreliable, temporary interests. The knitting within a knitting process facilitates such contradictory behaviors. A contrasting proverb underlines this: *Wiilkaa walaal ka lahow, walaalkaana wiil ka lahow* - "to protect yourself from your son, rely on your brother; for protection from your brother, rely on your son." Clan solidarity is encouraged by the following sayings: *Doofaar ficil la'aan ayaa lo cadaabaa,"* "a warthog without the guts to look after his kith and kin is sent to hell"; *tolkaaiyo kabtaadaba wa lagu dhex jiraa,"* rely on your clan's protection as you rely on your shoes."

A negative aspect of clan solidarity is captured by the following: *Tuug ha la dilee, yaa reerkoodi mari,"* as you shout 'Kill the thief!' remember, you risk revenge from his clan." Clan members are urged to participate, not to remain aloof from the struggles of their particular clan: *Tolkaa ama bar ka ahaw ama badhtanka kaga jiri,* "either lead or be led by your clan, but do not stand aside." Finally, a proverb reflecting the democratic impulse in pastoral democratic society: *Tolkaa taagta looguma taliyo,* "beware that your clan can never be governed by force." Under normal conditions of peace, most Somalis adhere to a mutual recognition code; such proverbs are part of the national cultural inheritance memorized and recited by all Somali clans (Nelson 1982).

"Why then do clans have so powerful an influence over their members that they can coalesce into clan or sub-clan groups in times of expectation or stress" irrespective, in many cases, of rational, life and death considerations (Drysdale 1994:70)? The answer partly lies in the concept of "clan and individual prestige" so widely shared especially among rural Somalis. I encountered this during numerous trips into Somalia's regions.[2] On several occasions, the conversations and folklore made me recall the Hegelian paradigm on lordship and bondage as interpreted by Alexander Kojeve (1969).[3]

Within the Somali context, certain marginalized groups who do not belong to the five major clan-families have accepted a situation of semi-domination in the Hegelian sense. These so-called "minorities" include Somalis of Bantu origins who live as agricultural cultivators around the main rivers of the south. Original city dwellers in what historically used to constitute Islamic city-states on the Red Sea and the Indian Ocean, as well as members of the shoe-making, tool-making and haircutting castes, all fall outside the pastoral and agropastoral clan system (Nelson 1982). In the past these groups, in their relations with the pastoral clan-dominated politics, have manifested an aspect of the Hegelian victim. Most of them have avoided politics and have focused on labor (agriculture, crafts and artisanship). The city dwellers have expended their energies in trade and commerce. They have demonstrated strong interest and abilities in sports, music and dance. Traditionally unarmed and lacking warrior traditions, they suffer a great deal during the current civil wars. Recently, some of them have been forced to arm themselves to defend their lives and rights and to project political organizations of their own (Drysdale 1994).

Within the Somali pastoral cultural context, which includes urbanized elements with pastoral backgrounds, what Fanon (1967) termed the "savage struggle" for recognition continues in its original form because no group has been able to enslave another in the Hegelian sense. Examples have been immortalized through classical Somali poetry. Actual historical rather than philosophical examples of the quest for recognition involve prestige as well as material needs, such as access to grazing grounds, water holes, salt-licks, etc. One example represents a typical case of the struggle for social justice and clan recognition. The conflict involved two sister clans belonging to the same clan-family (Isaq), and inhabiting the southern parts of Hargeisa in non-reciprocal recognition in the broad sense of the term implying denial of both status and customary material rights. During the late nineteenth century and early part of this century, the victimized clan waged continuous wars to free itself from such subjugation. Their gifted poet and leader, Farah Nur, composed several poems to inspire the struggles. The following is one of his best poems on the subject (cited in Andrzejewski 1964:134 and 136).

A Limit to Submission

> Over and over again to people
> I show abundant kindness.
> If they are not satisfied,
> I spread out bedding for them
> And invite them to sleep.
> If they are still not satisfied,
> The milk of the camel whose name is Suub,
> I milk three times for them,
> And tell them to drink it up.
> If they are still not satisfied,
> The homestead's ram

And the fat he-goat I kill for them.
If they are still not satisfied,
The plate from Aden
I fill with ghee for them.
If they are still not satisfied,
A beautiful girl
And her bridal house I offer them.
If they are still not satisfied,
I select livestock also
And add them to the tribute.
If they are still not satisfied,
'Oh brother-in-law, O Sultan, Oh King'
These salutations I lavish upon them.
If they are still not satisfied,
At the time of early morning prayers I prepare
The dark grey horse with black tendons,
And with the words 'Praise to the Prophet' I take
The iron-shafted spear,
And drive it through their ribs
So that their lungs spew out;
Then they are satisfied."

The long struggles ended in victory for Farah Nur and his clan. Later on, another sister clan from the northern parts of Hargeisa attempted to dominate Farah Nur's clan: the same bitter struggles ensured ending in victory for the poet's group. Victory means the politics of mutual respect and reciprocal recognition involving the three clans. This and several similar experiences offer lessons for Somalis if they are to avoid the current state of constant warfare and bloodshed.

The second example illustrates the case of clan warfare motivated by sheer hunger for prestige and even recklessness. The poet, Salaan Arrabey, composed this poem to prevent a war between two closely connected lineages of his clan which inhabits the Burao region in the north. Playing a mediator's role, he not only appeals to the potential combatants, he also threatens them: if they do not stop the war, he pledges to intervene with his sub-clan on one side. Excerpts from *Oh Clansmen, stop the war!* (Andrzejewski 1964:132 and 134):

You two lineages,
Hurling boasts for strength in each other's teeth;
  ....
And in defiance of our custom you killed,
And now if you start to devour each other
I will not stand aloof
But adding my strength to one side
I shall join in the attack on the other,
Oh clansmen, stop the war!

The poet ends by recalling examples of warfare between other, more distant Somali clans to add weight to his main argument: that it is in the nature of Somali society not to allow one clan to impose hegemony upon another. The example he cites concerns the Majeerteen clan (Darod clan-family), who tried to impose exploitative relations upon neighboring Hawiye clans. The poet is warning the potential combatants that the winner in the long run is bound to lose just as the Majeerteen lost against the Hawiye. This remarkable poem was able to avert a disastrous war between the two related sub-clans:

(Just as) the Majeerteen clan their glory,
And their tribute from the Hawiye people
And their regal staff, have lost,
  ....
In remote places
Facing the shore
They are forced to turn for sustenance to the fruit
 of the immature date palm,
And this is the path you are following (to the same end)
Oh clansman, stop the war!

Historically, the struggles for recognition involve not only intangibles such as prestige, as in Somali culture (this cannot be overemphasized) "prestige" constitutes a critical value: the quest for recognition transcends pure status to include recognition of social, cultural, political and economic rights. In other words, there is a solid material basis behind struggles for recognition. Accordingly, the state of non-reciprocal recognition portrayed in the master-slave dialectic assumes comprehensive and highly complicated forms. Clan warfare in Somalia today is partly a product of elite manipulation. However, elites are not monolithic and elite activities are not uniform. Certain types of elite activities succeed and fail in different periods (Saul 1979:391-423).

In order to avoid a simplistic reductionism, one must acknowledge aspects of clan consciousness that go beyond artificiality, that have a basis in historical, socio-cultural dynamics. Clan consciousness has a negative and positive side; during periods of class formation it manifests a trade union aspect, a shield in the struggle against a lack of proportionality under a process of uneven development. A cultural obsession with equality and recognition is an important aspect of Somali political struggles. Given the ongoing bloodshed and chaos, it is not easy to indicate which plays a leading role and which appears secondary until such time as we are able to gain a better historical perspective.

Clan identity is not inherently conflictual in a deterministic sense. It seems to come and go, rise and ebb in episodic cycles, rather than permanent patterns. In isolation from connections to the state's political system (Rothchild and Chazan 1988), these conflicts appear limited in scope and impact. The majority of them took place at sub-clan levels, some at inter-clan levels but not at inter-clan family levels. Conflict resolving mechanisms ensured the resilience of Somali society in the face of disintegration. A key element is the exercise of time honored principles of *Xeer* (Lewis 1961). Somali customary law and practice has survived parallel to Islamic and colonially inherited judicial systems. The collapse of the latter with the collapse of the Somali state, means that *xeer* is today the main pillar of law and order within the greater part of Somali territories (see Diblawe 1989).

SOURCES OF CLAN CONFLICTS

Within the Somali experience, ethnic conflict has only one axe to grind: clanism. While language and religion constitute basic axes of ethnic conflict in many parts of the world, language homogeneity in Somalia saves the country from linguistic wars, although bitter factional struggles accompanied the adoption of a suitable script for written Somali (Adam 1980). The 1972 decision in favor of Latin has received widespread approval. Most Somalis today write their language in Latin script.

Religious homogeneity has obviated, for the most part, the recurrence of Muslim-non-Muslim conflicts (Lewis 1955). During the turn of the century, colonial partitions gave rise to an angry process of rediscovered Islamic fundamentalism that led to violent struggles between the Sayyid Mohamed Abdullah Hassan's Dervish movement and British, Italian and Ethiopian forces (Sheik-Abdi 1993). The Sayyid's fanaticism led him to wage wars against "non-Dervish" Somalis; this tragic experience seems to have "inoculated" Somali society against a recurrence of the radical, politicized Islamic phenomenon. The current civil wars have witnessed a widespread search for personal roots in piety, a reformist Islamic renewal movement. It has also given rise to pockets of Islamic fundamentalism. A branch of the generic fundamentalist movement, the *Ittihad Al-Islami* (Islamic Unity) tried to take power in the northeast regions in June-July 1992. The clan militias of the political faction dominant in the area, the Somali Salvation Democratic Front (SSDF), aided by Ethiopian troops, were able to defeat the uprising at a cost of 600 lives. Ordinary Somalis appear to respond much more readily to elites who propagate clanism than those who advocate Islamism. Nevertheless, if chaos continues, fundamentalism in the long run may grow more powerful; as it has in 2006.

Max Weber offers an elastic concept of an ethnic group which is even more appropriate when applied to a clan: "a subjective belief (in) common descent ... whether or not an objective blood relationship exists" (cited in Horowitz 1985:53). If we recall the Hegelian notations, clan-in-itself and clan-for-itself, clanism therefore implies clan-for-itself or experienced clan consciousness. As a form of ethnicity, clanism depends on self-identification and not on objective categorization. Obviously, individuals define themselves partly in response to other people's perception of them. This is particularly critical in the Somali context where language, folklore, religion and physical traits do not provide "objective" differences. Clan groups experience internal differentiations leading, among other things, to the formation of urban and rural elites, traditional secular/religious elites and modern bureaucratic, military, intellectual and commercial elites (Diamond 1983). Clanism has a male gender bias in spite of traditions of widespread exogamous clan marriages. During clan conflicts, this rigid system discounts or treats as negative maternal and spouse links. What then, are the sources of clan conflicts within the Somali experience? These will be discussed in terms of:

- Elite Manipulation;
- Struggles for Social Justice and equality;
- Historical Memories;
- Environmental Pressures.

Elite Manipulation

To a very large extent, especially with regard to current civil wars, Somali elites have organized and led the conflicts. To do so, they have, in fact invented enmities. Most blame rests on military dictator Siyad and his governing elite. By opting to fight fire with fire, the elites of the various opposing factions share the blame. The view that selfish elites often manipulate ethnic/tribal/ clan feelings and attitudes for their own class interests was suggested by Frantz Fanon who stridently argued:

> We no longer see the rise of a bourgeois dictatorship, but a tribal dictatorship. The ministers, the members of the cabinet, the ambassadors and local commissioners are chosen from the same ethnological group as the leader, sometimes directly from his own family... This tribalizing of the central authority, it is certain, encourages regional-ist ideas and separatism. All the decentralizing tenden-cies spring up again and triumph, and the nation falls to pieces, broken in bits (1968:183-184).

Emphasizing the modernity of tribalism, Richard Sklar noted,

> it is less frequently recognized that tribal movements may be created and instigated to action by the new men of power in furtherance of their own special interests which are, time and time again, the constitutive interests of emerging social classes. Tribalism then becomes a mask for class privilege. To borrow a worn metaphor, there is

often a nontraditional wolf under the tribal sheepskin
(1967:6).

During the parliamentary era, civilian elites manipulated
clanism to win elections. The electoral system tended to exacerbate
intra-subclan tensions, while preserving clan relations at more or
less normal levels. The assassination of President Sharmarke by a
policeman from a neighboring group involved electoral corruption.
The civilian regime (1960-1969) failed due to its kleptocracy and
inefficiency rather than because of its clan-based politics.

Lewis (1990) and Laitin and Samatar (1987) have pointed out
that, Siyad's socialist rhetoric notwithstanding, the 1969 military
coup relied on an informal alliance of three Darod clans: President
Siyad's own Marehan clan, the Ogaden clan of his maternal side and
the Dulbahante clan of his son-in-law and Director of the dreaded
national Security Service (NSS). The clan element (with the acronym
MOD), lay relatively dormant between 1969 and 1978 as the regime
provided a script for Somali, launched urban and rural literacy campaigns, as well as self-help projects, to build schools, clinics, offices,
markets and playgrounds (Lewis 1979). In a top-down fashion, the
military regime "abolished" *diya*-payments and discouraged rural
clan warfare during this period.

Dependence on the USSR was reversed as a result of the 1977-
78 Ogaden War with Ethiopia. The USSR took Ethiopia's side as
Somalia sought American protection, importing at least 50,000
Cuban troops to push the Somali Army from the Ogaden. In
April 1978, a group of officers from a Majerteyn (Darod) subclan
attempted a coup, which failed. The regime began to rally clan
support and to adopt coup-proffing measures, including the creation
of several counter-insurgency forces based on the Marehan clan.
Siyad compelled Ogadeni refugees to join the army, which increased
from 37,000 in 1977 to 120,000 in 1982.[5]

The siphoning of aid to a repressive army increased donor mis-
trust, exacerbating the regime and society's economic difficulties.
Colonel Abdullahi Yusuf, who masterminded the 1978 attempted
coup, fled to Ethiopia to launch the Somali Savlation Democratic
Front (SSDF), the first armed, clan-based opposition group. In

due course, Siyad's brutal measures against his opponents fueled increasing opposition. The SSDF atrophied, but other opposition movements arose and were more successful in waging guerrilla war against the regime. The Somali National Movement (SNM), based on the Isaq clan-family in the north was finally able to undertake major military actions in 1988 to tie down government forces in the main towns while the SNM controlled most of the countryside. The savagery of the regime's ground and air response – massive civilian casualties estimated at over 50,000 – and the resultant refugee flows caused key western donors to severely cut their Somali aid programs (Bongratiz 1991).

Somali clans normally compete, occasionally they engage in conflict which includes violent warfare, but traditional mutual reciprocal relationships deter them from attempts at permanent domination. Siyad used Somalia's modern, well-trained and well-equipped army to impose hegemony, thereby transforming the unranked clan pattern into a ranked system. Among the measures employed, he provided arms and encouraged wars among rural populations between the so-called "loyal" clans and "enemy clans;" he practiced urban state terror of the kind associated with Latin American death squads; he violated the Somali balancing code and grotesquely distorted the clan arithmetic in the army, police and civil service.

Although Horowitz writes, "Reliable as they may be, relatives cannot be everywhere" (1985:553), Siyad's control mechanisms showed that they could "almost be everywhere." He appointed relatives and other loyalists to all strategic positions within the armed forces, civilian bureaucracies, and in political, social and cultural institutions. The so-called vanguard party, the Somali Revolutionary Socialist Party (SRSP) with its social organizations for youth, women, workers and peasants were all reduced to "spy and control" organizations. Siyad adopted the Russian "nomenklatura" system into "clan klatura" mechanism that warded off coup attempts from 1978 until January 1991.

An analysis of the military-police officers clan arithmetic shows vivid imbalances and distortions.[6] During the sixties, there was a rough balance between Hawiye and Darod officers. The paucity of Isaq officers represents their status as "enemy clan-family." In 1969, apart from Siyad himself, there was not a single other Marehan general in the army or police force. Analyzing the data at the manageable army and police generals level offers a telling indicator of "clan klatura" practices within the armed forces.

Clan Identification	Number of Generals in the Army/Police
Darod (Marehan alone 17)	56
Hawiye (Abgal 10, Habar Gedir 9)	25
Isaq	8
Rahanwin (Digil/Mirifle)	3
Dir (including Gadabursi)	2
Shiikhal (a religious lineage)	3
Ancient city communities	6
Total	**103**

In 1989, Hawiye dissidents formed the United Somali Congress (USC) with a military wing under General Farah Mohamed Aidid and a civilian wing under Ali Mahdi Mohamed, a businessman. At about the same time, some Ogaden soldiers and officers, in the north and south, defected to form the Somali Patriotic Movement (SPM) under Colonel Umar Jess and General Gabiyo. Aidid received the support of the SNM as he sought to establish his initial base in Ethiopia. As his forces approached Mogadishu, Siyad increased his arbitrary roundup and killings of Hawiye elements using terror as a weapon (Bongartz 1991). This generated bitter memories and culturally sanctioned demands for revenge among the victimized communities. This deflected the struggle into a Darod vs. Hawiye war, thereby intensifying the unfolding civil wars. As soon as Siyad departed from Mogadishu, Ali Mahdi declared himself "Interim President." The Aidid branch of the USC, the SNM, SPM and SSDF all condemned this unilateral action. The Italians, Egyptians and the UN (Boutros-Ghali) seemed inclined to back Ali Mahdi as his relations with Aidid deteriorated.

Esisodic warfare broke out in May and September, 1991; from November 1991 to February 1992 they fought full-scale wars turning Mogadishu into another Beirut, divided by a "green line."

All residual government functions – financial, cultural, judicial and administrative – collapsed. The army evaporated, the police disbanded and prisoners fled the jails. Aidid and Ali Mahdi launched mortar rounds against each other form their respective zones. It is estimated that 30,000 civilians died within four months and 300,000 of Mogadishu's inhabitants joined the ranks of displaced persons (Putnam and Nour 1993). The Aidid-Mahdi conflict is an excellent example of clan manipulation among the opposition elite. Personal ambitions mobilized and dictated clan interests.

The Habar Gedir clan of Genera Aidid and the Abgal clan of Ali Mahdi do not inhabit common territories. The Abgal occupy coastal territories adjacent to Mogadishu while the Habar Gedir come from Mudug region in north central Somalia near the town of Galkayo. Hence, they are not burdened by historical memories of previous conflicts. They are not only members of the Hawiye clan-family, but they are also both from a common Hawiye sub-branch, the Hiraab. Personal vendettas among the leading personalities were transformed into all-out clan warfare.

The UN helped to arrange a cease fire early in 1992. In January 1994, the Imam of Hiraab, Mohamed Imam Omar, convened a peace conference (a) to resolve all differences by peaceful means; (b) to forgive and forget damages already caused by war; (c) to return forcefully appropriated property to its owners; and (d) to open roads and guarantee their security. The Hiraab Treaty appeals to signatories to jointly prevent acts of violence by armed bandits and gangs who should be punished according to the Islamic Sharia (HAB) January-February, 1994:14.

Struggles for Social Justice and Equality

Employing the concept of elite manipulation as a major factor in clan analysis avoids falling into the trap of a single factor class analysis that clearly distorts realities. For example:

> If anything, it is a mark of *false consciousness* on the part of the supposed tribesmen, who subscribe to an ideology that is inconsistent with their material base and therefore, unwittingly respond to the call for their own exploitation. On the part of the new elite, it is a ploy or distortion they

use to conceal their exploitative role. It is an ideology in the original Marxist sense, and they share it with their European fellow ideologists (Mafeje 1971:259).

Within Somali historiography, this Marxist school of analysis is represented by Ahmed Samatar (1988), Aronson (1980), Swift (1979) and Abdi Samatar (1989). Their analysis is within the orbit of the global development/underdevelopment theory.

Writing within a similar approach, Kapteijns[7] argues that unlike the precolonial epoch, clanism is something grafted onto Somali society by, for example, British colonial divide and rule policies. Obviously, foreign "elite" manipulation of clanism began under the colonial centralized state. This school represents perhaps an understandable reaction to the modernization approach. However, its obsession with overcoming primordial sentiments within a single factor clanism analysis obscures other factors. I.M. Lewis (1961, 1979, 1988 and 1990), Laitin and Said Samatar (1987) subsume an anthropological determinism: analyzing clan conflicts takes on the flavor of "mass hysteria" of the followers. Complicated political behavior cannot simply be reduced to the straightforward project of a particular fraction of the petty bourgeois; neither is it the crude reflection of inherently irrational "mass hysteria."

The ingredients of clanism go beyond crude and cynical elite manipulation, beyond "false consciousness." Why is it that the masses voluntarily follow the elites not only during electoral politics, which is understandable, but also in prolonged armed struggles that involve risking one's life and even those of one's family and relatives? How come the Islamist elite in Somalia tends to lose to the clanist elite, as they too try to manipulate the masses through commonly shared religious sentiments? Clan consciousness is partially anchored in real socioeconomic processes and attains vitality in civil society. Reductionist clan/ethnic analysis focuses on kinship sentiments overlooking the historical and dynamic analysis of clanism/ethnicity and its dialectical linkages with the process of colonial and post independence class formation. In ex-colonial territories where capitalist penetration is relatively weak, distorted, and uneven, clan/ethnic forms of consciousness not only tend to prevail over embryonic forms of class consciousness, they also tend to reflect real social relations and the organization of civil society. In Somalia, clanism, at least in a positive group solidarity sense, is rooted in popular aspirations. The elites have a choice of channeling it towards constructive ends or unleashing destructive clan wars.

Defensive Clanism

Lack of authentic capitalism and industrial urbanization, accompanied by a lack of atomized individualism, leaves the individual an active member of organic subgroups existing between his family and the nation-state. In comparison to such groupings, the state appears abstract and fictitious. In such circumstances, clan consciousness plays a role in the defensive politics of prevention with regard to uneven professional/functional group and class formation. Clan/ethnic groups are likely to tolerate a process that is fair and, at the very lest, promotes equal opportunity in access to resources, whether access to grazing, water sources, jobs and educational opportunities, commercial contracts and promotions. "If the majority of any ethnic group falls into a single class status, one suspects that its members are being deprived of a chance for education or job training." Under peripheral capitalism and embryonic class formation, clans tend to assume trade union type functions providing dialectical linkages between class formation and clan consciousness:"...there are instances in which individual progress towards self-confidence and efficacy depends on an ethnic group's development as a community" (Enloe 1986:30-31,33).

The situation of the agropastoralist Digil-Mirifle clans situated on the relatively fertile zone between the Juba and Shabelle rivers offer a classical example of this phenomenon. Besides their relatively sedentary agropastoral traditions, they also happen to speak a distinctive dialect of the Somali language. Partly due to an attachment they have for their more productive homeland, they have not ventured as much into urbanized centers such as Mogadishu like members of the other clans. Accordingly, they have lagged behind in terms of modernity, as the Hawiye, Darod and Isaq clans developed a petty bourgeoisie increasingly involved in trade, professions and the various civil, army and police services. During the british Military Administration of virtually all Somali territories in the

Second World War they complained that the British were favoring the Darod and Hawiye elites.

They refused to join the main southern nationalist party, the Somali Youth League (SYL), formed in 1943. They formed their own party/union, the HDMS, with the acronym proudly proclaiming their clan affiliation; later they kept HDMS but adjusted the name to imply a constitutional, democratic party. At first, they wanted independence postponed to give their communities time to "catch up." They also raised the necessity of undertaking a census of the Somali population as a basic step of development and ensuring proportionality. They saw themselves as densely populated, while nomadic groups like the Hawiye and the Darod are widely spread out. As late as two years before independence in 1960, HDMS President Jelani Sheikh bin Sheikh reiterated in a speech to a party convention that "the party has become convinced that the only method of unifying the Somalis… is through a federal constitution which accords full regional autonomy" (Touval 1963:96-97).

When clanism attempts to impose a clan hegemony, defensive clanism unleashes struggles for social justice and equality best captured by Farah Nur's poem cited above: A *Limit To Submission*. The Isaq had to launch similar wars to free themselves from Siyad's Darod manipulated clanism. As early as 1981, he began to single out the Isaq for severe and prolonged punishment.[8] This gave rise to the SNM and the anti-clanism clanism struggles that followed. During the late seventies, Isaqs had welcomed Ogaden refugees from Ethiopia with open arms. Siyad's poisoning of clan relations now pitted Ogadenis against Isaqs: "Ogadeni refugees have been encouraged to take over the remains of Isaq shops and houses in what are now ghost towns. Thus, those who were received as refugee guests have supplanted their Isaq hosts, many of whom – in this bitterly ironic turn of fate–are now refugees in the Ogaden" (Lewis 1990:59). The Isaq revolt linked the elites and masses through real, shared consciousness of oppression leading to a vision of an independent Somaliland Republic. The Isaq facilitated the later revolt of the Hawiye and others:

> The grievances of ethnic groups frequently serve as cata-
> lysts for what eventually become supra-ethnic revolutions.
> A community which has been treated unjustly illuminates
> profound contractions within the entire political system
> – contradictions present but unseen until exposed in one
> group's poverty or oppression (Enloe 1986:224).

A final example of defensive clanism uniting the elite and masses
to fight perceived oppression is the June-October 1993 war between
General Aidid's Habar Gedir clan and the US/UN forces under
UNOSOM II. As soon as the US led Operation Restore Hope
(ORH) ended and UNOSOM II took over, the neutrality exercised
by ORH was dropped. A situation of ethnic civil wars requires international humanitarian intervention to function in the capacity of a
fair "referee and broker." Boutros Ghali and head of UNOSOM II,
Admiral Howe, had decided to "neutralize" Aidid as an obstacle to
"peace and nation-building" (Shoumatoff 1994). They threatened to
silence his radio station when his militia killed twenty-four Pakistan
UN peacekeepers on June 5. Howe offered $25,000 for his capture
or elimination; on July 12, Habar Gedir elders and other members
of the elite met in a prominent villa to discuss ways to engage in a
dialogue with UNOSOM. The villa was bombed by air and over
seventy leaders died.

This and other actions served to unite the clan behind the fugitive
Aidid. Siyad instigated rural wars against the Habar Gedir (Hawiye)
as early as 1982/1983 by pitting, on one side his own Marehan clan,
and on the other side, neighboring Majerteyn clans. These wars
of attrition pushed the clan into armed opposition as the elders
recalled General Aidid from India to lead their struggles during the
late 1980s. After defeating Siyad, they witnessed UNOSOM using
incredible force to bar them from political participation to set up a
new Somali order.

Their sense of justice was violated as rumors spread that
UNOSOM wanted to restore to power Siyad's clan if not Siyad
himself. UN peacekeepers and hundreds of Somalis died in urban
guerrilla warfare. The sense of being oppressed unleashed a powerful influence over members that they coalesced into a solid clan
fighting force. In early October, Habar Gedir militia forces killed

eighteen American Rangers and wounded seventy-five, obliging President Clinton to change policies. He sent special envoy former Ambassador Robert Oakley to begin a rapprochement with Aidid. As of March 31,1994, he pulled out all US forces from Somalia; UNOSOM pulled out by March 1995.

Historical Memories

Diamond correctly observes that elites do not "manufacture ethnicity out of whole cloth but rather, (can) exploit a profound cultural tendency for politics to be perceived and expressed in communal terms" (1983:469). The memories of previous clan conflicts for scarce resources, prestige or to attain equality and social justice, continue to burden the consciousness of the living. This is more so because conflicts have been captured in the immortal poetry of classical Somali poets: Farah Nur, Qaman Bulhan, Salan Arrabey, Abdi Gahayr and Ali Duuh (Andrzejewski 1964). Arrabey, Bulhan and Duuh have produced a "poetic combat," dealing with inter-clan conflicts during the late nineteenth century. Historical memories of a relevant nature are limited to clans sharing common pastures and water sources. Accordingly, the Abgal/ Habar Gedir conflict discussed above involves two groups who did not share such memories in their fight. Groups that share bad memories of previous conflicts also share good memories of peaceful coexistence. The conflicts were reconciled by the constant evolution and adaptation of specific *xeer* between the contesting parties (Diblawe 1989). Somalis believe that it is easier to mediate conflicts between those who have historical memories of fighting, rather than those who have never fought one another before. In most cases, previous peace contracts were likely to have been sealed by group marriages involving the previously warring parties.[9]

Environmental Pressures

Laba la hinjiyaba wa hunguri ki horreyn jirey; haddii la hakradane wa la isku his hibashadiisiiye. Roughly translated: "Of any two matters that you pick up, greed for material (hunger) needs must be given priority; if the distribution system is messed up, then a tremendously fierce and explosive war will ensure."

During periods of severe drought and famine, cultural sanctions tend to be ignored by groups that are desperately trying to survive. Various coping strategies come to play: moving to strange far-off places, appealing for help from distant relatives, conducting discounted marriages of young girls as well as raiding others for food. During the decline of the dervish movement, the famine was so severe that Somalis ate foods forbidden by the Islamic religion, such as types of wild animals, including warthogs (pork) and varieties of dead meat. It was also a period of chaos, clan wars and banditry. The world was shocked to see Somalis hijack food aid going to the Baidoa (Digil Mirifle) famine zone during 1991-1992. Obviously, some of this was due to modern bandits bent on stealing the food and selling it in Mogadishu and even far-off markets in Kenya and Ethiopia. Others stole the food as it passed their territories because they needed to hoard it for their own families and relatives. They had no way of knowing when it would stop flowing and the famine affected most parts of southern Somalia. During periods of extreme scarcities, conflicts are frequent, as each clan seeks to survive according to its power and wits. *Tol waxaa yaqan nin u taliyey ama tuugay* – "he who has either led his clan or begged sustenance from it, knows its members and qualities best."

PROSPECTS FOR DEMOCRATIZATION

It is useful to provide at least a working definition of democracy to compare with Somali political developments. Larry Diamond *et al,*(1988:xvi), provide a useful definition containing three main conditions: (a) competition among individuals and organized groups that is both meaningful and extensive; (b) a high level of political participation in the selection of leaders and policies through regular and fair elections; and (c) an adequate level of civil and political liberties.

By 1994, the northern Republic of Somaliland began to meet some of these conditions within its embryonic political processes and institutions. Southern Somalia is still groping to achieve sufficient reconciliations to ensure peaceful political cooperation. The five month war between General Aidid and the US/UN served to considerably delay this process. It began to pick up momentum by June 1993, when Aidid's branch of the USC within his Somali National Alliance (SNA) met with his old friend Colonel Abdullahi Yusuf, heading and SSDF delegation. This reconciliation conference, held in Mogadishu (formerly a hostile venue for the SSDF), issued its peace and cooperation declaration on June 4, 1993. On June 5, UNOSOM provoked the USC-SNA militia into the deadly encounter over the Mogadishu Radio Station.

The decentralized clan-based armed groupings that engaged Siyad's formidable army viewed themselves part of Africa's movement toward democracy, often called Africa's second struggle for independence. However; none of them anticipated the serious problems that would follow the military overthrow of Siyad. The war between Aidid's and Ali Mahdi's USC faction over the control of state power turned Mogadishu into another Beirut, thereby ensuring complete state collapse. To the northern SNM, Ali Mahdi "crowning" himself was seen as another instance of southern political arrogance. The straw that broke the camel's back occurred in May 1991 when they established the breakaway Republic of Somaliland creating an Eritrea type problem (Rothchild et.al.1983:199-232).

Siyad left Mogadishu but, unlike Mengistu, he did not leave the country until Aidid's forces finally chased him out in May 1992. Meanwhile, adopting lessons from RENAMO's (Mozambique) terrorist book, his forces continued to engage in spoiler raids, aimed at further destabilizing Mogadishu. These raids and counter raids went through the Digil-Mirifle territories around Baidoa. Most of these clans, especially the Rahanwin, were badly affected. They launched their own liberation movement (like the HDMS during an earlier epoch), the Somali Democratic Movement (SDM). However, they were not armed enough to withstand the onslaught. Siyad's forces in particular raided their camels, cattle, sheep, goats and crops, forcing thousands to flee deep into forests and mountains. Production ceased and a terrible famine ensued, terrible enough to launch Operation Restore Hope. The civil wars have induced most Somali groupings to launch their own proto-political organizations. Of the following list of these organizations, the first five are the relatively older ones. Each name is linked to its approximate clan affiliation:

1. Somali National Movement (SNM, Isaq, Republic of Somaliland)
2. Somali Salvation Democratic Front (SSDF, Majerteyn, Darod)
3. United Somali Congress (USC-SNA, Aidid, Habar Gedir and other Hawiye clans)
4. United Somali Congress (USC, Ali Mahdi, Abgal and other Hawiye clans)
5. Somali Patriotic Movement (SPM-SNA, Omar Jess, Ogaden Darod)
6. Somali Patriotic Movement (SPM, General Gabiyo, Ogaden and other Darod clans; recently however, the two have reunited as an Ogaden grouping under Jess)
7. Somali Democratic Movement (SDM, Digil-Mirifle/Rahanwin)
8. Southern Somali National Movement (SSNM-SNA Dir clans; previously aligned to the northern SNM)
9. United Somali Front (USF, Issa clan)
10. United Somali Party (USP, Dulbaante and Warsangeli, Darod clans)
11. Somali Democratic Alliance (SDA, Gadabursi clan)
12. Somali National Democratic Union (SNDU, other Darod clans)
13. Somali National Front (SNF, former President Siyad's Marehan organization, Darod)
14. Somali National Union (SNU, based on the ancient urban dwellers outside the clan system)
15. Somali African Muki Organization (SAMO, based on the so-called Bantu Somali sedentary farmers).

Practically all the clan and social groupings in the society have formed a political association. So far only the members of the Somali castes – Tumal, Midgan, Yibir– have not yet formed one. Those in Ethiopia have already done so: the Gabooye Democratic Front ("Gabooye" is a generic name for members of Somali traditional castes).

Given the scope and intensity of the civil wars, it would be unrealistic to expect the pro-democracy movement to regain its previous optimism and momentum in such a short time. For the southern third of the country, the so-called Triangle of Death, thousands of foreign troops had to deliver relief to save lives and to ensure that productive activities would resume their previous levels. For two-third of the country, including Somaliland, local committees utilizing *xeer* maintained law and order. Today these areas are ready to embark on reconstruction, provided they get relevant assistance.

The priority, especially for the south, is to turn swords into camel bells, to ensure peace and stability. To turn clan conflicts into peaceful competition would constitute a significant step in Somali political development. Present indications are that political development will not lead inevitably to centralized authority or to the old unitary state. There will be need for coordination, planning and maximization of scarce resources, but within a decentralized and somewhat fragmented state. The political posturing of the past four years has a deadly serious aspect: the need to establish institutions and structures that do not facilitate the dominance of one clan group over others. Historically speaking, Somali clans have been involved in their own unique forms of political development which "at bottom, means men's cultivation of forms for public power and authority that enable them to meet external challenges and internal needs. Ethnic groups are proving that nations do not have a monopoly on political development" (Enloe 1986:14). Somali clans have not only promoted political development, they have also shown themselves adept in the past with the intricacies of constitutionalism.

Historical Roots of Democracy

The current situation is one in which, with the full collapse of the state, Somalis have been obliged to rely on traditional *xeer*. A similar situation occurred in the sixteenth century when the Islamic state of Adal collapsed (Nelson 1982). From its coastal capital of Zeila, its famous leader, Ahmed Gurey, waged several successful wars against the Christian Abyssinian kingdom. In 1542 his highland enemies defeated his armies leading to the decline and collapse of Adal (Touval 1963). Oral traditions record the recurrent wars, famine, chaos and banditry (*shifta*) that followed.

A common response to the decline of public law was to revive and revitalize the *xeer*. The Isse clan (Dir clan-family) in particular produced an elaborate constitutions, Xeer Cisse (Iye 1991). The constitution bound together six sub-clans—three related by blood kinship and three "adopted" sub-clans. Having lived under the pluralistic state of Adal, they decided to transcend the concept of kinship based solely on "blood." Although blood kinship is pervasive, Somali genealogies also indicate examples of kinship by "contract" and through "fictitious" stories of origin. All the six sub-clans came to constitute the Issa clan through this legal instrument – all of it composed in poetic style to assist memorization. It was decided that the traditional clan leaders the *Ugaas* (other Somalis use *Suldan or Boqor)* would be chosen from the numerically smallest sub-clan of the six—which happens to be of the three "adopted" subclans in the original contract. The leader is a first among equals. The constitution provides detailed provisions concerning choosing the right *Ugaas* as well as dethronement.

A nonthreatening subclan was given, through the *Ugaas*, special prestige, recognition and responsibility in adjudicating claims and disputes objectively and fairly. It is claimed that this specially crafted social contract carried the Isse through the chaos and turmoil of the sixteenth centuries and continues to minimize and resolve intra-Isse conflicts. The *Ugaas,* like other Somali traditional leaders, presides over the decision-making body or assembly, the *shir* (open to all adult males of the clan). Since the decision taken would bind the whole *shir*, including opponents, the good leader seeks to accommodate the opposition along consociational practices to avoid pressures that might later divide the group. Above all, given the cultural obsession with pride, every effort would therefore be made to avoid a loss of face.

Recent Moves Toward Democracy

Reconciliations legitimize and facilitate political cooperation. Northerners have taken a grassroots approach to the process. Traditional secular and religious (local) elites, modern elites, and representatives of non-governmental organizations and ordinary citizens have participated in peace and reconciliation conferences held in virtually all the main towns: Berbera, Burao, Sheikh, Hargeisa, Erigavo and Borama. Elders play a leading role, and in their wisdom, Siyad's wars brought conflicts to civil society, and unless these are healed, there will be no mutual trust necessary to reestablish state organs. This approach has won the support of most of non-Isaq clans and the SNM was therefore able to transform Somaliland into a territorial project.

Following the 1992 conflict between two Isaq clan – the Isa Muse and the Habar Yunis – the Sheikh reconciliation *shir* went further in traditional practices: group marriages to demonstrate good faith were undertaken between the two ex-warring clans. In Mogadishu, grassroots meetings have just begun to appear (recall the Hiraab Treaty conference discussed above). Otherwise, the field has been dominated by elite level reconciliation meetings sponsored by foreign powers. In 1991, the Italian and Egyptian governments organized two conferences in Djibouti. General Aidid and his allies refused to attend because they detected attempts to legitimize Ali Mahdi's "coronation." The UNOSOM sponsored January 1993 Addis Ababa conference brought in all the fifteen political factions listed above (the SNM attending only as observers), but they could only agree on a ceasefire. The March 1993 Addis Ababa meeting included representatives of civil society, and agreed on a basic outline of transitional authority. Following Aidid's ordeal, an Addis Ababa III Conference took place (December 1993), but nothing much was achieved. The Egyptians called a Cairo meeting early in 1994, but Aidid and his allies once again boycotted this meeting.

CONSTITUTIONAL AND ELECTORAL MECHANISMS TO FORESTALL CONFLICT

SNM and Somaliland constitutional practices involve leadership rotation and electoral participation within a relatively bottoms-up approach; in the south, faction leaders hold power without electoral legitimacy. The SNM has proved to be the most democratic of the various insurgency movement. At its 1981 founding in London it elected Ahmed Jiumale from the Habar Awal clan as its first chairman. It raised its funds in a decentralized manner from local and expatriate members of Isaq clans and subclans. This saved them from coming under the control of Colonel Gadhafi, who funded the SSDF. It continued to hold elections regularly according to its constitution. Sheikh Yusuf Madar (also Habar Awal) won the next election; the third election was alleged to have been stolen by its military wing, headed by Colonel Abdulkadr Korsar. "However, the dominance of the military faction did not endure and, without any great acrimony or bloodshed, SNM again changed its leadership. A new civilian group was installed at the 1984 Congress" (Samatar 1988:155). Korsar (Habar Yunis clan) was replaced by the charismatic Ahmed Mohamud "Silanyo" from the Habar Jeclo clan, who had the distinction of being the only one who served two terms. In 1990, the SNM elected Abdurahman Tuur (Habar Yunis) as Chairman, who served as the first President of Somaliland.

The SNM Central Committee was made up of seats allocated according to traditional proportionality involving the eight "sons" of the clan-family founder, Sheikh Isaq constituting therefore, the main clan branches of the Isaq: Toljaclo, Ayub, Arab, Habar Awal (Saad Muse and Isa Muse), Garhajis (Habar Yunis and Idagale), Muse, Sanbul and Imaran (constituting the Habar Jeclo alliance).[10] The SNM Central Committee was enlarged early in 1991 to include, on a proportional basis, representatives of non-Isaq clans in order to serve as the parliament or National Assembly of the Somaliland Republic. Membership became pruned and refined enough to constitute a seventy-five member House of Elders (*Guurti)* and a seventy five member House of Representatives, a total of 150 for the northern parliament. (This may be the first time in post-colonial Africa that traditional elders were given such power and prestige). The House of Elders will handle clan conflicts and will strive to ensure reconciliations and peace. It will also scrutinize legislation to see to it that it does not violate Islamic principles. There is also talk about forming an Administrative Council of Elders as an advisory body to help the administrative day-to-day handling of clan conflicts.

The British colonial administration of Somaliland left records and precedents that were used to arrive at Isaq/non-Isaq proportionality. The 1960 elections conducted under the British utilized winner-take-all electoral districts. The British tried, however, to organize electoral districts in a way to ensure an outcome that reflected clan proportionality. Out of the thirty-three parliamentary seats for the territory, Isaqs won twenty-one seats, non-Isaq won twelve seats (a rough proportion of two to one). The SNL and UNF represented Isaq led and supported political parties, they polled fifty-four and thirty-four percent of the popular vote; the non-Isaq USP polled twelve percent. Former Somaliland President Ibrahim Mohamed Egal, as head of the SNL, became first northern Premier on June 26, 1960, just before unification with the south on July 1st. The Gadabursi, who hosted the Borama reconciliation and constitutional conference that ended in May 1993, asked for the formula to be slightly revised to give them more seats. Isaq clans volunteered to lose seven seats which were added to their ratio. The Habar Yunis have not felt satisfied with their eight seats and they have pushed for further reforms. To make their demands felt, they have boycotted sessions of the new parliament. The current clan composition of members is as follows:

Habar Awal	16
Garhajis (Habar Yusnis & Idagale)	16
Arab	13
Ayub	6
Toljaclo	4
Habar Jecolo and allied clans	33
Sub-total for Isaq	**88**
Dulbahante (Darod)	23
Warsangel (Darod)	9
Gadabursi (Dir)	21
Isse (Dir)	9
Sub-total for Non-Isaq	**62**
Total	**150**

The Borama Peace and Reconciliation Conference lasted from January to May 1993. The length itself represents an indigenous rhythm. At first, it set out to reconcile clan differences, then it laid out constitutional guide-lines: there will be a president, vice-president and assembly constituting two houses, the court system will function independently of the government. The 150 body assembly served as the electoral body to elect the president, Egal (by 99 votes) and the vice-president, Abdurahman Au-Ali, from Borama. The incumbent President, Abdurhaman Tuur, and former Foreign minister Umar Arte also ran, but they lost. This transitional government was given until may 1995 to organize a referendum and to establish a commission to prepare a draft constitution.

Somaliland's major problem is that no country has so far recognized it. A Supreme Court has been established and the rule of law has begun to be exercised; groups of citizens have sued the administration for violations of contracts. Political parties were to be allowed in the next phase, however, groups are able to informally organize clan and sub-clan groupings as political lobbies and to participate in elections. Freedom of expression and freedom of the press thrive, though it is a relatively crude press. Publications criticize the government through poems, proverbs and cartoons. "With the hope that the rule of law can be made uniform and predictable in Somaliland, a group called lawyers for Civil Rights in Hargeisa aims to supplement the use of customary law and *Shari'a* by presenting to the government proposed legal codes that are also based on useful precedents from Somaliland and British law" (Leatherbee 1994).

As early as January 1993, UNOSOM wanted to pressure Somali elites to set up a juridical Somali state, oblivious of the fact that such pressures contributed to the prolongation of the civil wars. The March 15-27, 1993 Addis Ababa Conference resisted pressure to form a centralized state and adopted a regional autonomy approach based on Somalia's eighteen regions (actually 13 minus the 5 northern regions): each is to establish a regional administrative council, police forces and judiciaries, as well as district councils, leading Somali observers to comment that the Conference decided to turn Somalia into eighteen Somalilands!

Avoiding the issue of forming an immediate national government, Addis II recommended the formation of a Transitional National Council (TNC) of three representatives (including one woman) from each region, five additional seats for Mogadishu, and one representative from each of the fifteen political factions (a total of 74 members). UNOSOM finally backed this regional autonomy approach and speeded up the process, especially after it freed its energies from the General Aidid debacle. By January 1994, UNOSOM assisted in the formation of fifty-three district councils out of eighty-one (excluding Somaliland), and eight out of thirteen regional councils (again, excluding Somaliland) (HAB v 6:16).

In 1986, Somalia, Ethiopia, Sudan, Kenya, Uganda and Djibouti established the Intergovernmental Authority on Drought and Development (IGADD), headquartered in Djibouti. The OAU and President Clinton asked Ethiopian President Meles Zenawi to play the leading role in promoting Somali peace and reconciliation. In March, at the Nairobi IGADD Summit (Eritrea is now a member), the East African leaders invited President Egal and all the factional leaders. Egal continued to participate as an observer. The other factions engaged in intensive informal consultations ending in a formal agreement. They agreed to hold a formal National Conference in Mogadishu in May 1994 to elect a President, several vice presidents, a prime minister and formally launch the TNC. The northern SNM had been invited. However, President Egal and his government condemned such talks as violating Somaliland's constitutional status and procedures.

This incident does, however, indicate the emergence of elite politics and maneuvers in line with the pledge to abandon the logic of force for the ethic of dialogue. For some time, the leaders entertained the notion of a Council of Presidents involving a series of rotating presidents, but they seem to have dropped this idea for the time being. Any coordinating body that will serve as a transitional government will have to be based on the principle of a multi-clan grand coalition.

It was Professor Arthur Lewis, in his thought-provoking book, *Politics in West Africa* (1965), who first recommended that Africans drop the winner-take-all electoral principle and form grand coalitions, as a more realistic way to operate African governments:

> One can alter the constitutional rules for forming a government: for example, instead of the President sending for the leader of the largest party to form a Cabinet, the rule may tell him to send for the leader of every party

which has received more than 20 percent of the votes, and divide the cabinet seats between them, or such of them will cooperate... To write the coalition idea into the rules of forming a government in place of the present government versus opposition idea would itself be quite a step forward.

Consociationalist Solutions

From ideas such as those of Arthur Lewis, Lijphart (1977) and other European political scientists have formulated a "consociational" theory of democracy that seeks to avoid the pitfalls of the majoritarian, winner-take-all mode. Somali studies scholar and political scientist David Laitin (1990) has argued that Somalia is in an excellent position to evolve its own unique version. Somaliland has already taken several steps towards a consociational or power sharing democracy (see Steiner 1991). The facilitating conditions are there: no clan-family or clan can hope to dominate/impose a hegemony. (Siyad tried, using the huge national army which has since evaporated and there are no plans to establish another one). The clans have recognized leaders who have, at least in the past, cooperated with one another. Traditional Somali society endorses the principal of proportionality as discussed above. It is also tolerant of the use of a mutual veto for any group that considers a proposed measure vital to its survival and wellbeing. Segmental autonomy, to allow each group sufficient resources, may be achieved through the principle of territorial regional autonomy/federalisms, which has already been formally endorsed. Many Somali clans are territorially concentrated and in multi-clan regions, so the principle of proportional power-sharing may be applied. (Horowitz 1985). Civil service, commissions, committees and other bureaucratic appointments will be implemented on the basis of merit criteria and proportionality. Consociation practices would facilitate clan organizations and clan competition, and would, hopefully, discourage violent clan conflicts.

There are a number of enabling factors that need to be mentioned. Somalia's emerging consociational democracy needs to put a premium on the emerging private sector in order to reduce conflicts by keeping the public sector relatively small, lean and efficient. Clan competition within the private sector does not give rise to the tensions one finds in the public sector. A vibrant, small-scale private sector has mushroomed, unhindered by the nationalizations, the parastatals, the price controls and the rentierstate regulations of the Siyad military dictatorship. A great deal of the emerging private sector is in the hands of women, most of whom have played remarkably constructive roles during the catastrophe.

UNOSOM had been asked to establish local police forces that would be accountable to district and regional bodies. Somalia's more democratic future will be better safeguarded if the present consensus not to establish a new central army is maintained. A non-profit sector led by indigenous Somali non-governmental organizations has developed and needs non-dependency assistance from international non-governmental organizations (INGO's). State collapse and the civil wars have given Somalia the opportunity to rely on remarkable forms of self-reliance that need to be built on, to produce a society that is relatively free from neocolonial dependencies.

For long term socio-economic development, Somalia, like her neighbors, will have to rely on an emerging Horn of Africa common market. Relations with Ethiopia, Djibouti and Eritrea are good, and relations with Kenya have improved considerably during the past months. Earlier, General Aidid had accused Kenya of supporting pro-Siyad forces. The old Somali irredentist policy has been thoroughly discredited because Siyad had converted it into a tool of his attempted Darod domination. When he failed in his military attempt to join the "Ogaden" into Somalia, he turned to using Ogadenis to "colonize" northern Somalia. During the 1960s Somali irredentism was popular because the five pointed star seemed to offer something for many of Somalia's clans (Drysdale 1964).

What is journalistically termed the "Ogaden" is actually a vast territory containing several clans besides the Ogadenis. The Gadabursi and Issa in the western half of Somaliland have clansmen in Djibouti and even larger populations in what is today Ethiopia's Region 5. Sizable Isaq populations occupy the Haud and Reserve Area of Region 5. The Ogaden, other Darod and Hawiye clans, as well as numerous smaller clans occupy the rest of Region 5. Northern Kenya has Darod, Hawiye, Dir and other clans. This is why

Somali irredentism was widely popular until Siyad discredited it by turning it into a Darod affair.[11] Another reason for good Ethiopia-Somali relations is that most of the key leaders in Somalia/Somaliland launched their movements from within Ethiopia and received Ethiopian support.

CONCLUSION

The challenge for Somali political development is to transcend violent clan conflicts and move toward peaceful clan competition. Clans cannot simply be wished away; the current situation represents a basic realism that clans exist, and that they need to be harnessed and gradually modified to promote positive political developments (Diamond 1987). Siyad's Machiaveliansim considered clan organization illegal while he surreptitiously armed clans to wage savage wars. Clan consciousness is sometimes based on self-identification, on a "subjective belief in common descent" which, as the Isse clan example shows, is sometimes based on a mutual defense "contract," rather than on an objective blood relationship.

Utilizing a psychocultural dimension, we have analyzed selected proverbs and poetry emanating from precolonial and early colonial instances of clan conflicts. Elite – both government and opposition – manipulations provide the major source of clan conflicts. Colonial elites first introduced this practice within a centralized state leaving a divide and rule legacy to be exploited by the post-independence elite. Military dictator Siyad carried the practice to outrageous levels through the provision of abundant modern (Darod) hegemony. Armed opposition groups used defensive clanism and military bases in Ethiopia to overthrow the viciously clanist regime. Clanism operates in a defensive manner for those struggling for social justice and equality – the elite and masses are bound together by consciousness of shared oppression, which is significantly different from forms of "false consciousness" artificially manufactured by a cynical elite. Under peripheral capitalism, uneven class formation produces a unique dialectic of class and clan (see Saul 1979:394-423). Historical memories and environmental pressures (disasters) facilitate clanism as a group phenomenon.

Clan Conflicts: The Invention of Enmity

In the post-Cold War era, with its rhetoric of a new democratic world order, democratic governance is increasingly becoming the basis for international economic and social assistance. Somalia, both north and south, needs priority assistance to conduct urgent voluntary mass disarmament.

The UN seems to have conducted significant demobilization in Mozambique, while it has lagged behind in Somalia and Somaliland. Youthful clan militias with guns need training programs and various other incentives to be able to reenter civil society without their arms. After careful screening, some of them could be recruited as part of the new locally accountable police forces.

In the south, the political situation continues to pose dangers of violent clan conflicts, especially in the Mogadishu and Kismayu area. More than half the political factional leaders, including Mohamed Farah Aidid (USC-SNA), Abdullahi Yusuf (SSDF), Umar Jess (SPM-SNA), Abdi Warsame (SSNM) and Umar Masala (SNF), were senior military officers in Siyad's army. However, due to the clan factor, today none of them can conquer Somalia militarily. Creating a government necessitates compromise and the formation of multi-clan coalitions along consociational lines. This would prove to be "strong men consociationalism," requiring the eventual introduction of the electoral principle and leadership rotation, for the transition to evolve toward consociational democracy. Perhaps the post-Cold War democratic order would serve as incentive for such a transformation.

The Republic of Somaliland, on the other hand, is positively moving toward "power-sharing, decision-making through consensus, respect for autonomy, and acceptance of differences" (Leatherbee 1994). A recent *Fund For Peace* human rights and democracy assessment for the Sudan, Ethiopia, Eritrea, Djibouti, and Somaliland, concluded as follows:

> In fact, that the SNM leadership would acquiesce to *Guurti* direction is in accord with the party's long-time reputation of being 'one of the most democratic movements in the Horn of Africa' ... Unlike in the other four countries examined in this article, there are powerful checks on the power of the executive in Somaliland. The power of the

clans, demonstrated in their reluctance to turn control of the national airport in Hargeisa and seaport in Berbera over to the national government, indicates ... potential resistance to the state ... Whatever its future relationship with Somalia may be, if Somaliland keeps to its present path of cautious consensus-building and respect for local and regional autonomy, preparing for free and fair elections at the end of the transitional period in 1996, and extending the rule of law to prevent the type of criminal behavior that most notably victimizes women, then the future for civil society and human rights there may be the most hopeful in the Horn of Africa (Leatherbee 1994).

Post-transitional elections pose serious dangers to both Somaliland and Somalia. After all, it was election corruption that partly paved the way for Siyad's military coup in 1969. The 1960 elections in British Somaliland were organized on the basis of first-past-the-post: the results were most unfair to the NUF which polled 34 percent of the popular vote and won only one seat! The leading party, the SNL, polled 54 percent of the vote and won a majority of twenty seats. The non-Isaq USP party polled 12 percent of the vote and won twelve concentrated seats.[12] The 1964 and 1969 elections were based on a crudely devised proportional system that left much to be desired. Today, Somali constitutionalists can have access to a variety of tested mathematical formulae for achieving an array of consociational objectives (Horowitz 1991:163-203)

It is important to resist choosing once again the failed 1960 model simply because people happen to be acquainted with it. This almost happened during the Djibouti conference, when old exiled politicians called for reactivating the 1960 Constitution which, even during the 1961 referendum, had been rejected by the northern regions. The current situation calls for both constitutional and electoral innovation. Regional territorial arrangements may transfer competition to the levels of even more homogeneous sub-clans and sub-subclans. Once the ruling to form parties is passed, the propensity to form clan based parties will manifest itself. Hopefully many of them will constitute multi-clan coalitition, sometimes pitched at the level of crisscrossing subclan alliances. The Somali experience can benefit from a variety of innovations in federalism, regional autonomy and electoral systems which are now available.[13]

The electoral system should deflect clan parties from contesting "divisive elections, which produce feelings of permanent exclusion on the part of those who are ascriptively locked out of office" (Horowitz 1985:681). One alternative, of course, is to continue and refine the system of indirect electoral pooling practiced in Somaliland. Otherwise, a new electoral system needs to (1) prevent clan domination; (2) induce clans to behave moderately; (3) encourage inter-clan and intra-clan negotiations and bargaining; (4) prevent the permanent exclusion of any resulting minority; and (5) reduce the disparity between votes won and seats won (Horowitz 1985:632). Above all, the new electoral system must encourage the formation and preservation of multi-clan coalitions along the lines advocated by Professor Arthur Lewis (1965). Such an approach will allow Somali political development to continue to evolve from violent conflicts to peaceful competition.

Notes

1. The five clan-families into which the Somali nation is divided (Isaq, Hawiye, Darod, etc.) and even their respective clans and subclans are generally too large, too widely scattered, and too unwieldy to act or serve as effective legal, organizational or corporate political units. The modern context of party political competition does, of course, provide a new significance to such extended kinship links. Within the series of diffuse attachments the most binding and most frequently-mobilized loyalty is the "*diya*-paying group." This unit's size varies from a few hundred to a few thousand men. An injury done by or to any member of the group implicates all those who are party to its treaty. According to Somali traditional law (*xeer*), if a man is killed, blood compensation stipulates a payment of a hundred camels. The *diya*-paying group of the victim would collectively claim the damage due from the killer's group. Obviously highly decentralized, the process emerges from the pastoral ecology and facilitates considerable collaboration within the group. For a pastoral society, in which self-help provides an effective sanction for redressing wrongs, the *diya* unit permits the resolution of political issues between groups. Despite the formal security of the colonial and post-colonial state, the security of the individual pasto-

ralist's person and property depends ultimately upon his membership in a *diya*-paying group. Nevertheless, over and beyond this unit, other wider kinship alliances can form and flourish.

2. Between 1981-1987, I conducted several tours into most of Somalia's eighteen regions as head of SURERD, a rural development non-governmental organization.

3. Hegel argued that what sets man apart from the natural world is the desire for recognition. This desire is pre-eminently human; that is to say, it is found only in self-conscious and rational beings. Self-consciousness is, therefore, an incomplete state for the human who requires recognition from another, equally self-conscious existence. However, this human search for recognition involves dangerous contradictions since reciprocity is often denied. Kojeve demonstrated that this longing to gain, but not give recognition to others, which characterizes pure self-consciousness, leads to a conflict of "pure prestige." Man is not certain of his value unless others admit it; yet what he requires of them he is himself not willing to yield. The encounter for recognition must therefore, be understood as a struggle in which one, or both participants risk all, even their physical lives, to gain recognition from the other. If one of the two parties in the struggle for prestige is killed, the other no longer obtains effective recognition; if both die, neither of the two is recognized. The one who saves his biological life by recognizing and submitting to the other, becomes the slave to the other, the Master. Kojeve's interpretation goes on to affirm that labor for the Master fashions in the slave a new being; the slave comes to see himself in the product he has created.

4. Interviews conducted with the supporters and opponents of the movement in Basaso and Gardo, March-April, 1994.

5. Interview with Colonel Abdillahi Kahin in Toronto, August 1 and 3, 1992.

6. Interview with Abdirahman Osman Raghe, who let me copy these figures from his notes during the *Fifth International Congress of Somali Studies,* College of the Holy Cross, Worcester, Mass, December 1-3, 1993.

7. See a recent example, Lidwin Kapteijns, "The catastrophe and Culture," presented at the *Fifth Internnational Congress of Somali Studies,* College of the Holy Cross, Worcester, Mass., December 1-3, 1993.

8. Perhaps the most bizarre aspect of this oppression has been the middle of the night arrest of forty-seven young Isaq civil servants and University lecturers in July 1989. They were working loyally in Mogadishu,

far from their rebellious regions. To demonstrate the power of state terror, Siyad had them taken to an empty Jasiira beach where they were slaughtered in cold blood and buried in mass grave. This is but one of several incidents that finally caught the attention of international human rights organizations.

9. These assessments were obtained during interviews conducted in Hargeisa and Mogadishu, June-August 1991 and in the Bari (Bosaso) region during March/April 1994.

10. Interviews and conversations with Ibrahim Meygag Samater, last chairman of the SNM Central Committee, especially during the *Fifth International Congress of Somali Studies,* College of the Holy Cross, Worcester, Mass, December 1-3, 1993. He kindly supplied me with most of the information pertaining to the SNM and Somaliland Republic. The information in the following section all derives from these interviews and conversations.

11. Donald Horowitz (1985:286-287) misses the multi-clan nature of "the Ogaden" and therefore, the real reason for the relative popularity of Somali irredentism during the 1960s.

12. Interview with Ibrahim Meygag Samater, see note 10.

13. For this discussion of electoral systems, I am indebted to Horowitz (1985 and 1991).

References

Adam, Hussein M. *The Revolutionary Development of the Somali Language.* Los Angeles: Occasional Paper No. 20 for the African Studies Center, University of California, 1980.

Andrzejewski, B.W., and Lewis, I.M. *Somali Poetry.* Oxford: Clarendon Press, 1964.

Aronson, Dan. R. "Kinsmen and Comrades: Toward a Class Analysis of the Somali Pastoral Sector." *Nomadic Peoples.* 7 (November 1980).

Bayart, Jean-Francois. *The State in Africa: The Politics of the Belly.* London: Longmann, 1993.

Bongartz, Marie. *The Civil War in Somalia.* Uppsala: Current African Issue II, Nordiska Afrikainstitute, 1991.

Bulhan, Hussein. *Crisis.* 1(11) (November 1989):2.

Cassanelli, Lee. *The Shaping of Somali Society.* Philadelphia: University of Pennsylvania Press, 1982.

Chazan, Naomi and Donald Rothchild, eds. "Patterns of State-Society Incorporation and Disengagement in Africa." In *The Precarious Balance: State and Society in Africa*. Boulder, CO: Westview Press, 1988.

Diamond, Larry. "Class, Ethnicity and the Democratic State: Nigeria, 1950-1966." *Comparative Studies in Society and History*. 25(3) (July 1983): 457-489.

Diamond, Larry. "Review Article: Ethnicity and Ethnic Conflict." *Journal of Modern African Studies*. 25(1)(1987): 117-128.

Drysdale, John. *The Somali Dispute*. New York: Praeger, 1964.

Drysdale, John. *Whatever Happened to Somalia? A Tale of Tragic Blunders*. London: HAAN Associates, 1994.

Enloe, Cynthia H. *Ethnic Conflict and Political Development*. Boston: Little Brown, 1973. Lanham, Md.: University Press of America, 1986.

Fanon, Frantz. *Black Skin, White Masks*. New York: Grove Press, 1967.

Fanon, Frantz. *The Wretched of the Earth*. New York: Grove Press, 1968.

Galaydh, Ali Khalif. "Democratic Practice and Breakdown in Somalia." In Dov. Ronen, ed. *Democracy and Pluralism in Africa*. Boulder, CO: Lynne Rienner Publishers, 1986,

Glickman, Harvey, ed. "Issues in the Analysis of Ethnic Conflict and Democratization Processes in Africa Today." In *Ethnic Conflict and Democratization*. 1995.

Horn of Africa Bulletin. January- February 1994.

Horowitz, Donald L. *Ethnic Groups in Conflict*. Berkeley: University of California Press, 1985.

Iye, Ali Moussa. *Le Verdict De L'arbre*. Dubai: International Printing Pres, 1991.

Kojeve, Alexandre. *Introduction to the Reading of Hegel*. New York: Basic Books, 1969.

Laitin, David. "A Consociational Democracy for Somalia." *Horn of Africa*. XIII (1&2) (January- March and April-June 1980).

Laitin, David and Samatar Said S. *Somalia: Nation in Search of a State*. Boulder, CO: Westview Press, 1987.

Leatherbee, Leah and Bricker, Dale. *Consensus and Dissent: Prospects for Human Rights and Democracy in Horn of Africa*. New York: The Fund for Peace, January 1994.

Lewis, Sir Arthur. *Politics in West Africa*. London: Allen and Unwin, 1965.

Lewis, I.M. "Sufism in Somaliland: A Study in Tribal Islam." *Bulletin of the School of Oriental and African Studies*. 17 (3) (1955).

Lewis, I.M. *A Pastoral Democracy*. London: Oxford University Press, 1961.

Lewis, I.M. "Kim Il-Sung in Somalia: The End of Tribalism?" In *Politics in Leadership*. Shack, William A. and Cohen, Percy S., eds. Oxford: Clarendon Press, 1979.

Lewis, I.M. *A Modern History of Somalia: Nation and State in the Horn of Africa*. Boulder, CO: Westview Press, 1988.

Lewis, I.M. "The Ogaden and the Fragility of Somali Segmentary Nationalism." *Horn of Africa*. XIII (1 and 2) (January-March and April-June 1990).

Lijphart, Arendt. *Democracy in Plural Societies*. New Haven: Yale University Press, 1977a.

Luling, Virginia. "The Other Somali-Minority Groups in Traditional Somali Society." In *Studies in Humanities and Natural Sciences. Proceedings of the Second International Congress of Somali Studies- University of Hamburg, August 1-6, 1983* Vol. 4. Labahn, Thomas, ed. Hamburg: Helmut Buske Verlag, 1984.

Mafeje, A. "The Ideology of 'Tribalism'." In *The Journal of Modern African Studies*. 9 (1971): 253-261.

Mukhtar, Mohamed H. "The Emergence and Role of Political Parties in the Inter-river Region of Somalia from 1947 to 1960." In *Proceedings of the Third International Congress of Somali Studies, (May 1986 at the University of Rome)*. Annarita Puglielli, ed. Rome: Il Pensiero Scientifico Editore, 1988.

Nelson, Harold D. *Area Handbook for Somalia*. Washington: USGPO for Foreign Area Studies, The American University, 1982.

Putnam, Diana B. and Nour, Mohamood. *The Somalis: Their History and Culture*. Washington D.C.: The Refugee Service Center, October 1993.

Rothchild, Donald and Olorunsola, Victor A. *State Versus Ethnic Claims: African Policy Dilemmas*. Boulder, CO: Westview Press, 1983.

Samatar, Ahmed. *Socialist Somalia: Rhetoric and Reality*. London: Zed Books, 1988.

Samatar, Abdi. *The State and Rural Transformation in Northern Somalia, 1884-1986*. Madison: University of Wisconsin Press, 1989.

Saul, John S.. *The State and Revolution in Eastern Africa*. New York: Monthly Review Press, 1979.

Sheikh-Abdi, Abdi. *Divine Madness: Mohamed Abdulle Hassan* (1856-1920). London: Zed Books, 1993.

Shoumatoff, Alex. "The 'Warlord' Speak." *The Nation*. April 4, 1994.

Sklar, Richard L. "Political Science and National Integration- A Radical Approach." *The Journal of Modern African Studies*. 5(1) (1967).

Steiner, Jurg. *European Democracies*. New York: Longman, 1991.

Swift, Jeremy. "The Development of Livestock Trading in a Nomad Pastoral Economy: The Somali Case." In *Pastoral Production and Society*. Cambridge: Cambridge University Press, 1979.

Touval, Saadia. *Somali Nationalism: International Politics and the Drive for Unity in the Horn of Africa*. Cambridge: Harvard University Press, 1963.

CHAPTER 5

INTERNATIONAL VERSUS LOCAL ATTEMPTS AT PEACEBUILDING

A series of Somali civil wars have led to state collapse and layers of complicated problems. Like Chad in 1980-2, Somali state collapse in 1991-2 essentially resulted from a factional civil war among the United Somali Congress (USC) guerrilla victors who had overthrown the previous brutal Siyad Barre regime; a war that caused the demise of all the branches of central government. The capital, Mogadishu, became a city divided by armed barricades, resembling Beirut during the Lebanese civil war. Somali minorities escaped by sea to Kenya and Yemen recalling Vietnam's boat people. Chaos and anarchy engulfed Mogadishu, making it the epicenter of Somalia's problems. The situation in northern Somalia, former British Somaliland, which declared a de facto secession under the Somali National Movement (SNM), reflected similarities to the problem of Eritrea with Ethiopia. A deeper tragedy lay in the formerly peaceful Bay region inhabited by the large, yet poorly armed Rahanweyn Somalis. The war came to them simply as a result of their geography. Siyad Barre left Mogadishu but did not leave the country as Mengistu did. He barricaded himself and his remnant loyalist troops in his home region of Gedo, from where he launched spoiler wars like Renamo in Mozambique. What ensued were continuing civil wars between General Aidid's USC and Siyad's remnant forces fought mostly on Bay (Baidoa) territories. Journalists termed Bay's plight Somalia's Bosnia. The devastating man-made famine that resulted led to the international community's humanitarian intervention in Somalia in the years 1992-5.

One could speculate about various possibilities for external intervention to rescue Somalia from destruction. According to Ali Mazrui: 'Ideally, Somalia should have been saved by fellow Africans – a kind of Pan Africana, Africans policing themselves or policing each other. It has been attempted in Liberia by a West African force drawn from several nations... A Second preference would have been a rescue of Somalia by members of the Organization of the Islamic Conference (OIC), a kind of Pax Islamica... A third preference for the Somali resuce would have been under the League of Arab States – a kind of Pax Arabica or Pax Arabiana... A fourth preference would have been a truly multinational task force to both pacify and feed Somalia, a kind of Pax Humania which would combine troops from carefully and sensitively selected countries.'[1] Perhaps the UNOSOM situation in 1994-5, after the departure of most American and European forces, mirrors somewhat Mazrui's fourth option. The fact remains that when foreign intervention to avert the Somali catastrophe came, it was a US initiative under the umbrella of the United Nations. 'What we have instead is a Pax Americana – a primarily American force. It is essentially a Pax Americana with a UN fig leaf.' In the post-Cold War era, with socio-economic difficulties facing most states, the prospects for a single power (other than the United States) to save a collapsing state have diminished considerably. It gives support to the proposition that the more complete the collapse of state, the greater will be the role and magnitude of foreign intervention aimed at reconstruction. The magnitude and complexities of Somali problems led the OAU, the OIC, and the Arab League to maintain a cautious posture, concluding that it was not realistic to attempt an intervention. The OAU lacked political will and resources while the OIC and the Arab League lacked political will.

STATE COLLAPSE

Around January 1991 and during the ensuing months, Somalia experienced a cataclysmic event, virtually unseen since the Second World War. It was not simply a military coup, a revolutionary replacement of a decayed and ineffective dictatorship, or a new, radical regime coming to power through a partisan uprising. Somalia's collapsed state represented the literal implosion of state structures and of residual forms of authority and legitimacy, and the situation has lasted for over almost two decades. In some respects, the country seems to have reverted to a nineteenth-century status: no internationally recognized polity; no recognized national administration exercising real authority; no formal countrywide legal and judiciary system; no national banking and insurance services; no national telephone and postal systems; no national public services; no national educational and health systems; no national police and public security services; and no reliable electricity or piped water services. Most of the so-called officials serve on a voluntary basis and are often surrounded, in a number of places, by disruptive, violent bands of armed youths.

Like all collapsed states, the Siyad military state disintegrated because it could no longer perform the functions required for it to pass as a state. Siyad Barre's brutal and arbitrary repression and his concentrations of power in the hands of his clan elite led to the whole country rising up against him, using their own clans as organizing bases. Such armed clan-based protopolitical organizations were created as the Somali National Movement (SNM, for the northern Iraq clan-family), the Somali Salvation Democratic Front (SSDF, for the Majerteen, Darod clan-family), the United Somali Congress (USC, for the Hawiye clan-family), the Somali Patriotic Movement (SPM, for the Ogaden, Darod clan-family), and so forth. By 1993 there were about twenty-eight such clan-based political fractions. As Marina Ottaway put it, 'Competition becomes turf war among political organizations trying to keep each other out. A tragic example is offered by Somalia, where the fragmentations of the elite after the demise of Mohamed Siyad Barre led to the emergence of warlords fighting with each other for exclusive control over territory.'[2] Elite fragmentation has led to political paralysis and continuing conflict or at best negative peace in the central (Mogadishu) and southern (Kismayu) parts of the country. Territorial fragmentation has also led to enclaves of positive peace and progress.

The phenomenon of state collapse represents a major challenge to developmental social sciences. The Siyad case shows a close relationship between state collapse and the role of rogue leadership. A critical cause lay in the mismanagement , pillage of resources, brutal military repression, and abuses by the dictatorial regime that left the majority of the population without a stake in the existing system. Under Siyad Barred, Somalia became one of the most indebted states in Africa, with a debt service ration of over 180 per cent and a meagre revenue base. From a historical perspective, Somali state collapse also represents a mismatch between a seemingly strong military state and an amorphous Somali civil society. The problem is not between the state as such, or in the abstract, and concrete Somali civil society; rather, it involves the particular Siyad military state. It is a case illustrating the hypothesis that tyranny, in the end will destroy its own state. The Cold War sustained Siyad's military regime but in due course, clan-based opposition groups rose up to challenge Siyad's military dictatorship at a time when the end of the Cold War reduced the opportunities for extracting military, technical, and financial resources from external sources. As a result, Somalia became the perfect illustration of the state-civil society contradiction and its implosion, precisely because the Cold War had imposed an exceedingly heavy military state on a decentralized, relatively democratic civil society that was able to survive on meagre resources.

MISSED OPPORTUNITIES

Could the Somali catastrophe have been anticipated and prevented, or at least limited? What pre-emptive measures were appropriate to confront the causes? Ambassador Mohamed Sahnoun, the UN's Special Representative to Somalia, raised these issues forcefully in his publication, *Somalia: The Missed Opportunities* in which he concludes: 'if the international community had intervened earlier and more effectively in Somalia, much of the catastrophe that has unfolded could have been avoided.'[3] I hope to dwell on lessons and avoid recrimination. I have tried to base my comments on what was known at the time in order to approach the policy-maker's point of view. I have limited the discussion to selected major instances, which meet the criteria for a missed opportunity. In my judgment, this includes the period of the switch from Soviet dependency to American hegemony (1977-8), the 1988 civil war in northern Somalia, and the scramble on the eve of Siyad's fall in 1990-1.

Following the 1977-8 Ogaden War, Somalia switched sides from being a close ally of the Soviet Union to coming voluntarily under American hegemony. During this period of high tension and flux, the United States missed the opportunity to impose conditions that would have redirected Somalia toward a somewhat different political trajectory. The Americans relied on the IMF and the World Bank to press for market reforms and economic liberalization while remaining silent on political liberalization and issues involving human rights. Interestingly, the United States did delay implementation of the agreement on military assistance from 1978 till 1980 because of continued Somali military activities in the Ogaden. In the end, it was Siyad who blinked and restrained such activities in order to receive US military assistance. A clear sign of Siyad's vulnerability to outside pressure is manifested by the offer he finally accepted from the United States. As an opening bid in the negotiations over the former Soviet military facilities, he demanded $2 billion over a ten-year period, but a take-it-or-leave-it offer from the United States obliged him to accept a meagre $40 million over a two-year period.[4]

As an observer at the time, I was aware that the regime fully expected to receive not only new economic directives but also pressures for political reforms as the price of its switch to the US camp. Instead, the regime was allowed to get by with insignificant cosmetic reforms, including a meaningless constitution and a bogus election. Perhaps the two most salient reasons for lack of political and diplomatic response then were the overriding concerns of a Cold War mentality and an obsession with economic reforms at the cost of all other reforms. Perceptions of the costs involved in taking action often dim a policy-maker's receptivity to an early warning of an impeding catastrophe. However, in 1977-80 the visible signs did not call for a unilateral military intervention; US and international actions could have limited the problems through military and economic sanctions and diplomatic pressure for tough political reforms.

In May-June 1988 the international community received a crystal clear warning of the impending Somali tragedy in the form of a large and explosive insurrection in northern Somalia. The Ethiopian president, Mengistu Haile-Mariam, and Siyad Barre signed a peace agreement in 1988, intended to prevent armed movements directed against their governments from using each other's country as a base. As a result, Mengistu told the Somali National Movement (SNM) that they could seek refuge in Ethiopia but they could no longer use his country as a base for military attacks on Somalia. The SNM returned home to northern Somalia where they launched a military campaign against Barre. Siyad's response was vicious; he launched full-scale military and aerial campaigns destroying many cities, towns, and much of the infrastructure in the area. An estimated five thousand people belonging to the northern Isaq clan-family were reported to have been killed in May 1988 alone; about fifty thousand more lost their lives and many more were injured over the following months as revolt and repression spread throughout the region. Over half a million people either crossed the border in the Haud area of Ethiopia or were displaced within northern Somalia. These tragic events were covered by the global media and even in a series of reports by agencies of the US government and by human rights organizations and should have served as a warning signal.[7] There is some evidence to indicate that the US Congress would have supported a drastic cut in all military and economic aid in order to apply pressure for significant political reforms. The Pentagon, however, opposed it and actively lobbied against a change in policy, based on its interests in gaining access to military facilities and the so-called regional security issue.

A third window of opportunity opened up in 1990, on the eye of Siyad's fall from power. The Djibouti conference, analyzed below, represents cases of misused opportunity involving Italian and Egyptian responses that were misconceived, harmful, and highly inappropriate given the circumstances. By 1990, armed rebellion had spread like wildfire in most of Somalia's regions and districts, and the international press began to refer to President Siyad Barre as the Mayor of Mogadishu. Nevertheless, Italian and Egyptian officials maintained a single-minded effort to continue and retain a political role for Siyad Barre. The opportunity came with the rise of the Manifesto group – a Mogadishu-based civilian opposition movement. The rapid successes of the armed opposition movements encouraged the latent civilian opposition to rear its previously timid head. On 15 May 1990 they launched a protest and issued a Manifesto. This manifesto was signed by 144 well-known members of the post-independence elite: politicians of the parliamentary civilian era, ex-officials of the Siyad regime, well-known religious leaders, business leaders, traders, as well as professional/intellectual elements (lawyers, doctors, teachers, and other academics). They established a thirteen-person committee to organize a national reconciliation conference. The committee was headed by Abdullah Osman, the first elected president of Somalia, and Sheikh Mukhtar Mohamed Hussein, a former president of the elected Somali parliament. They called for a peaceful end to the civil wars and for a national conference to launch constitutional changes and guide the nation towards electoral politics and a multiparty system. They advocated the establishment of an interim, power-sharing coalition government to pave the way for multiparty elections. Unfortunately, Siyad's reaction could not have been more predictable. The regime jailed forty five manifesto signatories, although Italian and Egyptian protests led to their release after a few weeks. Nevertheless, distorted Italian and Egyptian strategies and tactics led them to misuse this window of opportunity that could have led to political reforms that might then have limited the catastrophe. On this issue, Italian political scientist Novati is both succinct and blunt:

> While Somalia was ravaged by civil war, hastening the downfall of Siyad Barre's regime in a dramatic crescendo of bloodshed and despair, Italy sought once more to manage the crisis by offering her good offices. The aim was to effect an orderly transfer of power to a large coalition of forces, parties and persons in which Siyad Barre would continue to play an important transition role in order to avoid, it was argued, a dangerous power vacuum. A self-fulfilled prophecy, Siyad's enemies firmly refused to join such a deal, pleading that the President should be personally responsible for crimes, malpractice and political chaos. An eleventh hour reconciliation conference, co-chaired by Italy and Egypt, was called in Cairo but it was doomed from the start and at the last minute was canceled. General Aidid wouldn't forget the activism of Boutros Boutros-Ghali, then foreign minister of Egypt, to 'save' Siyad. The flight of Siyad Barre from Mogadishu deprived Italy of her best card. The setback was definitive. A regime Italy had tried stubbornly to preserve over twenty years as a token of stability was in shambles. The

University, the jewel of Italian technical assistance, was destroyed and vandalized.[5]

Some observers felt that the Djibouti conference, held in June and July of 1991, constituted another missed historical opportunity. I do not think so; the Djibouti effort was bound to fail even before the conference doors had opened. For one thing, Djibouti was the brainchild of the distorted Italian and Egyptian strategy. During the 1989-90 period, they insisted that foreign powers still had to work with the Siyad regime to create transitional political structures that would facilitate 'stability for a successor regime.' The most positive role the Italians and Egyptians could have played at this point would have been to prevent the Renamo-like spoiler wars and Bosnia-like tragedy in Bay by offering Siyad the incentives to quit Gedo and go abroad into exile. Confusing wishful thinking with rational analysis, their efforts failed and continued to fail after the Djibouti conference had ended. Perhaps involvement of the United States, considered then more impartial than Italy and Egypt by many Somalis, and the United Nations could have produced a relatively better outcome. However, the United States ignored Somalia and concentrated its diplomatic efforts on ensuring a peaceful transition from Mengistu Haile-Mariam to Meles Zenawi in Ethiopia. Somali observers felt bitter: after all, they argued, Ethiopia was a Soviet problem while America was significantly responsible for the Somalia's mess.

THE DECISION TO INTERVENE

After showing much reluctance and discouraging others (including the United Nations) from intervening, the lame-duck first Bush administration decided to launch a humanitarian military intervention late in 1992. Why did the Americans refuse to intervene when the circumstances were more appropriate and waited until it was almost too late? Liberal writers and left-wing circles accused the United States of imperialist motives. Some argued that it intervened to protect actual or potential oil resources. However, a number of US oil companies (Conoco, Chevron, for example) were granted exploration rights during Siyad's rule and even earlier. Besides, during this period, most of the Somali elite either incumbent or in opposition, had generally manifested pro-American attitudes. From a pragmatic perspective they would have welcomed the investment and involvement of US companies as the best guarantee of efficient exploration, production, and access to global markets. It did not make sense for US companies to impose themselves militarily where they would obviously have been welcomed. Had this been a significant motive, the United States would surely have intervened before or just after Siyad fell, not twenty-two months later. Moreover, when military intervention came, none of the US and UN troops were deployed any where near the major areas of oil exploration in the northeast and in the de facto Republic of Somaliland.

The United States intervention, some alleged, was motivated by the need to combat the threat of Islamic fundamentalism financed by Sudan and Iran. Since 1991, Somaliland had both witnessed pockets of Islamic fundamentalism symbolized by the Islamic Unity group. During that period, their strength lay in northeast Somalia where they tried to gain power but were evicted by the SSDF and a coalition of clan-based forces, assisted by Ethiopian troops. Their strength since US and UN forces left, lay in the Gedo region in southwest Somalia near the Kenyan and Ethiopian borders. That this is not a significant issue is demonstrated by the fact that US and UN troops entered Somalia and departed without staging even minor skirmishes with the fundamentalists in Gedo; those in the northeast were too far from their area of operations. Later on, Ethiopian forces have conducted several forays against the Gedo area fundamentalists at the behest of the secular, clan-based Somali National Front (SNF) organization.

Other writers raised the issue of access to Somali military bases. However, as argued above, our knowledge of Somali elites tells us that they would not have denied the Americans access to military base agreements. The most attractive Somali military installations consist of the Berbera naval and airport facilities in the self-declared Republic of Somaliland. The elites who control Somaliland, according to our information, would only have been too glad to renew Americans access to the Berbera base and facilities, in exchange for recognition or for economic assistance. As of March 1994, US troops and as of March 1995, UN forces had left Somalia without deployment anywhere near the Berbera base. Besides, 'even if one accepts the globalist rationales for ensuring US military access to the region, the Somali bases were unnecessary in the light of other, more extensive, facilities readily available in the region.'[6] An illustration of this is the fact that the massive deployment of U.S. troops and equipment associated with Operation Desert Storm in Kuwait in 1991 did not need the naval facility in Berbera. A more sophisticated version takes the redundancy argument mentioned above and argues that, even though the United States in this highly technological post-Cold War era does not need Somali bases, it simply wished to deny their access to hostile regional powers such as Iran, Sudan, and Iraq. Once again, the evidence is simply not there: intervening forces have come and gone without deployment to protect Somali military bases.

The least satisfactory explanations are those derived mainly from the old Cold War context of the US strategic interests. These represent echoes of the general experience of American foreign policy towards the Third World which was shaped by the necessity to control and protect the extraction and supply of raw materials and /or insure access to military bases. Even if one cannot resist the conclusion that American foreign policy has historically been driven by economic and/or strategic determinants rather than by humanitarian considerations, one has to admit that the Somali intervention was a unique phenomenon. Bush administration officials argued that the United States had to intervene because of the 'massive proportions' of the tragedy and because the United States had the means to 'do something' about it. This global vision explanation argued that Somalia could enhance both US and UN credibility in the post-Cold War era, a case study of President Bush's New World Order.[7]

Those who use globalist explanations go on to point to the convergence of vision between Bush's New World Order and the new United Nations Secretary-General Boutros-Ghali's commitment to assertive multilateralism: 'Secretary-General Boutros-Ghali has an ambitious agenda for peace, through which he plans unprecedented UN involvement in peacemaking, peacekeeping, and peace enforcement. He is convinced that the UN now has an opportunity to achieve the great objectives for which it was established...'[8] There is no doubt that when Bush finally took the decision to intervene, the Secretary-General and the UN spared no efforts in its implementation.

However, early in 1991-92 the United States' mission to the UN did its best to keep the Somali case off the Security Council agenda. The shortcomings of the globalist interpretations have more to do with timing. 'In other words, why did Bush decide to launch Operation Provide Relief during August 1992 as opposed to July 1992 (or earlier), and why did he decide to launch Operation Restore Hope only after (as opposed to prior to) the presidential elections of November 1992?'[9] The dynamics of US electoral politics played a critical role in providing us with a more satisfactory explanation.

Another view advanced to explain the decision to intervene is based on the structural dynamics of American politics. The end of the Cold War has created at least two opposing groups. On one hand are those who want to transcend militarism to promote domestic social progress at home under the slogan of 'the peace dividend.' On the other hand are those who argue that the post-Cold War fragmentation and diffusion of power among multiple actors have made the contemporary situations even more dangerous and volatile. In the unstable, anarchical international system, the United States need to retain its military establishment in place. In other words, the United States needed the large Somali intervention for its military establishment to retain its size and expenditures.

Obviously globalist and structural militarist explanations were used in retrospect to rationalize the decision but not to trigger it. Domestic politics explanations involve the role of the media, non-governmental organizations (NGOs) and the US Congress. By 1992 the effects of state collapse manifested themselves in a devastating man-made famine and a brutal multi-sided civil war which collectively claimed the lives of at least three hundred thousand men, women and children (roughly 25-30 per cent of all children under the age of five). At its peak in 1992, the magnitude of human suffering in Somalia was overwhelming: out of a total estimated population of eight million, approximately 4.5 million Somalis required urgent external assistance. Of those, some 1.5 million people were at immediate risk of starvation, including one million children. American television screens carried the humanitarian disaster in Somalia to saturation point. The sense of urgency about the Somali crisis filtered from the media to the public and Congress, significantly raising pressures on the Bush administration.

The growing media, public, and congressional pressure provided, nevertheless, only a partial explanation for the reversal in US policy. For example, on 3 August 1992, a bipartisan resolution advocating a tangible humanitarian response overwhelmingly passed the Senate; the same bill was adopted by the House of Representatives on 10 August. The most sufficient explanation for President Bush's decision to intervene has to do with the presidential politics in an election year. Therefore in his October 1992 address to the United Nations General Assembly, Bush declared that the Pentagon would prepare the US military for a new and more active role in peacekeeping efforts in the New World Order.[13] It is important to observe that his NSC staff began serious preparations for the Somali intervention only *after* Bush lost his re-election bid. 'In an effort to leave office on a high note, President Bush finally decided that something had to be done about humanitarian disaster in Somalia.'[10] His harsh critics saw the dispatch of American troops to Somalia as a cynical effort on the president's part to deflect domestic and international criticisms for his abject failure to act in Bosnia. In retrospect, the US-led multinational force represented possibly a convergence of interests between Boutros-Ghali and President Bush.

A CRITIQUE OF OPERATION RESTORE HOPE (ORH)

Security Council Resolution 794 of 3 December 1992 authorized the United States to lead a Unified Task Force (UNITAF) code-named Operation Restore Hope (ORH) under chapter VII of the UN Charter. Chapter VII sanctions the use of forceful means to enhance UN objectives, in this case the delivery of relief supplies to starving people in Somalia. The resolution gave UNITAF the right 'to use all necessary means to establish as soon as possible a secure environment for humanitarian relief operations.'[11] Resolution 794 authorized the deployment of 24,000 American troops to Somalia; the initial cost of the operation to the United States was estimated at $500 million. More in line with his royal exit aspirations than with his New World Order vision, President Bush wrote

Boutros-Ghali to underline that the missions was 'limited and specific: to create security conditions which will permit the feeding of the starving Somali people and allow the transfer of this security function to the UN peacekeeping force.' At another point he seemed somewhat aware that the situation was more complicated and, stated that, 'Our mission is humanitarian, but we will not tolerate armed gangs ripping off their own people, condemning them to death by starvation.'[12] He contradicted himself further by declaring that US troops should depart from Somalia by the time of the inauguration in January 1992 – a forty-day span that did not allow for the time it takes to settle them on the ground.

Another consequence of the absurd six-week timetable President Bush proposed meant that the US army had to remove the critical civil affairs and military police training components from the ORH program. 'This was unusual; civil affairs officers are specialists in foreign cultures and are used for liaison with local communities. The U.S. military deployed approximately 1,000 civil affairs officers to Panama in December 1989 and about 300 to northern Iraq after the Gulf War. Under UNITAF, the numbers ranged from 7 to 30.' This meant that UNITAF was crippled from the start; it was not able to mount a viable program to demobilize armed youth, train a Somali police force, and revive the legal and court systems. The international intervening force was also doomed to fail because it lacked a credible exit strategy. One key lesson the United States learned from this failure in Somalia led to the positive situation in Haiti, where 'the United States reverted to the immediate and effective use of civil affairs units. In addition to civil affairs troops, more than 800 police advisers were sent to Haiti. Shortly after the initial landing, the United States began a police recruitment and training program.'[13] Under ORH, the Australian force had a civil-military affairs unit and was able to achieve tangible success in rebuilding Baidoa's and Bay's police forces and strengthen its civil society.

At its peak, UNITAF strength reached approximately thirty-seven thousand troops, including eight thousand on ships offshore. The United States provided the largest contingent by far, with a peak strength of about twenty-eight thousand marines and infantry. About nine thousand troops from over twenty countries joined ORH. For example, France provided twenty-five hundred French Legionnaires from neighboring Djibouti, Australia sent nine hundred elite soldiers, while Pakistan contributed four thousand soldiers, some of whom became embroiled in conflicts with General Aidid's faction.

ORH was implemented in four phases. The first involved the United Nations Task Force, UNITAF. Phase four involved the handoff from UNITAF to UNOSOM II. The troops were deployed in 'the triangle of death,' an area between a quarter and a third of the whole country and located between Somalia's two main rivers, the Shabele and the Juba. Boutros-Ghali's pleadings that troops be deployed in most parts of the country, including the northeast and the northwest (Somaliland) were understandably ignored by the United States and the other members of the Security Council.

There is no doubt that prior to 1992, and even after, ORH and UNOSOM represented the most radical and ambitious operations that the United Nations had undertaken in a sovereign state. Since Somalia did not present a military threat to surrounding states, this represented the first time ever that the United Nations organization had intervened in purely domestic affairs involving a humanitarian crisis. The aim was to restore peace, order, reconstitute the state, and promote socio-economic development. The Security Council showed that it was now freed from the paralysis of the Cold War epoch, when the United States and the Soviet Union often blocked Security Council action by their veto. For the first time the Security Council authorized enforcement action under chapter VII of the Charter, bypassing article 2, paragraph 7, which prohibits interference in the domestic affairs of a sovereign state. The world confronted a concrete case of the clash between two international principles: respect for the state sovereignty versus the imperative to protect life, to safeguard human rights. The decision goes beyond Somalia since it has potential for much wider application.

It is misleading to conclude that the US/UN humanitarian intervention was a complete failure. The UNITAF/ORH operation permitted the distribution of relief food to previously famished populations. It has been estimated that at least 250,000 lives were saved during the emergency. However, the operation did no achieve its maximum objectives – that is, reconstituting a viable political system and facilitating democratization and development. Nevertheless, it did achieve as much as could be hoped for under the circumstances; it created an environment that was tangibly better than what would have existed without it, at least in certain aspects.

As soon as ORH was on the ground, throughout central and southern Somalia, looting, extortion, and attacks on relief workers dropped sharply. Operations began to shift from emergency relief to development programs, including the revival of agricultural production, restocking livestock herds, restoring some of the country's shattered services and infrastructure. Relief continued to command high priority since 1.5 million Somalis continued to be estimated as still at risk from malnutrition and disease. In March 1993 the United Nations unveiled a comprehensive Relief and Rehabilitation Program for all of 1993, budgeted at $159 million. It included projects ranging from the resettlement of displaced persons and refugees to restoring health, sanitation, water, and administrative services. By 1994 some 130,000 refugees had come back to Somalia from camps in Kenya. The exodus of refugees to neighboring countries began to dwindle. Seeds and agricultural tools were distributed by UN agencies and NGO's. There was a really good rainfall in 1992-3, helping to increase local food production and facilitating the emergence of markets. While relief continued to receive top priority, greater emphasis was being placed on rehabilitation and reconstruction. The mechanism to carry out such activities involved the Civilian-Military Operations Centre located at UNOSOM headquarters: nearly one hundred participants met daily for briefings from the UN agencies, the Red Cross, and NGO's, as well as representatives from UNITAF headquarters and the military commands.

It is on the political front that the international humanitarian intervention met the insurmountable challenges. The United States had no evident reason to favour any one of the several armed factions, and most Somalis continue to believe this in spite of the conflict that ensued. Errors do occur in the conduct of such operations, including those that belong to the inherent structure of the situations in which the intervening (international) forces find themselves. Normally, the intervention freezes the military situation, and thus prevents factions currently victorious or on the offensive from pressing home their military advantage. The intervention therefore favours and aids the faction with the weakest military position that manipulates the intervening force against its rivals. General Aidid had succeeded in defeating President Siyad and his remaining forces and chasing them from Somalia into Kenya in May 1992. Siyad's son-in-law, General Morgan, and loyalist troops, began to cross back into Somalia in November-December 1992, timing his armed faction's movements with the arrival of UNITAF-ORH.

Ambassador Oakley, President Clinton's representative to Somalia during ORH, reports that 'Morgan's forces had been moving toward Kismayu when UNITAF landed in December. They moved back to near the Kenyan border, but after the Addis Ababa cease-fire agreement they began to move south.' Following discussion with UNITAF officers, Morgan 'sounded reasonable and compliant, seemingly reconciled to keeping his forces outside the city,' toward Kismayu in the south.[14] In Kismayu, Morgan's SNF faction confronted Omar Jess's SPM faction allied to General Aidid and his USC-SNA (Somali National Alliance):

> In February 1993… an anti-Aidid faction managed to seize part of Kismayu by a *coup de main*, catching UNITAF peace keepers by surprise. When Aidid's ally, Omar Jess, tried a similar trick a few days later, peacekeepers were on their guard and managed to foil it. From Aidid's point of view, it was hard to avoid the conclusion that UNITAF had sided with his opponents, but if this particular event had not occurred to create that impressions, another incident would have had the same effect.'[15]

General Aidid and his allies believed that there was outright UNITAF-Morgan collusion against Jess. At that point, UNITAF troops in Kismayu were mostly from Belgium. Aidid and his angry supporters mounted demonstrations outside the US embassy compound in Mogadishu. Aidid was also angry at the Nigerian government for having granted asylum to Siyad Barre, and so followed the protest demonstrations with an attack on Nigerian UNITAF forces. 'The arrest of Colonel Jess by UNITAF as he tried to drive from Mogadishu to Kismayu, heavily armed and without permission, only rubbed salt into the wound. More protests and demonstrations followed. Though not through anti-UNITAF actions by the SNA stopped for a while as cooperation resumed, the Kismayu events marked the beginning of bad blood between General Aidid and UNITAF; it had all the ingredients for 'clanizing' the United States and the United Nations.

THE WAR WITH GENERAL AIDID

The United Nations later mission, UNOSOM II, was mandated explicitly to include enforcement powers, and Boutros-Ghali appointed American Admiral Jonathan Howe as his new special representative. International intervention confronted two broad strategies: one, working with the existing forces, mostly warlords, as a critical source of legitimate authority whose cooperation must be sought; the other, encouraging new institutions and leaders by promoting Somali civil society. Mohamed Sahnoun, as a special representative of UNOSOM I, felt that this complicated solution did not call for an either/or policy and he tried his best to pursue a two-track strategy. Ambassador Oakley, representing President Clinton under ORH, leaned heavily on the first strategy and got on very well with all the so-called warlords, especially General Aidid in spite of the suspicions that had begun to emerge. Admiral Howe did not seem to have a strategy; instead he rapidly developed an obsession which he shared with Boutros-Ghali. As John Drysdale and others have argued, Ghali and Howe became convinced that peace and a government could only come to Somalia once Aidid was removed from the political scene.[16] Two cardinal aspects of leadership for such unprecedented operations are the ability to think and act strategically, and the personal aptitude to absorb relevant aspects of indigenous history and culture as well as the diplomatic skills to work effectively with all other actors involved in the peace-building effort. Admiral Howe and his team did no appear to have such qualities.

An attitude of confrontation with Aidid (probably mutual at this point) had set in; the issue became how to find an incident that would provoke him. On the morning of 5 June, Pakistan UNOSOM soldiers were sent to inspect Aidid's armaments near his radio station at very short notice. UNOSOM had already targeted his radio as hostile to UNOSOM's mission. An armed confrontation between this UNOSOM unit and Aidid's militia left twenty-four Pakistani soldiers dead. Did General Aidid give the order to kill UNOSOM troops or was this a spontaneous act undertaken by his militia in the heat of tensions and hostile suspicions? There is no clear answer to this question. Under Howe's leadership, UNOSOM took precipitate military action in response to this attack. A far better response would have been to call for an impartial investigation by an esteemed group leading to a judicial decision arrived at in a fair and transparent manner. Before any such assessment had been undertaken, UNOSOM and the United States fixed blame on Aidid and launched an operation to either capture or kill him. Wanted posters with Aidid's picture were displayed all over south Mogadishu, and a price of $25,000 was placed on his head. A clandestine American-led military operation was launched against him. The Italians recommended isolating Aidid while at the same time recognizing and dealing with other leaders of his clan and its protopolitical organization, the Somali National Alliance (SNA). Boutros-Ghali and Howe rejected their suggestions, rebuked them for their initiatives, and deployed them out of Mogadishu.

Elders and other prominent personalities from Aidid's Habar Gedir clan met on 23 July 1993 to assess their situation and explore various options. US/UNOSOM helicopters bombed the building on the grounds that Aidid could be attending the meeting. As it turned out Aidid did not attend and at least fifty-four Habar Gedir clan members, mainly civilians, were killed without provocation. Such activities led to the perception that UNOSOM was simply another 'rival clan.' Aidid's hand was in fact strengthened among his clan members, who perceived UNOSOM's activities as an attack against their entire clan. As long as this new external threat persisted, Habar Gedir clan members decided to rally behind Aidid. The clan took heavy casualties while inflicting serious damage and paralyzing the whole UNOSOM mission and operations. From June to October 1993, the hunt for Aidid put a hold on most of UNOSOM's work at reconciliation and reconstruction. In October 1993, Aidid's faction shot down at least two US helicopters and in the ensuing combat, eighteen American soldiers were killed, one was captured, and over seventy-five were wounded. This prompted President Clinton to shift both American and UN policy back to politics and diplomacy, as he ordered an end to the manhunt. Even though the hunt for Aidid was aborted, UNOSOM II had been so discredited that it was subsequently unable to play an effective role as interlocutor in the Somali civil wars.

LESSONS LEARNED AND LEGACY

One can draw preliminary lessons from these experiences. While assisting a country devastated by ethnic conflicts, it is important for international intervention to avoid overt political activities that favour one side over another. This is not a question of neutrality, but an effort to achieve impartiality to the best extent possible. The Somali case invariably draws our attention to the primary responsibility of leadership in fomenting and sustaining civil wars and also, in initiating and nurturing peace. Leaders have the choice as to whether to manage or exploit ethnic/ clan cleavages. A number of warlords promoted actions and decisions that have perpetuated Somali civil wars. Even though environmental and structural factors played crititcal roles, what actions leaders decide to take is what ultimately matters. Sahnoun and Oakley's diplomatic instincts allowed them to be flexible and judicious; Howe was rigid, stubborn, and mediocre. A mix of factors led to incorrect UNOSOM decisions: incompetence, personal vanity and ambition, a short-term orientation, and bureaucratic infighting. The leadership of such large operations much be carefully chosen. There is a need for an overall strategy for peace-building. With sophisticated, sensitive, pragmatic, and nuanced leadership, the two strategies outlined above could be synchronized and pursued with the long run aim of civilianizing most of the leaders and demobilizing the clan militia. The design and implementation of a peace-building strategy should be guided by considered, professional decisions that are responsive to the local cultural and political conditions.

The issue of disarmament also shows that UNOSOM lacked insight into the general situation. To have succeeded, UNITAF/ UNOSOM's disarmament strategy would have needed a comprehensive, multidimensional approach: a demobilization program to provide job-training for the youthful militias; a serious program to train and equip police forces; and a program to equip and restore the courts and legal justice system. The funds the Security Council allocated for UNOSOM troops could not be used to support such developmental efforts. The handful of justice and police systems UNOSOM was able to establish had been reduced in size or disappeared after UNOSOM II's financial support evaporated. On its own initiative, the northern Somaliland Republic has carried out a successful demobilization and disarmament program. Northeast Somalia, or Puntland, has achieved similar success including the establishment of a police training school. UNOSOM promoted elite level reconciliation conferences in Addis Ababa and Nairobi. The Addis Ababa conference of 15-27 March 1993 resisted UNOSOM pressure to form a centralized state and adopted a regional-autonomy approach. UNOSOM finally backed this plan and speeded up the establishment of regional and district councils as an exit strategy. As of 1994, UNOSOM had assisted in the formation of fifty-three district councils out of eighty-one (excluding Somaliland), and eight out of thirteen regional councils (again, excluding Somaliland). The legacy of these institution-building efforts is mixed. Those that survive are in the process of being incorporated into wide clan-based authorities. Others have been subsumed by alternative indigenous institutions that have emerged without donor support. The UNOSOM method of establishing district and regional councils was based on a top-down approach, rather than being locally generated. UNOSOM was always eager to announce the number of district councils formed, a reflection of its 'product' rather than 'process' orientation. Qualitative rather than quantitative processes that would have eventually led to authentic local governance would have provided a sounder policy to pursue.

Paradoxically, even though UNOSOM moved to support decentralization in Somalia, UNOSOM itself was highly centralized in Mogadishu. It should have been decentralized, with strengthened offices in the various zones and a small mobile headquarters in Mogadishu. Somali civil wars and territorial fragmentation had, de facto, diminished Mogadishu's previous hegemony. In this way, UNOSOM could have avoided becoming hostage to events in a particular part of the country, as it did in Mogadishu. UNOSOM had to learn to overcome serious coordination problems. In military affairs, certain units, the Italians for example, continued to seek directives from their own national capitals rather than from UNOSOM headquarters. UNOSOM tried to create entirely new divisions to carry out its development-oriented mandate, rather than seeking to incorporate the efforts and harness the expertise of UN agencies, particularly UNDP, to assist in institution-building and economic reconstruction. There were ups and downs in coordination with humanitarian agencies and the press; this function was later routinized in the form of daily UNOSOM-NGO-press briefings and information exchanges. UNOSOM invested tremendous political capital in the reconciliation process involving factional leaders. Highlighted conferences involving these elements took place in Addis Ababa and in Nairobi. The UN placed a great deal of pressure on the factional leaders to reach agreements quickly, since its own mandate was of limited duration. All such factional elite conferences both before and after the demise of UNOSOM II have failed. Unfortunately, UNOSOM ignored the need to support, simultaneously, grassroots peace and reconciliation conferences like the one that was held in Borama, Somaliland. In such conferences, more indigenous methods of reconciliation were applied, and sufficient time was allowed for agreements to be reached. One of the negative legacies of UNOSOM is that it did not give much attention to and provide support for areas that were more stable and peaceful, such as Somaliland and Puntland.

The lack of a comprehensive and consistent strategy meant that the UNOSOM mission faced serious difficulties in pursuing an appropriate sequence of actions: Should, for instance, reconciliation and institution-building precede or follow disarmament? Should re-establishment of law and order (e.g., police) precede establishment of local or national authority or follow it? There was no reason not to pursue a two-track reconciliation process: bottom-up and top-down. However, for a bottom-up approach to succeed, demobilization and disarmament would have to be pursued consistently and energetically. This would have provided the necessary political space for civil society. Unfortunately, UNOSOM did not have either a clear strategy or resources. Continuity in both policy and personnel, which is essential for the success of a peace operation, was lacking. Investment in indirect peace-building, such as the promotion of business, professional, and communal associations, is a critical element in building a web of bridges across conflict lines, and should be a major component of future peace operations, with appropriate budget and expertise. UNOSOM had a negative impact on both Somali political and economic life. UNOSOM's massive presence caused indigenous and sustainable Somali employment to decline while an artificial service sector mushroomed. At the same time, UNOSOM preferred to import many items that were in fact available in local markets.

The international community's preference for local NGO's rather than local business, led to a mushrooming of inauthentic Somali 'NGOs'. All this led to resource-driven mentalities and opportunists and a revival of the culture of dependency of the Siyad era. Had UNOSOM been in the business of promoting sustainability, its approach would have resulted in a series of initiatives, beginning with institution-building assistance to Somaliland, which had formed its own civilian government, followed by efforts in the Puntland areas and other relatively stable clan-controlled zones. The strategy involves building on the stable and authentic cases and expanding to surround and eventually include more and more of the war-torn areas.

UNOSOM and the war with Aidid left a significant and broader legacy in international affairs: it dimmed, some would say extinguished, ambitious dreams for a New World Order.[17] Proposals advocating the creation of a separate UN standing military rapid response mechanism were put on hold and, even though Boutros-Ghali failed to win a second term as UN secretary-general for other reasons as well, it was also evident that he was made the scapegoat for the Somali debacle. The United States promptly drew the wrong conclusions from the Somali experience and delayed the Haiti mission to restore elected President Aristide when Haitian mobs bearing Aidid's pictures demonstrated before US ships. The United States went so far as to prevent or delay others from taking humanitarian action. Obviously Rwanda became the tragic outcome of the wrong reading of the Somali lessons. As Thomas Weiss observed:

Somalia cast an ominous shadow on Washington, where the Clinton team and the commander in chief in May 1994 issued Presidential Decision Directive 25 (PDD25). Supposedly the remaining superpower had 'wisely retreated from the overly sanguine expectations held by the administration when it begun its term.' The first real test of the policy was Rwanda. As one senior State Department official close to human rights policy quipped during an off-the-record discussion, 'It was almost as if the Hutus had read it.' The new restrictive guidelines made it possible for the United States not only to remain on the sidelines but also to prevent others from getting involved while genocide proceeded apace.[18]

The Somali experience has also thrown new light on debates about Africa's 'juridical' versus 'empirical' sovereignty and rhetoric about recolonization and trusteeship: 'As anachronistic as it may seem, we need to consider ways to recommit countries (like Somalia) to the good offices of the UN Trusteeship Council.'[19] The war with Aidid's faction (actually only one clan out of a potential hundred) shows the recolonization advocates must be willing to pay a heavy price in casualties and must possess unlimited resources. There is, after all, a residual empirical sovereignty in African civil society even after the collapse of the state. Should the society choose to reject foreign intervention, recolonization, or absorption into another state, this residual sovereignty is manifested in the resistance movement and the sacrifices involved.

Let us recall that the most positive and dramatic legacy of the US and UN involvement and that of their NGO partners in Somalia was the success in defeating a man-made (civil war-induced) famine. Reaching a peak in 1992, the magnitude of human suffering in the triangle-of-death zone was overwhelming, as captured and transmitted by the international press. More than 250,000 lives are estimated to have been saved during the famine emergency. There has been no recurrence of a famine of even half such a magnitude.

THE POST-SIYAD ENVIRONMENT

There are several lessons to be learned from the Somali experience. UNOSOM came to admit that the roots of the Somali crisis were much deeper than originally believed. Further, the international community and the UN lacked adequate knowledge of Somalia and the UN did not have adequate means and institutional mechanisms for learning about the country. The most critical aspect of this knowledge consists of a deeper understanding of the nature and mechanisms of Siyad's dictatorial rule and the emergence of various manifestations of anti-Siyadism. This is the dialectic that shapes the post-Siyad environment. The collapsed state has also produced unique formations as well as survival and coping strategies. Powerful new forces make it virtually impossible for foreigners and Somalis to revive the old collapsed state. So great was Siyad's malevolence and abuse of power that virtually all Somalis now hold a deep-seated fear and distrust of any centralized authority. Any notion of a central army is met with bitter hostility. An Islamic revival draws its inspirations from the need to resist Siyad's anti-Islamic measures. Donor-driven attempts to bring a quick-fix unitary form of government actually have prolonged the civil wars and facilitated fragmentation. UNOSOM could have delved deeper into Somali society to appreciate certain enabling conditions that reflect a new spirit that is reconstructing a new Somalia – one which is prepared to accept a shorter-term modus operandi at district, regional, and even zonal levels as an efficient and necessary step towards building the national coherence that donors, and most Somalis, seek. Future prospects could involve a federal and confederal state or even two states, depending on the wishes of the people involved..

The immediate impact of UNISOM II's departure did not result in the violence that many had predicted. During the post-UNOSOM period, donors have become more pragmatic and flexible. They have come to provide rehabilitation assistance in a more decentralized manner-to units of variable size, as long as they provide security and effective local counterparts. With the collapse of UNOSOM-sponsored institutions, a few authentic entities, including authoritative local lead-institutions, have emerged. With the distortionary effect of UNOSOM no longer present, the process of both political and economic transformation has been facilitated. In certain places, including northern Mogadishu, alternative institutions have emerged without external support. One such significant institution has been the Sharia court movement. A number of these Sharia courts have effectively performed policing and judicial functions. Such indigenous initiatives provide the framework for what one might call enabling conditions or factors. UNOSOM's admitted lack of knowledge of Somali culture and politics prevented it from grasping the dynamics of these enabling factors which, in turn, offer 'leverage points' to initiate constructive action.

It is now possible to list a number of enabling conditions upon which sound governance for Somalia could be built.

- *Autonomism*: A spirit of regional and zonal authority pervades Somali society and ought to be enhanced and formalized. In Somaliland, this spirit of autonomy has been pushed, by specific circumstances, to attain the extreme form of de facto independence.

- *Power-sharing*: People seek broad-based power-sharing both as an echo of the pastoral past and as a key to a more participatory future. This aspiration should be reinforced and information be provided about various power-sharing models.

- *Decentralization*: People favour decentralization and devolution of power. The UN and even the faction leaders were obliged to pay lip service to this preference at the March 1993 Addis Ababa conference.

- *Role of Women*: Women are playing an increasingly prominent and constructive role in Somali society, both at home and in the diaspora. They have been building bridges between hostile clan groups. Supporting their efforts enhances reconciliation and lasting peace.

- *Islamic revival*: There were pockets of Islamic fundamentalists on the margins of Somali Society as of the 1990's (the Gedo region bordering Ethiopia and Kenya). For most Somalis, however, a spirit of revivalism reflects core values, based on the Somali Sunni tradition of avoiding radical politicized Islam. Somalia's Islamic revival promises to strengthen civil values and institutions of civil society and should be reinforces. Unlike the centrifugal politics of clan division, Islamic beliefs and behaviour manifest a latent centripetal political tendency of integration.

- *Market economy*: With the demise of Siyad's controlled economy along with its numerous parastatals, the post-Siyad period has witnessed a vibrant, free, and unregulated economy. Its growth should be encouraged and facilitated. However, there is also a need to encourage the development of necessary and select regulations to protect the environment and to protect resources for future generations.

- *Local adaptation*: The civil wars and the resulting lack of goods and services that used to be imported have fostered a spirit of innovation and self-reliance. This creativity needs to be encouraged and expanded.

- *Traditional institutions*: The new environment has also obliged Somalis to resort to their rich cultural traditions and institutions to handle grazing and agricultural systems, conflict mediation, legal adjudication, and a number of other related functions. Somaliland has provided an example of innovative governance by establishing a National Assembly with two houses, one of which, the Guurti or House of Elders, comprises traditional clan and religious elders. Traditional law – the *xeer* – is now widely practiced in both rural and urban areas. Traditional law and practices are part of the support system needed to make new settlements effective and sustainable.

- *Free Press*: The pre-Siyad Somali Republic was well known for having a tradition of an irreverent free press. The tradition has returned. Mogadishu has fourteen private newspapers while Hargeisa in Somaliland has about four. They present various perspectives on the current situation in the Somali language. A number of them are often critical of the political elements, often using cartoons to drive home their points. All of them would be more effective with training and technical assistance. Free speech and open debate have to be encouraged to promote lasting peace, accountability, and the gradual civilizing of the political elite.

- *Regional links*: Independent Somalia, with its policy of irredentism, engaged in confrontational and hostile relations with Ethiopia and Kenya. All that has changed as relations with neighboring states have improved greatly. There is, however, a minor danger signal posed by Ethiopia's forays into parts of Gedo to combat pockets of Islamic fundamentalists.(Unfortunately, this has culminated in the 2006 outright invasion of Somalia by Ethiopia).

Somalia is gradually healing, but it remains a fragmented entity. The northern zone, ex-British Somaliland, has proclaimed itself the independent Republic of Somaliland. The northeast zone, now called Puntland, is seeking only internal autonomy in a future Federal Republic of Somalia. After the departure of UNOSOM II the Rahanweyn and related clans of Bay, Bakool, and parts of Gedo and Lower Shabelle regions formed a governing council for the Digil Mirifle. This is another example of civilianization and autonomy process. Unfortunately, this process in Bay was interrupted by Aidid's invasion of the area in September 1995. The Rahanweyn have continued to organize against Aidid with the formation of the Rahanweyn Resistance Army (RRA) and the struggles persist. While the Somaliland, Puntland and, hopefully, Bay zones have managed to control violence and ensure the establishment of relatively peaceful societies, strongman (warlord) solutions continue to prevail in Mogadishu with Hussein Aidid, Ali Mahdi, Musa Sudi, and Osman Ato; and in the Kismayu and Lower Juba areas with Siyad's son-in-law General Hersi Morgan, General Gabio, and Ahmed Omar Jess. Post-UNOSOM factional leader conferences have been held in Addis Ababa, Nairobi, Sanaa (Yemen) and Cairo, but they have all failed to achieve reconciliation and coordination.

These contrasting outcomes of positive peace in northern Somalia and at best negative peace in central and southern Somali can, in part, be accounted for by the different approaches adopted towards negotiations. In the north peace has been built upwards from local Somali development on the ground, while efforts in the south have frequently been the result of externally-injected, top-down approaches. The former is best represented by the Borama conference held in February-May 1993, while the latter is captured in the Djibouti-hosted, elite-oriented conference of 1991 and, more recently, 2000.

It was at the Borama conference that peace was restored in Somaliland. Considerable time was spent adjudicating clan conflicts and disputes between neighbours since peace and reconciliation were considered primary tasks. Discussions were held on the major provisions of an anticipated constitution and it was recommended that the structure of government be based on a president/ vice-president model rather than a president/ prime minister one. The conference also recommended the strict separation of the judiciary from executive and legislative powers and bodies, and formally endorsed a National Assembly or Parliament consisting of two chambers: a Council of Elders and a lower popular Chamber of Representatives. On an interim basis, both of these were to exist together with a president (Isaq), vice-president (non-Isaq from the Borama area), and a cabinet selected by the president, who was to be sensitive to issues of merit and clan representation.

The Guurti, or Council of Elders, was to be chosen according to traditional rules of protocol, historical precedent, and proportionality. The Borama conference elected an electoral body of 150 (elders, politicians, SNM cadres, civil servant and civil society leaders) who went on to conduct competitive elections resulting in the selection of veteran politician Ibrahim Mohamed Egal as the second Somaliland president (Abdurahman Tuur was president from 1991-1993) and veteran SNM leader Abdurahman Aw Ali as his vice-president. As a variant of liberal democracy, consociationalism stresses process over product. It is indeed an irony of history that the person delegated in 1960 to consummate union with ex-Italian Somalia is today charged with the task of guiding Somaliland out of that union! Somaliland claims to favour radical decentralization. Indeed, it regained its independence in 1991 with a vigorous civil society that obstructed the formation of a coherent and efficient central state. It took the wily veteran Mohamed Egal to win the credit of bringing the state back in. Finally, popular country-wide elections for local and national bodies, including presidential elections, were being held during January and May 2003. With Egal's death, two of his former ministers each from different clans, competed to replace him. In the end, Dahir Riyale Kahin, who had served under Egal as vice-president, was elected president.

Somaliland has thus brought an end to generalized fighting and introduced an atmosphere of trust and confidence. It has created a number of political institutions and political arrangements, some of which, like the Guurti, are highly original. It has fostered a relatively open and inclusive political culture. The mini-civil war (within Somaliland) of 1994-5 demonstrated that the evolving arrangements and political culture were capable of fostering reconciliation among previously warring communities and thus helping to build a sense of common identity.

The experience elsewhere was quite different. In 1991 President Hassan Guled, with Italian and Egyptian support, called the first Djibouti conferences as soon as Siyad had fallen from power. In May and again in July 1991, the Italian and Egyptian governments backed the USC faction of Ali Mahdi and the Manifesto Group in organizing two conferences in Djibouti with the objective of forming a national government. The Aidid USC group and the SNM refused to attend. This top-down approach was intended to confirm Ali Mahdi as interim president and reject Somaliland's independence. The July conference advocated reviving the 1960 constitution and its 123-member Parliament for an interim period of two years, with Parliament electing a president nominated by the USC.

This attempt at parachuting state power from Djibouti to Mogadishu proved unworkable. Ali Mahdi was too impatient to await the parliamentary nomination process; he had himself sworn in soon after his return. The method of filling Parliament seats was never spelled out. Ali Mahdi renominated the northern (Isaq) politician Omar Arteh as a prime minister, but his eighty-three ministerial appointments could not obtain parliamentary and full USC approval. The two leaders hoped to obtain quick injections of foreign aid to be able to function. They ignored the realities of post-Siyad Somalia. Open warfare and banditry had made Mogadishu ungovernable, and they ignored the spirit of decentralization and autonomism at large in post-Siyad Somalia.

Djibouti I (1991) and Djibouti II (2000) share common characteristics and a few superficial differences. Both were top-down projects privileging the modern elites: ministers, politicians, civil servants, military and police officers. Whereas Djibouti I favoured the elites of the parliamentary pre-1969 era, Djibouti II was overwhelmed by the predominance of Siyad-era elites: numerous ministers, diplomats, civil servants, police and military officers (including many of the most notorious). That is why the constitution that was approved included the Siyadist principles of a unitary centralized state. Djibouti I did not claim to involve civil society representatives, while Djibouti II included a certain number of representatives of civil society.

Djibouti II elected Adbulkassim Salad Hassan as the president of Somalia. In kinship terms, he is a relative of the late General Aidid. Specifically he is of ayr (subclan), Habar Gedir (clan) and Hawiye (clan-family). He was one of the few long-serving ministers under Siyad. His many portfolios included information and interior. Paying lip service to clan power-sharing, he appointed as prime minister Dr Ali Khalif Galied, a Dulbahante, Darod from eastern Somaliland. A veteran of Siyad's service, he was once minister of industries. His deputy is a distinguished veteran of Siyad regime, a minister serving for many years as minister of fisheries. Osman Jama is from the Habar Yunis, Isaq clan-family. Hasan Abshir, from the Issa Mahamud, Mijertein,Darod clan-family, first served as the new minister of natural resource, and then went on to become the prime minister, having replaced Dr Ali Khahf Galied. He worked closely with Siyad, once as a mayor of Mogadishu. There are few in this newly proposed cabinet who have not worked closely with former dictator Siyad Barre. Djibouti II has established a Transitional National Government (TNG). Headed by former ministers of General Siyad's discredited regime, the new 'government' includes notorious figures as well as others almost unknown to the Somali public.

Professor I.M. Lewis, a longtime student of Somalia, described this intervention in Somalia's internal affairs by the UN as 'extremely untimely.' Professor Lewis argues that prior to the Djibouti conference the situation in Mogadishu and the south was relatively calm, with signs that local peace-making efforts (the only kind that ever work in Somalia) were producing results, and the model for local state-formation provided by Somaliland and Puntland in the north was attracting increasing attention in the turbulent south. Now thanks to the UN intervention, the scales are tipped again toward violence. With the provocation of the new faction, it is difficult to see how serious bloodshed can now be avoided.

Somalia is indeed made up of two distinct parts. One, involving Somaliland, Puntland, and Bay and constituting the largest part of the country, forms a zone of peace. Here, there exists a dynamic process of peace-building in which civil war antagonists have learned to resolve their differences nonviolently, developed a common set of objectives and a common identity, and moved towards the creation of a just society. Elsewhere, in the capital of Mogadishu and the central regions, in Kishmayu and Gedo in the south and southwest, the situation is not nearly as stable. At best, it can be described as a condition of negative peace, where violence, if not effectively controlled, is at least limited. If genuine peace is to be consolidated in the south, it will likely arise from spontaneous developments from civil society, such as it did in the north.

THE TRANSITIONAL FEDERAL GOVERNMENT (TFG)

US troops pulled out from UNOSOM and from the Somali chaos in 1994; UN troops followed in 1995. Thus began the era of warlords with their fiefdoms. The UN continued to provide humanitarian assistance and continued efforts aimed at putting the Somali state back together; it continued to call for top-down elite conferences in Ethiopia and Kenya. The UN failed 14 times. In 2000, the Djibouti government sponsored a Somali conference that ended with a Transitional National Government with Abulkassim Salad Hassan (Hawiye, Habar Gedir), as President and Dr. Ali Khalif Galied (Darod, Dulbahante) as Prime Minister. This government remained symbolic and did not survive by 2003. Finally, the UN sponsored another elite level conference in Nairobi, Kenya. This time Ethiopia put its full weight behind the exercise. Most of the participants were Siyad era functionaries, ministers, politicians, civil servants, military and police officers; some businessmen, selected women and NGOs, Many of the participants were exiles living in the Somali Diaspora.

This conference with selected not elected representatives, in November 2004 came up with Transitional Federal Institutions (TFI). They issued a Transitional Federal Charter (TFC); a legislative branch, Transitional Federal Parliament (TFP) and an executive branch, the Transitional Federal Government (TFG). The Ethiopians lobbied hard to elect as President, Adbullahi Yusuf (Darod,

Majerteen); and obliged him to appoint a Pro-Ethiopian Prime Minister, Ali Mohamed Ghedi (Hawiye, Abgal); a connection of Prime Minister Meles himself. For the next two years, the TFG remained a symbolic government with no capital within Somalia and riddled with factions. Mogadishu remained the fiefdom of the warlords. The TFG at first tried to establish a temporary capital in Jowhar, north of Mogadishu, but finally settled in Baidoa. On February 26, 2006 the parliament first met in the city of Baidoa, 260 kilometers northwest of Mogadishu. The Transitional Federal Parliament gives 61 seats to each of Somalia's four major clan-families decreed as Hawiye, Dir (supposed to include Isaq), Rahanweyn and Darod. The 4.5 formula designates the "fifth" to represent Somali and non-Somali minority clans for a total of 275. The President and the Parliament are to serve for 5 years.

The Speaker of the Parliament was chosen because he was not Pro-Ethiopia. Earlier on, some members of The Parliament relocated to Mogadishu in spite of the Jowhar-Baidoa choices. When the Union of Islamic Courts (UIC) captured power, united and pacified Mogadishu; the Speaker, Sharif Hassan Sheikh Aden proposed negotiations with the UIC. The other moderates and constitutionalists within the TFG also favoured negotiations. The UIC jihadis and the extremist-militarist wing of the TFG decided to opt for military confrontations and, with the help of Ethiopians troops, the latter won. The Speaker and other moderates were expelled and decided to go into exile in Eritrea. The only significant political action since the formation of the TFG has been to invite Ethiopian military power to impose its authority on Somali politics and society. In spite of the rhetorical calls for national reconciliations, the TFG has constantly postponed the dates proposed for such reconciliations – which they still view at the level of elites, not the grassroots. Ethiopian military intervention was facilitated by the jihadi Islamists who played into the hard-line global anti-terrorism policies of the Bush doctrine and its proxy-ally PM Meles Zenawi. Ethiopia and the United States said that the Somali Islamic movement, is under extremists who are harboring terrorists, including three suspects in the 1998 bombing of the US embassies in Kenya and Tanzania. Up till now, the TFG has not opened the political system to allow for popular expression of resentment, frustrations, and anger. The TFG and Ethiopian troops are pursuing the nasty politics of petty clan revenge come hell and high water. Poor independent Somalia: it evolved from semi-anarchy, to diabolical tyranny, to anarchy, separation, and decentralized tyranny of warlords, a temporary authoritarianism of the jihadi Islamists and a neo-Siyad tyranny of the TFG. One can expect that continuing and growing violence is the most likely outcome.

Notes

1. Hussein Adam and Richard Ford, eds., *Mending Rips in the Sky: Exploring Options for Somali Communities in the 21st Century,* (Lawrence, NJ: Red Sea Press, 1997), 9-10.

2. Marina Ottaway in I. William Zartman, ed., *Ripe for Resolution: Conflict and Intervention in Africa* (New York: Oxford University Press, 1995), 236-7.

3. Mohamed Sahnoun, *Somalia: Missed Opportunities* (Washington, DC: United States Institute of Peace, 1994), xiii.

4. Samuel M. Makinda, *Seeking Peace from Chaos: Humanitarian Intervention in Somalia* (New York: International Peace Academy Occasional Paper Series, September 1993), 55.

5. Giampaolo Calchi Novati, 'Italy and Somalia: Unbearable Lightness of an Influence,' in Adam and Ford, eds., *Mending Rips in the Sky,* 567.

6. Peter Schraeder, 'The Horn of Africa: U.S. Foreign Policy in an Altered Cold War Environment,' Middle East Journal 46, no. 4 (1992), 17.

7. Terrance Lyons and Ahmed I. Samatar, *Somalia State Collapse, Multilateral Intervention and Strategies for Political Reconstruction* (Washington, DC: The Brookings Institution, 1995), 33-4.

8. Makinda, *Seeking Peace from Chaos,* 59-60.

9. Schraeder, 'The Horn of Africa,' 18.

10 Walter Clarke and Jeffrey Herbst, eds., *Learning from Somalia: The Lessons of Armed Humanitarian Intervention* (Boulder, CO: Westview Press, 1997), 8-9.

11. *The United Nations and Somalia*: 1992-1996 (New York: United Nations Department of Public Information, 1996), 214.

12. Cited in John R. Bolton, 'Wrong Turn in Somalia,' *Foreign Affairs* 73, no. 1 (1994), 60; see also Lyons and Samatar, *Somalia State Collapse,* 34.

13. Clarke and Herbst, *Learning from Somalia*, 9, 35.

14. Robert Oakley and John Hirsch, *Somalia and Operation Restore Hope: Reflections on Peacekeeping and Peacemaking* (Washington, DC: United States Institute of Peace, 1995), 76, 77.

15. Christopher Clapham, 'Problems of Peace Enforcement: Some Lessons from Multinational Peacekeeping Operations in Africa,' in Jakkie Cilliers and Greg Mills, eds., *Peacekeeping in Africa* (Cape Town: Institute for Defense Policy, 1995), 2: 146.

16. John Drysdale, *Whatever Happened to Somalia? A Tale of Tragic Blunders* (London: Haan Associates, 1994), 4.

17. Boutros Boutros-Ghali, An *Agenda for Peace: Preventive Diplomacy, Peacemaking and Peacekeeping* (New York: United Nations, 1992).

18. Quoted in Clarke and Herbst, *Learning from Somalia*, 207-8.

19. Robert Rotberg, quoted in ibid., 233.

CHAPTER 6

SOMALILAND IN CONTRAST TO ERITREA

"Somaliland" has reasserted the separate existence it had as the colony of British Somaliland before independence and union with the former Italian Somalia in 1960. It has avoided the devastation of warlordism that has afflicted the rest of Somalia through compromise politics between clan elders. However, its de facto statehood since 1991 has not received the international recognition accorded Eritrea in 1993. The experiences of Somaliland and Eritrea in the circumstances of their post-colonial union with other entities, in their liberation movements and in their current politics are contrasted. It is suggested that there can be mutual learning from Somaliland's consociational, ethnic democracy and Eritrea's "radical social democracy", of an eventual, orchestrated multi-partism that eschews ethnic and religious divides.

[The member States affirm]… respect for the sovereignty and territorial integrity of each State and for its inalienable right to independent existence (Charter of the Organization of African Unity (OAU), Article III, Paragraph 3).

It will take much courage for the OAU and its members to champion this unorthodox but politically beneficent reality. But once it gains local acceptance, bilateral and multi-lateral donors must harken to the needs of the Eritreas and Somaliland republics in precisely the same manner as they have the Baltic republics and other new European states (Michael Chege).

On 24 May 1993, Eritrea conducted an internationally monitored referendum to determine its future status; the vote was overwhelmingly for independence. The United Nations, the US, Ethiopia, Italy immediately recognized the new state. From May 1991, Eritrea had enjoyed autonomy but, two years later it was able to garner international recognition which "invests it with a personality in the law of nations" (Visscher, 1968: 175). Former Italian and British colonies in Somalia gained independence and formed the Somali Republic in 1960. On 17 May 1991, the resistance movement and important groups in the former northern British colony, dissolved the union and declared formation of the Republic of Somaliland. This entity has since existed bearing characteristics generally attributed to a "state" but devoid of international recognition. Somaliland's leaders still ask why recognition of their statehood has been withheld.

This chapter seeks to probe such comparisons and provide a considered overall assessment. It offers some historical, constitutional/legal context before comparing and contrasting the two liberation movements and their implications. These comparisons with Eritrea allows us a deeper grasp of the Somaliland situation by illustrating its uniqueness and salient peculiarities.

It also offers a perspective on a general issue post-cold war Africa is bound to confront: how far the principle of territorial integrity should be subordinated to what some consider a higher principle – the principle of self-determination. From the point of view of the Organization of African Unity (OAU), self-determination is to be exercised only once, at the time of decolonization from European domination, and it is not subject to continuous review. The emerging post cold war environment is beginning to nourish a new thinking that is both flexible and pragmatic. Kenyan intellectual Michael Chege recently reignited old Africanist debates with the perspective: "There is nothing remiss about altering state frontiers in the nobler interests of domestic tranquility and sustained economic growth, which are now so scarce in these lands" (Chege, 1992:153).

This chapter will sustain such debates: useful insights into the operation of the principle of self-determination and its problematic elements could be gained by an analysis of Somaliland's and Eritrea's comparative claims to political sovereignty. African states are more likely to confront movements demanding regional autonomy and implying federalism or neo-federalism than those demanding outright secession. However, the crucial difference involves historical timing: recent experience suggests militarist suppression of regional autonomy movements could transform them into separatist movements.

This comparison has also policy implications for the new states: Eritrea and Somaliland could learn from each other's experiences. From Somaliland, Eritrea could gain greater sensitivities and flexibility in matters involving ethnic/clan issues; Somaliland could profit from Eritrean methods to evolve class and other cross-cutting identities and institutions. Both Eritrea and Somaliland can learn from Somalia's multi-party parliamentary era (1960-1969). The article provides greater details on Somaliland and only summary analysis of Eritrea because there is hardly any serious publications on Somaliland while publications on Eritrea excel in both quantity and quality.

HISTORICAL AND CONSTITUTIONAL BACKGROUND

The British created the Somaliland Protectorate in the 1880's as a source of food and water supplies for their colony of Aden across the Red Sea. Aden provided a major port and harbor facilities for British commercial and navy ships on the strategic route between England and the "jewel" colony of India. British Somaliland consists of a cooler plateau, including the capital Hargeisa, and a hotter, humid coastal zone where its main port, Berbera, is located. However, nowhere is the diversity of climates and culture as great as in Eritrea. The people are homogenous in language, religion (Islam) and customs: social pluralism manifests itself in clan rather than ethnic cleavages. A majority belongs to the Isaq clan-family subdivided into several clans; on the eastern border are two clans of the Darod clan-family, the Dulbahantes and Warsangelis; on the west are two Dir clans, the Gadabursi and the Issas. Under British rule, a small urban elite formed, led by educated and trading factions which established civic associations and eventually political parties. Somaliland has a territory of 67,000 square miles, slightly larger than Eritrea's 50,000 square miles; however, its approximately three million population is roughly the same as Eritrea's. Somaliland has ample pastoral resources threatened by environmental degradation; there are also hopeful possibilities of uncovering oil. Limited areas of agriculture exist, while fishery resources are yet to be explored to their fullest extent.

Somaliland's unification with southern Somalia to form the Somali Republic involved different steps from those taken to unify Eritrea into Haile Selassie's Ethiopian Empire. In all Somali territories the struggle for independence assumed a multi-party form in spite of the relatively homogeneous nature of Somali society. In 1943, during the British Military Administration of most of the Horn of Africa (including ex-Italian Somaliland and Eritrea), a nationalist party was born – the Somali Youth League (SYL) which came to dominate southern Somali politics and to advocate Pan-Somalism and irredentism. The leading nationalist party in British Somaliland was established in 1945 as the Somali National Society which, in 1951 adopted a new name, the Somali National League (SNL). The two parties shared similar objectives as they also did with parties that rose to challenge them in their respective territories (Touval, 1963:85).

At least one southern opposition party, though it subscribed to independence as the main goal, differed somewhat radically from average Somali nationalist parties of the period. The Hizb al-Dastuur Mustaqil al-Somali (Somali Independent Constitutional Party, HDMS) represented the Digil – Mirifle clan-family, more dependent on agriculture than pastoralists elsewhere settled between the two main rivers, the Shabelle and Juba, with Baidoa as their main city. This is the area that recently suffered a man-made famine prompting US/UN humanitarian military intervention. This clan-family speaks a different dialect of Somali and practices a somewhat different way of life due to their agro-pastoral environment. The HDMS pursued regional autonomy and federalism. As late as 1958, HDMS President Jelani Sheikh bin Sheikh, reiterated in a speech to a party convention that "the party has become convinced that the only method of unifying the Somalis... is through a federal constitution which accords full regional autonomy" (Touval, 1963:96-97).

According to one account, when the British Somaliland delegation came to Mogadishu for union negotiations, HDMS leaders approached them and impressed them on the need to opt for federal arrangements. Northern Premier Mohamed Ibrahim Egal went back to Hargeisa to advocate a gradualistic approach, but other politicians organized demonstrations against him as a "power hungry opportunist". The two Somalilands rushed headlong into immediate union – unconditional, unitary and poorly prepared. The UN voted to move up Somalia's independence date from 2 December to 1 July 1960. The British Government went on to announce that the British (northern) Somaliland Protectorate would become independent on 26 June 1960, five days before the independence of the UN Trustee-ship territory of (southern) Somalia. This hasty decision put incred-ible, undeserved pressure on the politics and administration of the two territories. No committee had been appointed and charged with the official responsibility for drafting the legal instruments for the Union, and there was hardly any time for consultations (Contini, 1969:9).

It was anticipated that a representative of the independent northern Somaliland and southern Somaliland states would formally create the Union through the signing of an international treaty. The north drafted an Act of Union, had it approved by its legislative body and sent it to Mogadishu. Following approval by the legislative assembly in the south, it was to be signed by two respective repre-sentatives. The southern assembly never passed the proposed Act. However, it passed its own Atto de Unione, significantly different from the northern text. The following summary of the legal loose ends surrounding what Touval has termed the "precipitate Union is offered by Rajagopal and Carroll (1992:14) as follows:

> (a) The Union of Somaliland and Somalia Law did not have any legal validity in the South; (b) the approval "in principle" of the Atto de Unione, which was different from the above text was legally inadequate; (c) the declaration of independence by the Provisional President was legally invalid since no Act of Union had been signed prior to his election, in accordance with the Constitution.

The *de facto* union experienced a lot of problems. Right at the outset, the Somali sense of proportional balance was ignored. The south provided the capital city, the anthem, the flag and the con-stitution. The parliament elected a southern president who nomi-nated a southern prime minister. His cabinet included four north-ern ministers out of fourteen. Southerners occupied key ministries such as Foreign, Interior and Finance. The ex-northern premier was appointed Minister of Education. The posts of Army Commander and Police Commander went to the southern officers; a northern became head of the Prison Division of the police and the Assembly elected a northern deputy as its first president. The north gave up the possibility of joining the British Commonwealth while the south openly flaunted its links with Italy. Italian legal experts drafted the Constitution in an undisguised attempt to graft Italian multi-party democracy on to independent Somalia. Before the British had agreed to grant independence to Somaliland, Italian officials had finalized the Constitution. Northern politicians and lawyers had virtually no chance to make even marginal changes in the draft.

Eritrea is located along 1,000 kms on the west coast of the Red Sea on the Horn of Africa. Somaliland (the term utilized here to refer to former British Somaliland) is similarly located, separated form Eritrea by the Republic of Djibouti – formerly French Somaliland. Eritrea's modest land surface offers a great range of environmental and ethnic variety: highlands, deserts, the savannah and the severe volcanic ecology of South Arabia and the Djibouti zone; some areas suitable for agriculture, others for pastoralism. Eritrea consists of several ethnic groups: the highland Tigrinyans, for example, are culturally linked to the Tigray of Ethiopia and they both profess Coptic Christianity though some of them profess Islam. The Bejas on the coast and bordering the Sudan, and the Afar in the south, are Muslims by religion and pastoralists by occupation when compared to the farming highlanders. The Afars live in Eritrea, Djibouti and Ethiopia. Eritrea is a pluralist society of farmers and pastoralists from diverse ethnic groups, languages, and religions.

Italy colonized Eritrea and the southern part of Somali territories, Italian Somaliland. With southern Somalia, therefore, Eritrea came to share similar colonial administrations including armed forces, educational systems, official languages as well as selected aspects of urban life, architecture and cuisine. Those who have visited both Asmara and Mogadishu have noticed such similarities. Under Italian rule, Eritreans developed a modest working class and a miniscule trading elite and with these elements, early forms of modern national consciousness. Civic associations including trade unions flourished until they were suppressed by Haile Selassie in the 1950's and 1960's (Trevaskis, 1960).

After the defeat of Italy, the UN took up the fate of Eritrea and debated three options: (1) union with Ethiopia, (2) federation with Ethiopia, and (3) independence preceded by a ten year trusteeship under UN administration as was the case with ex-Italian Somalia. Haile Selassie obtained strong US lobbying support to link Eritrea to Ethiopia in exchange for a military base at Kagnew in Eritrea. The UN rejected option (1) and (3) and opted for (2) federation. It did not take long before Selassie made it crystal clear that for him options (1) and (2) are one and the same; he had no tolerance for "legislature" or a division of powers and totally ignored all constitutional elements of the UN pact.

THE POLITICS OF UNION

Technically, the Ethiopian-Eritrean federation lasted from 1950 to 1962 when the Emperor unilaterally annexed Eritrea as an Ethiopian province subject to his brutal, dictatorial rule and ended all hopes implied in the status of federal autonomy. The exodus of Eritrean elites opposed to the union accelerated. In 1961 they established the Eritrean Liberation Front (ELF) from which, in 1970, a more ideologically self conscious Eritrean People's Liberation Front (EPLF) emerged. Both groups engaged in hit and run tactics during their early years. The fall of the emperor in 1974 brought some hope in that the new Mengistu regime proclaimed itself socialist in orientation and consolidated strong military and diplomatic links with the USSR and Cuba. Before long it became clear that Mengistu did not even intend to revive the abolished federation. He sought huge amounts of Soviet arms in order to crush the Eritrean resistance movement. The long struggle served to integrate ever widening circles of the population transforming it from a series of episodic military confrontations to a popular people's war (Selassie, 1980).

The politics of the Somali Union are in two main phases: multiparty parliamentary politics giving room for negotiations and bargaining processes, and oppressive militarist polices under Siyad Barre. A few months after independence, northern irredentist nationalist feelings began to sour. The resultant resentments in the north were overwhelmingly manifested in the referendum on the Constitution on 20 June 1961. The SNL vigorously campaigned against the Constitution and advocated a boycott. Suffrage included all adult men and women, the latter voting for the first time. Estimates indicate that the north had a population of 650,000 in 1961; only 100,000 persons voted indicating that at least half the electorate boycotted the referendum. In addition, out of the just over 100,000 recorded votes more than half opposed the Constitution (Lewis, 1965: 172, 219 and note 5). The major cities of the north – Hargeisa (72%), Berbera (69%), Burao (66%) and Erigavo (69%) – all returned negative votes. In southern Somalia, the HDMS and at least two other opposition parties campaigned against the Constitution; however, the Government recorded more than one million eight hundred thousand votes in favor of ratification. An insignificant village called Wanla Weyn not far from Mogadishu is reported to have registered a yes vote higher than the total northern vote! This gave Northerners a new political term, *Wanla Weyn* used somewhat pejoratively for all the Southerners. It is more than a geographic label, it is a Somali equivalent of Tammany Hall that implies "those who fear central government, those who participate in or condone political corruption." This is one of a series of events that convinced Northerners that their political culture is different from that of the south.

The newly formed Government did not pay heed to the warnings and in December 1961, the recently united Somali Republic experienced the first attempted military coup in sub-Sahara Africa. Sandhurst-trained lieutenants of the former (British) Somaliland Scouts resented the Italian trained commanding officers imported from Mogadishu. Led by the popular Hassan Keid, northern officers felt corporate interests, personal ambition and regional grudges ignited following the "precipitate union". The abortive military coup had unmistakable secessionist objectives; however, the people, not yet ready for a radical break with Mogadishu, opposed it and it failed. Paradoxically, the absence of a legally valid Act of Union assisted their defense at their trial. The judge listened to different arguments but decided to "acquit them on the basis that, in the absence of an Act of Union, the court had no jurisdiction over Somaliland" (Rajagopal and Carroll, 1992:14)

During the first five years or so, the Union experienced serious difficulties in amalgamating different administrative, judicial, and economic systems. A written form for Somali was not decided until under military rule in 1972. The post-independence bureaucracy, therefore, resembled the Tower of Babel: English, Italian and Arabic were all used as official languages in the haphazard manner. When UNESCO and other significant donors influenced the Government to adopt English in a unified educational system, southern civil servants were enraged and this exacerbated regional tensions. Northerners resented the involvement in politics of the civil service in the south; they believed it had learned about bureaucratic and political corruption from the Italians. In the north, songs and poems began to appear criticizing the Union. In one of these composed in 1964 by poet and song writer Ali Sugule, entitled " Let me remind you", he argues that the north would have gained better political and economic advantages had it refused to join Mogadishu until all the missing Somali territories joined. Somaliland's natural cultural and economic hinterland consists of Ethiopian Somaliland and Djibouti.

Northern politicians tried to manipulate the existing party and government system to reduce the inequalities experienced. Former Premier of the north, Mohamed Ibrahim Egal, resigned from the cabinet and formed a new opposition party, the Somali National Congress (SNC) together with veteran southern opposition politician, Sheikh Ali Jiumale. The 1964 national elections were the country's first post-independence elections. Out of a total of 123 parliamentary seats (33 for the north, 90 for the south), the SYL won 54, the SNC 22 seats, the HDMS won nine seats and a left-leaning opposition party, the Somali Democratic Union (SDU), won 15 seats. The impatient and ambitious Egal decided that, given unequal financial and other resources, it was very difficult to defeat the ruling party, SYL. Soon after the 1964 elections, he joined the SYL and supported former Prime Minister Abdirashid Ali Shermarke in his 1967 presidential elections against incumbent President Aden Abdullah Osman. The new President nominated Mohamed Ibrahim Egal as first northern Prime Minister of the Republic. Egal raised the number of cabinet ministers as he sought to include every major clan-family, as well as some members of his former party, SNC. As

the post-independent years passed, national political parties degenerated: a general atmosphere of cut-throat competition, corruption,
incompetence and irresponsibility afflicted the nation. Things got
out of hand during and after the 1969 elections; the semi-demo-
cratic system began to teeter on the verge of collapse, and anarchy.

Conflicts with Ethiopia over the fate of Somalis living under the
imperial flag, led the civilian leaders to Moscow for what they deemed
adequate military assistance. Eager to obtain a strategic foothold in
black Africa, the USSR obliged and helped Somalia create one of
the largest and best equipped armies in sub-Sahara Africa. While
visiting drought-stricken areas in northeast Somalia, President
Sharmarke was assassinated by a policeman on 15 October 1969.
The parliament gathered on the evening of the 20th to choose his
successor. During the early hours of 21 October 1969, Commander
of the Somali National Army, Mohamed Siyad Barre engineered a
successful coup and Somalia came under military rule.

For Somaliland, semi-colonial oppression came with Siyad's military regime. Though highly centralized and authoritarian, initially
the regime promised a series of socio-economic reforms under the
banner of "scientific socialism". In 1972, the Supreme Revolutionary
Council decreed the Latin script as the orthography for Somali and
conducted urban and rural literacy campaigns. For a while it seemed
that Somali nationalism had reached its peak. Even in those calmer
days, Siyad showed that he was more willing to deprive the north of
its fair share of development funds and projects. The area came to
rely mostly on its local and foreign-based business and professional
elite. Then, Selassie fell, and the Ethiopian civil war tempted Siyad to
invade Ethiopia to "liberate" the Somali-speaking region (so-called
Ogaden) by military force. Cold war logic reigned supreme. The
Soviets had trained a Somali army that Siyad increased to 37,000 at
the onset of the Ethio-Somali War of 1977-78. The US had trained
and equipped a larger Ethiopian army. New Ethiopian leader Mengistu brought Ethiopia under Soviet patronage as Somalia switched
sides and came under the US umbrella.

Siyad dropped his socialist façade and adopted clanism (tribalism) as a manipulative tool to continue to hold on to power after
a Soviet led Cuban-Ethiopian offensive pushed his army from the

Ogaden. By 1982, he had built the army into a force 120,000 strong for internal repression. In rural areas he encouraged clan based massacres by his notorious specialized military units. He singled out the Isaq clan-family in Somaliland for neo-fascist type of punishment. Somali scholar Ian Lewis confirms this from his own eyewitness account:

> From the early 1980's, the north was administered by increasingly harsh military rule with savage reprisals meted out to the assumedly pro SNM local population who were subject to sever economic, as well as political harassment. The north, as I saw when I last visited it in 1985, began to look and feel like a colony under a foreign military tyranny (Lewis, 1990:58).

Semi-colonial subjugation helped rekindle collective self-assertion which the northern clan-based opposition movement, the Somali National Movement (SNM) channeled into the declaration of the Somaliland Republic soon after the Siyad dictatorship fell in 1991.

THE DIALECTIC OF MILITARY AND SOCIO-POLITICAL ASPECTS

The long drawn out Eritrean struggle is too well known to need detailed recounting. It began episodic ambushes in the 1960's, but by the 1975-77 Eritrean armed struggles were able to open extensive liberated zones supported by external links in nearby Sudan and elsewhere: a gradual metamorphosis of the military struggle led to the crystallization of a counter-government with an active social program – operating clinics, schools, courts and political education campaigns (Gebre-Medhin, 1989). From episodic hit and run military tactics, the EPLF was able to transform its small-scale military operations into a full-scale people's war. Some of the Somali armed opposition movements never graduated beyond episodic ambushes. The northern movement (SNM) transformed its armed struggles to a people's war only during 1988 and after. The major southern armed group, the United Somali Congress (USC) led by General

Aideed, was only able to do so at what was literally the last minute, the 1990-91 period.

Struggles against the Siyad dictatorship came to be symbolized by clan-based decentralized armed opposition groups operating from sanctuaries in Ethiopia. After failing in an anti-Siyad coup in 1978, military officer Abdullahi Yusef automatically fled to Ethiopia where he established the Somali Salvation Democratic Front (SSDF). This movement, which was later atrophied, made a pioneering contribution: it showed others coming later, that Siyad's military rule could be challenged by armed groups based in Ethiopia. Following the SSDF's decline period of hit-and-run tactics, Siyad was able to entice many of its ex-fighters in Ethiopia to return and constitute the spearhead of his brutal wars against the Isaq in the north, and later against the Hawiye in Mogadishu. By 1990-91, the SSDF was reduced to a phantom organization, though it is now active once again in northeast Somalia. It is the proto-political organization that serves an official role in those regions.

The Isaq based Somali National Movement (SNM) formed in 1981, first tried to organize a movement from London but soon decided to move to Ethiopian Somali towns and villages close to the border with the Somali Democratic Republic. The SNM, it is alleged, was repulsed by Qaddafi and was forced to rely mostly on funds raised monthly by the Somali (Isaq) communities in the Gulf, in other Arab states, East Africa, and in various western countries. This self-reliant method gave the movement relative independence, and obliged it to be accountable to its numerous supporters. Accordingly, it evolved a more democratic approach: it held popular congresses periodically during which it has elected its leaders and evolved its policies. So far, only one leader has been elected to serve two terms (four years) – the energetic Ahmed Mohamed Mahamud "Siilanyo". Leadership rotation has been an article of faith. It held six or seven elections from 1981 to 1990. Contradictions among its leaders and supporting clans are handled politically not militarily. The SNM claims it bargained with Mengistu purely as a matter of political expediency. The SNM played an indirect role in the formation of the USC, an armed movement based on the Hawiye clan-family which inhabits the central regions of the country including the capital city of Mogadishu. It also encouraged a group of Ogaden soldiers who defected from Siyad's army to go to the Kismayu area and join their clan members in forming the Somali Patriotic Movement (SPM).

By the mid-1980's Somali armed opposition movements were more like the youthful ELF rather than the disciplined EPLF. Led by externally based leaders, they were engaged in hit-and-run tactics. To a greater extent than the EPLF, the ELF had a leadership that led the struggle from foreign capitals where they were involved in fund-raising and information activities. Later on most of them were removed from their positions and replaced by leaders who were field fighters. By 1987-88 many of the SNM leaders abroad began to establish themselves in the field. By then they had become aware that they might lose their influence to field fighters. Dictators Mengistu and Siyad met in Djibouti in January 1986 on the occasion of the first summit launching the Inter-Governmental Authority on Drought and Development (IGADD). The two states opened negotiations aimed at normalizing their relations. The SNM was alarmed and began to discuss alternative options. In 1988 the Ethiopian-Somali agreements were signed and Siyad disbanded his puppet anti-Ethiopian organization, the Western Somali Liberation Front (WSFL). His main object was to induce Mengistu to destroy the SNM. The Ethiopian dictator turned out to be more Machiavellian than Siyad on this issue: he did not disarm the SNM as Siyad had hoped. He told them to wind up military activities from Ethipian soil but that they could go on living as political exiles. Siyad achieved the opposite of what he wanted. The SNM decided to take all the forces in their command and launch surprise attacks on government garrisons in the main northern Somali cities of Hargeisa and Burao.

Siyad used aerial bombing and heavy artillery to chase about one million of the population in Isaq territories into refugee camps across the border into Ethiopian Somaliland. These momentous events finally brought the SNM into close, organic links with the population whom it claimed to represent. In addition to the SNM Central Committee, they were obliged to constitute a Council of Elders (*Guurti*) which proved most effective in resolving dispute, supervising the fair and just distribution of food and other assistance, recruiting fighters for the various fronts, and after the fall of the Siyad dictatorship, took the lead in disarming the mischievous young volunteer fighters, the so-called children's army. Siyad's brutal counter offensive only reestablished his huge army's control of the main cities, most of the countryside came under SNM control. By 1998 then, the SNM had liberated zones which were analyzed by Basil Davidson as "proof of nationalist fighting movement's efficacy, a demonstration of what is to come after victory, but also a vital means of achieving that victory" (Davidson, 1969:117-18).

The SNM military campaign of 1988 constituted an offensive so surprising and tactically destructive that the enemy was rendered incapable of careful, planned and effective resistance. Prior to this, the SNM utilized terrorist hit-and-run tactics, including selected assassinations of government officials and the freeing of political prisoners from maximum security jails. The guerillas made effective use of superior knowledge for hiding, sniping, sudden ambushes, quick escapes, timed to produce the greatest possible psychological effects. After 1988 the SNM, for all practical purposes, came to constitute a counter-government with all the responsibilities that go with the transformation.

The SNM tried its best to coordinate its use of violence with organization, propaganda and information, although here, its record fell far short of that of the disciplined EPLF. However, it did subordinate violence as a means to clearly stated political ends. The Siyad's oppressive military machine, on the other hand, used violence for war and for internal repression without any attempt to subordinate it to the overall objectives and operation of which it was a part. This element became even more pronounced following SNM's strategic occupation of the north: sheer joy in sadistic excess, not even chastened by expediency, meant that the military regime deserved the label "fascist or neo-fascist". The shocking destruction of Hargeisa and Burao (Somalia's second and third largest cities, for example, does not seem to correspond to any rational political or military objectives. Had Siyad's aim been to win and turn Hargeisa into an Ogadeni settler-city, as some alleged, he would definitely have needed houses to shelter them instead of the horrendous rubble confronting Somalilanders in 1991. Had he felt unable to win the war militarily, then surely he should have pursued a compromise with

Isaq leaders and elders. According to some, this was what a minority of his advisers were advocating but a number of those advocating comprises were jailed in the critical 1982-84 period. In 1991, Somaliland refugees returning from Ethiopia could not believe the scale of the destruction they encountered; the shock strengthened their resolve to support the independence proclamation.

A contrast between the EPLF and SNM military organization offers insights into their socio-political orientations. They both have in common the policy in which politics must command arms and not vice versa. The SNM recalls a brief period when its armed wing led by ex-Somali National Army officers took over the organization, but that was never allowed to last very long. The temporary putsch was led by a former military officer of the Somali National Army, Colonel Abdulkadr Kosar, who used to participate in OAU Liberation Committee military training programs. Apart from this, albeit crucial factor, the two movements differ in several ways. First of all there is the time factor which facilitates a ripening or maturing process: the ELF was active as of September 1961; its splinter organization, the EPLF, emerged in 1970 and subsequently came to exercise hegemony and rule Eritrea since mid-1991.

In a much more decisive way than the SNM, the EPLF attracted strong, consistent support from professional and working class Eritreans abroad. These exiled groups created organizations for fundraising, policy research and public education abroad. Women are said to constitute over a third of the EPLF army, while in the SNM small groups of women served mostly as nurses or in related auxiliary services. In areas under its control, the EPLF initiated remarkable experiments in social transformation and land reforms. The SNM has had no "class struggle" approach partly because Somaliland has no significant agrarian based class formation. The EPLF stressed mass political education while the SNM approach on this was "superficial". It is important to stress that this is not due to ignorance, neglect or sheer laziness; on the contrary, it is due to the EPLF, with its radical Marxist origins, wishing to go beyond "flag independence" by transforming civil society itself. The SNM tends to accept its own civil society and to rely on its elders and its politics of compromise. The EPLF provided vanguard oriented village and social organizations for democratic participation. The SNM relied on surviving traditional and neo-traditional structures involving clan elders and religious notables. Thus, embryonic forms of radical social democracy in Eritrea and clan-based power-sharing or consociational democracy in Somaliland began to emerge during the very different number of years of armed struggle.

Upon capturing ample supplies of Soviet made heavy armaments in 1984, the EPLF transformed its guerilla army into a formidable, disciplined, well organized national army crucial in the 1992 onslaught against Mengistu's forces and the capture of Addis Ababa. The SNM never graduated beyond a guerilla army into a conventional army though it has an ample supply of officers trained in conventional warfare. Its longer disciplined and organized experience has given the EPLF charismatic leaders and a core of dedicated cadres. The SNM has striven for "consensual leaders" partly because Somali pastoral society tends to shun "charismatic" leaders – in spite of Siyad's brutal attempt to impose his own savage and distorted brand. The EPLF congresses are run and directed by militants. Somali pastoral democratic tradition which often militates against military discipline and efficient administration, dictates that SNM congresses be open, at times chaotic, always full of surprises, because they are full of compromises. The potential danger facing Somaliland: pastoral "anarchy"; that facing Eritrea: "vanguard authoritarianism". French researcher Gerard Prunier who traveled within SNM liberated territories and attended the February-March 1990 SNM Congress held in Bale Gubadle, offers similar insights.

> The first remark that comes to the mind when one travels through the SNM-held areas is what a perfectly well-adapted guerilla force it is – and what a poor regular army. The SNM is a close expression of the people... it is as much at home in its environment as the ubiquitous camel (1990-91:112).

Prunier noted that the SNM suffered from poor logistics, poor discipline and strategic incoherence (this third defect is probably a corollary of "pastoral democracy"). Lacking the heavy armaments of the EPLF, the SNM most mechanized equipment is ironically called a "technical" – recoilless riffles and Zug automatic cannons mounted on Toyotas or other four-wheel drive (pickup type) vehicles, made world famous by media coverage of Mogadishu violence. The questions of poor logistics is crucial: from a political economy point of view, this is what prevented the SNM from transcending its decentralized, voluntary, clan recruited guerilla militia phase into a centralized, disciplined army. Prunier concluded:

> My estimate of the SNM (the real figures are "a military secret" but my feeling is that nobody really knows them) is that is has about 4,000 regulars. But that figure means little, since it can bring together, in about a week's time, ten times that number of fighters. In a pinch, every man (and even some women – I have seen them) can become a fighter. The problem is how to feed these people. Dispersed they survive more or less well in their respective areas; brought together, they quickly starve. Nowhere is there a sufficient store of food to enable a ten or fifteen thousand men army to stay together more than four or five days. And even if such a store of food existed, there would still be the problem of bringing it where it would have to be used (1990-91:112-13).

The Somali environment and resources favors organizational as well as survival strategies based on decentralization, often extreme decentralization. The political cultural context included the segmentary clan system and anarchistic individualism. It is true that material conditions hinder the development of a centralized army just as they obstructed the development of a centralized Somali state throughout history. It is also true that contemporary Somali public opinion is against the formation of a strong central army. Most of the Somaliland contacts interviewed during 1991 advocated the formation of decentralized locally-controlled police forces whose recruitment takes into account issues of merit, proportionality and clan balance. Many rejected the idea of a new "army"– as a reaction to Siyad's brutal army and in awareness of the socio-economic issues raised above. They favor popular militias to be raised as and when needed, drawing upon the SNM experience. Another consequence of SNM clan sensitivities is the belief that a clan cannot be "liberated" or "developed" by another clan. Thus, during the war, non-Isaq deserters who sympathized with the SNM were encouraged to operate alongside the SNM, but form their own units and eventually, their own organizations. Each clan must learn to liberate itself. Even among the clans constituting the Isaq clan-family, the SNM encouraged wide political and military space under its loose umbrella to avoid petty conflicts. Asked why the SNM did not fight with its allies in southern Somalia, an SNM volunteer responded in a realistic, self-critical mood: "Who knows, we might behave as badly down there as THEY have up here" (Prunier, 1990-91:119). The key concern is "never again" to let *them* "behave badly" in the north.

IMPLICATIONS FOR DEMOCRATIZATION

Power Sharing Democracy

The democratization form compatible with SNM experience may be termed consociational or power-sharing democracy (Steiner, 1991). Power-sharing facilitates reciprocal recognitions in societies fragmented by ethnic, clan, religious and/or linguistic cleavages. Consociational democracy (industrial versions of which are practiced in Switzerland, Belgium and Austria for example) recognizes and acknowledges ethnic, clan or religious cleavages in constituting cabinets and parliaments, while civil service and army recruitment are conducted on the basis of both merit and proportionality – utilizing mechanisms similar to those of affirmative action procedures in the US. Attempts at forming governments on the basis of grand coalitions are encouraged to reduce competition and potential conflicts. Each significant subgroup is allowed the right to veto legislation that is directly against an issue which it considers vital to its survival and well-being. Leaders must be endorsed by their own particular group in order to reflect the legitimacy needed to broker binding inter-group decisions and undertakings. In this connection, recent Oromo Liberation Front allegations that the new Ethiopian regime is creating "artificial leaders" for the Oromos and other ethnic groups could, in the long run, jeopardize Ethiopia's embryonic experiment with "ethnic democracy" Since Ethiopia is so much larger in size and population than Eritrea and Somaliland, its initial attempts to establish consociationalism have appeared clumsy and confusing.

Size also obliges Ethiopia to favor federalism and local autonomy to give consociationalism an implementation chance. On the other hand, the TPLF with its vanguard party experience, may be tempted to imitate Eritrea with its class oriented radical social democracy. Consociationalism is often strengthened by federal structures, decentralization and local autonomy.

Ethnic or clan based power-sharing democracy is facilitated if the groups involved share a common vision and common history (in this case the history of British Somaliland as a separate entity, memories of inequities with the south and Siyad's military oppression), the various groups occupy more or less defined areas and share similar perspectives on external threats. None of the groups exercise hegemony, they are more or less equal. It is also important that the Ethiopian and Somaliland experiments in "ethnic democracy" not be overwhelmed by staggering socio-economic burdens. Ethiopia receives considerable external assistance but Somaliland has not even received its share as allocated by the UN. Problems are bound to arise if such a state of affairs is allowed to continue for long.

During its early years, the SNM represented an elitist, external, armed guerilla band claiming to represent the people in the north – the Isaq community in particular. Following their 1988 occupation of the north, Siyad's savage air and artillery attacks caused most of the urban population to flee to rural areas as displaced persons; a sizeable group of about 800,000 crossed the Ethiopian border to merge as refugees in several camps: Harchin, Dulhaad, Bele Abokor, Balyeleh, Harta Sheikh, Haror and Rabaso. In and around these camps, as well as among the internally displaced, the SNM began to emerge from the Isaq population. It is within this context that the elders – secular, clan leaders and the religious – came to play critical roles in organizing the distribution of food aid and other forms of relief, in adjudicating disputes and in recruiting fighters for the SNM. They came to form a Council of Elders, or *Guurti* in Somali which, as time passed, grew in importance. It came to constitute one of the two legislative houses proposed in the constitution drafted for Somaliland. The *Guurti* reached it pinnacle early in 1993, when it called a Grand National Reconciliation Conference in Borama (a non-Isaq town) and helped elect independence era leader Mohamed Ibrahim Egal as the second President of the *de facto* Republic of Somaliland. In order to make a whole series of binding compromises, the Borama Conference lasted from February until May of 1993. In composition and functioning, the *Guurti* derives its inspiration from traditional Somali power-sharing style. In this way, consociationalism could facilitate an evolution to multipartism, as became the case.

The February-May Borama Conference conducted several tasks. It spent considerable time adjudicating clan conflicts and disputes between neighbors since it views peace and reconciliation as its primary task. It discussed the major provisions of an anticipated Constitution and recommended, for example, that the structure of government be based on a President/ Vice-President model rather than a President/ Prime Minister model. They recommended the strict separation of the judiciary from executive and legislative powers and bodies. They formally endorsed a National Assembly or Parliament consisting of two chambers, a Council of Elders and a lower popular Chamber of Representatives. On an interim basis, both of these latter exist together for sometime with a President (Isaq), Vice-President (Non-Isaq from the Borama area) and a Cabinet selected according to the initiatives of the President but sensitive to issues of merit and clan representativeness.

The *Guurti* is chosen according to traditional rules of protocol, historical precedent and proportionality. During the 1990's, Somaliland tried to avoid the pitfalls of direct, competitive multi-party elections that negatively politicized clanism and produced chaos and the military coup during the 1960-69 period. Elections to the lower chamber consist of a series of mini-elections involving the groups and subgroups that are party to the Somaliland experiment. These have resulted in a chamber dominated by modern elites: former politicians, businessmen, teachers and other civil servants, leaders of women's and other civil society organizations. At a recent regional meeting of a council of elders in Erigavo (eastern zone) participants recommended that, in the future, the Guurti be given more powers than the popular lower Chamber. The Borama Conference elected an electoral body of 150 (elders, politicians, SNM cadres, civil servants, and civil society leaders) who went on to conduct competitive elections resulting in the election of veteran politician Ibrahim

Mohamed Egal as the second Somaliland President (Abdurahman Tuur was President from 1991-93) and veteran SNM leader Abdurahman Aw Ali as his Vice-President. As a variant of liberal democracy, consociationalism stresses process over product: disappointed SNM leaders were encouraged to accept the results and bide their time until the next elections in two years time. A majority of the population – the elders in particular – have confidence in Egal as an experienced leaders and wish to give him a second chance. It is indeed an irony of history that the person delegated to consummate union with ex-Italian Somalia is today charged with the task of guiding Somaliland out of the union!

Radical Social Democracy

Radical social democracy frowns upon ethnic, clan, religious and related cleavages, even prohibiting using such labels or forming organizations on their basis. It tends to stress a social class perspective to transcend primordial cleavages. The EPLF version has a participatory democratic vision which may not prove easy to sustain in the long run. While Somaliland encourages unbridled market mechanisms, Eritrea appears bent on experimenting with its own form of planned or at least guided economy, though markets will be allowed to play economic roles.

The EPLF has declared that multipartism is an issue in the long run. At their recent Third Congress (February 1994), however, they have indicated that such a transition might take a further four years. Radical social democracy tends to lean towards one partyism. It favors popular participation in various levels of decision-making and administration and policies favoring distributive equity among the people. Radical social democracy encourages ongoing democratic participation in cooperative farms, social organizations for women, youth and professionals, trade unions, schools and universities, as well as within the armed forces and the ruling party. EPLF's revolutionary experience not only facilitated such participation, it was indispensable for its success. Will the people sustain such high levels of popular involvement several years from now?

Radical and social democracy tends to put a premium on exceptional leaders and dedicated cadres. However, as time passes, the tendency towards ordinary if not corrupt leaders tends to emerge

– the "banalistation" of politics (Bayart, 1993:228-259). In relying on the spontaneous virtues of revolutionary leaders, radical social democracy tends to overlook the need to establish detailed systematic checks and balances of power. While radical social democracy neglects electoral competitions and related mechanisms, it stresses the substantive issues – emancipation of women, combating poverty, broadly based participation and social transformations. Consociational democracy concentrates on procedures and mechanisms, as well as elaborates traditional protocol in its Somaliland version, partly at the expense of democratic content.

One hopes Somaliland's evolving consociational democracy will be blessed with at least a reasonable number of responsible and socially aware political parties and leaders with a vision of development that included broad social benefits. Otherwise, development efforts would degenerate into a crude sum of individual entrepreneurial actions with large net costs to society. Once a stable power-sharing democratic system is in place, consistent efforts have to be made in order to both *conserve* and *transcend* ascriptive clan identities – otherwise a pastoral democracy would eventually degenerate into pastoral anarchy. Unless Eritrea develops greater sensitivities to consociational issues which could prove critical given its natural diversity and sociocultural, ethnic and religious pluralism, then the EPLF could find itself sitting on the slippery slope leading towards authoritarianism or conflict.

And now we must confront what could turn out to be a critical question: what would happen if minority groups, in their turn, tried to secede from these new entities? Does the right to self-determination cease to exist at "independence"? Both movements challenged this before, but how about now that the dagger is pointed at them? This is already partly the case with Eritrea and the Afars. To try and give a detailed answer to this intricate issue would require analysis of at least the following factors: vision, ideology and basic beliefs; resources, including organizational capacity; military capabilities and legal/diplomatic status. Both countries are very poor, however Eritrea's infrastructures have not been as devastated as those of Somaliland. Eritrea hopes to rapidly develop its resources to provide for all national minorities. Somaliland would offer a free market, an opportunity to use virtually open borders to trade from and to East Africa, through Somalia, Djibouti, Ethiopia and from and to Yemen, Saudi Arabia and the Gulf.

We have already seen how even the SNM militia army is based on clans controlling their own particular territories. On the issue of military capabilities the differences between Eritrea and Somaliland are vast. However it cannot be automatically assumed that the availability of military capacity in Eritrea would automatically lead to militarist policies and practices. The leader is in many ways a relatively free agent of history: it is he who will, ultimately, have to make the *ethical* choice between conceding or denying others the right to self-determination for which he and the nation had sacrificed so much during violent years of struggle. He also has several options short of repression and seccession.

Eritrea has a clear advantage over Somaliland with regards to international recognition. In May 1993, Eritrea translated *de facto* into *de jure* statehood. With such a status change some numerous economic and political advantages, including having one's borders proclaimed sacrosanct. Therefore, what should happen if the Afars, for example, struggle to unite with their kin group across borders into Ethiopia and Djibouti and Eritrea refuses: the international community would support and aid Eritrea, should it opt for coercive policies. Should such a scenario unfold, we can say that the wheel has come around full circle. Perhaps the best antidote against secession is democracy: federalism helps but it only can be strengthened and made more effective through democratization. Northerners were angered and bitterly disappointed by the 1960 Somali Union, but they did not opt for secessionist politics because they felt open parliamentary politics gave them a chance to right some of their felt wrongs during the 1960-69 period. Siyad's military regime offered no such hope pushing them to armed self-determination and secession.

Political decentralization along federalist lines is of course no panacea. *To be effective it must be underpinned by democratic principles and institutions.* These must include, above all, scrupulous observation of individual rights and the rule of law, safeguards for minorities and the separation of political power to check the rise of autocrats' (Chege, 1992:152)(emphasis added).

CONCLUSIONS

The 1960 temporary secession of Katanga from the then Congo (Zaire) was engineered by white settlers and international mining and financial interests. Biafra represented an elite preemptive strike which eventually fizzled out once it became clear that the Nigerian army was not bent on Ibo genocide; on the contrary, Biafra was welcomed back into the Nigerian federation. Eritrea's and to a lesser extent Somaliland's claims to self-determination are grounded on a historic consciousness of oppression. Unlike Biafra and Katanga, Eritrea and Somaliland also have stronger juridical claims: each had existed for eighty years or more as a distinct colonial territory. In this sense they are within the spirit, and the Eritrean's would also claim, the letter of the OAU code. Even though Somaliland as a historical project commenced with the defensive military actions of the overtly oppressed Isaq clan, simplistic clan claims have been radically altered through articulation in territorial terms – facilitating power-sharing negotiations with non-Isaq clans within the territory as was achieved in Borama and other reconciliation conferences. A territorial approach also allows the SNM to avoid any suggestion about incorporating the sizeable Isaq population within the Haud and Reserved Areas of Ethiopia's Region 5 (Markakis, 1990).

At the international level, both law and state interests confer a powerful advantage to the existing states. The recent collapse of communism has allowed Western states to break this state sovereignty taboo in an enthusiastic rush to recognized the dismemberment of the USSR, Yugoslavia and Czechoslovakia. Other parts of the world, especially Africa where the OAU code continued to exert its influence, have not been treated by the same standards. Prior to recent events, Bangladesh provided a rare case of a secession that won international recognition. This was due to geography – East Pakistan (Bangladesh) separated by Indian territory from West Pakistan – as well as the decisive intervention of the Indian army and India's diplomatic offensive. Compared to Somaliland, Eritrea had presented an impressive and energetic justification for separation aimed at external audiences – mostly sympathetic organizations and circles within Western societies. However remarkable, they were not enough to win international recognition. This came about through the most compelling argument of all – outstanding military success. Somaliland also won military success allowing it to proclaim a *de facto* Republic. During its long struggle, Eritrea was able to assist an ally in the neighboring Ethiopian province of Tigray, the TPLF. As the Mengistu regime decomposed, TPLF forces in coalition with other Ethiopian People's Revolutionary Democratic Front (EPRDF) forces and backed by organized EPLF troops, armored units and tanks, moved on to capture the capital Addis Ababa itself and install an EPRDF government. Outstanding military success, principle and kinship (the Tigrinya element) paved the way for Eritrean recognition by the new Ethiopian regime. Once Ethiopia itself stood ready to sanction the separation, the OAU ruling became irrelevant.

The clan structure and operations of Somali society could not permit the SNM to play a similar role with groups like the USC in the south. A "clan does not liberate another clan" has been an SNM principle. Somaliland, like Eritrea, would like to separate with the blessings of Mogadishu which has yet to constitute a recognized central authority. There are important elements in the south who are sympathetic to the issue of autonomy (not independence) for Somaliland. It is possible that north-south conflicts could flair up again, creating a Yugoslav type scenario which could be highly influenced by the military and diplomatic posture of Ethiopia. An Eritrean-type scenario constitutes a second option. Should international opinion lean towards this solution, Somaliland would have to conduct a just and fair popular referendum to earn the international legitimacy now enjoyed by Eritrea.

For want of a better expression, a third option could be termed the confederal solution: a two equal states arrangement representing greater autonomy than say the federated state of Quebec. Internally, Somaliland may constitutionally have a President (who may automatically assume the title of First Vice-President or even Co-President of the Confederation). Somaliland would have and control its own police forces (army, in case armies are established); it would have its own separate parliament, cabinet and civil service.

Somaliland could be admitted to United Nations membership (following the precedent of the Ukraine and Byelorussia, for example). Somaliland would gain virtually all the substance of an independent state retaining slim, practical links: currency, passports, jointly shared foreign embassies. It is beyond the focus of this article to pursue such speculations. It is up to the peoples of Somaliland to exercise their hard won *de facto* self-determination the best way possible. Meanwhile, however, it is important to narrow the gap in political cultures. Since 1991, while Somaliland has rotated leaders through elections and solved conflicts through extended negotiations, the south has been dominated by warring warlords. There are pockets of local power sharing authorities in southern Somalia but the overall situation is held hostage (the capital city in particular) by intense faction fighting – a form of decentralized Siyadism. And so the final outcome in Somaliland remains indeterminate. Somalilanders hope that, in the long run, the *de facto* situation may become irreversible.

The United Nations has an inbuilt hostility toward dismemberment of states which are full members. Thus, the UN has been reluctant to provide Somaliland with the assistance its problems deserve. Following its debacle against General Aidid, the UN has shown more flexibility towards Somaliland: referring to its government as "the Egal Administration" instead of the previous "community leaders of the northwest". In one of his Reports to the Security Council, the Secretary General Boutros Ghali observed:

> I am aware of the very delicate question of the secession proclamation in the north... The development of UNOSOM to the north would not prejudice in any way the decision of the Somali people on their national future (Ghali, 1993:21).

Few states in Africa are economically "viable" in the strict sense of the term. Political rather than economic viability criteria were used to recognize most of the states that seceded since 1989. However, a discussion on democratic possibilities for Eritrea and Somaliland cannot ignore linkages with socio-economic developments. Perhaps one day both countries may discover oil and other mineral resources, but until they do, the spectre of serious underdevelopment will continue to haunt them. Long-range economic viability depends on the creation of a Horn of Africa Commonwealth or Common Market – an example of the potential fission of national borders based on free choice, reciprocal recognitions and mutual advantages. The Commonwealth would consist of the following core countries: Ethiopia, Eritrea, Djibouti and Somalia/ Somaliland. Until recently, good relations exist between all these countries. Ethiopia forms a natural and potentially wealthy hinterland for Eritrea, Djibouti and Somalia/ Somaliland. A coordinating organization has already been formed in 1986 consisting of the core plus Kenya, Uganda and the Sudan – the Inter-Governmental Authority on Drought and Development (IGADD), renamed IGAD.

In evolving a radical social democratic state, the EPLF relied on its long military and socio-political experience as well as its Marxist background. It is also a response to guiding a country as diverse as Eritrea which contains about nine major ethnic groups and three religious traditions. Some of the ethnic groups (the Afars, for example), have traditional structure similar to the Somalis; the Tigrinya on the other hand, have had centralized politics like the Amhara. Radical social democratic institutions attempt to penetrate and influence all equally. Hopefully, Eritrea will resist moves to quell pluralism; tolerating ethnic identities could turn apparent problems into assets. Should significant propositions demand it, Eritrean leaders would be wise to allow for multi-partyism well before the four year deadline. Bringing self-determination to Eritrea would be incomplete unless, like Somaliland, the citizens are able to exercise the basic right to rotate their leaders regularly and freely.

Somaliland, a relatively homogenous society like Botswana, is able to evolve its modern polity through an adaptation of relatively uniform tradition of religion, institutions, laws, languages, and attitudes. The country has experienced an Islamic revivalism but not radical fundamentalism due to the lack of mature, charismatic fundamentalist leaders and, even more important, due to the potency of the clan factor in Somali politics. SNM fighters called themselves *mujahidins* – those waging Islamic Jihad. This was good for morale. Pockets of fundamentalists exit but not yet sufficient to create a critical mass. How will they be involved in party politics should they choose to participate? Marxism, on the other hand, hardly penetrated SNM ruling circles and political thought. Once the break with USSR came in 1978, the most well-known Somali Marxists went to Aden, then South Yemen, where they formed a party; others went to Addis Ababa to work with the SSDF; only a handful joined the SNM. They played no significant role though some of them may yet establish a social democratic party during the anticipated multi-party phase. Somaliland must be brought to learn that democracy involves more than power sharing procedures; there is need to evolve policies and institutions that can combat poverty, that facilitate women's emancipation, children's welfare, minority rights, regulating the unbridled private markets as well as tackle and resolve other substantive issues. The issue of recognition and non-recognition aside, Eritrea and Somaliland have their special experiences to offer each other and to offer others in Africa who are willing to learn.

A Clash of Vision and of Political Culture

Somaliland has not been free of social tensions boiling into civil wars. Conflict flared in 1992 between the military and civil wing of the SNM. This was adjudicated at the Grand Borama Conference. A faction advocating federal relations with Somalia ignited another more serious conflict from November 1994 to October 1996, displacing over 180,000 people. This was adjudicated by another Grand Conference held in Hargeisa. Once again it was the Guurti, supplemented by Diaspora delegations and leaders of civil society, those who played critical roles. Once again, complaints about unfair clan presentation laid behind such grievances. From 1997 onward Somaliland enjoyed a long period of peace that lasted to this day. In Somaliland's vision, conflicts are bound to occur; the critical issue is to evolve a political culture of mediating tensions and contradictions.

In the years that followed, Somaliland turned its attention to the transition between caucus type indirect elections and toward secular and direct, one-man, one-vote democratic order. The 1997, Hargeisa Grand Conference – this time compromised half of parliamentarians and half of clan elders – replaced the earlier Borama Charter with a provisional Constitution. In May 2001, the Constitution was ratified by 97 percent cast in a national referendum. This result was seen by insiders and outsiders as approval of Somaliland independence and a repudiation of rule from Mogadishu.

The new Constitution obtained its baptism by fire when President Egal died in May 2002, on a visit to South Africa. The transition went uncontested and proceeded in accordance with the Constitution: Vice President Dahir Riyale Kahin served for the remainder of the presidential term.

The second phase in the transition consisted of holding direct local elections in December, 2001. But before this phase, a complimentary phase was initiated: adopting an electoral law and establishing the National Electoral Commission (NEG). Six political parties contested the local elections. The Guidelines state that only the top three would qualify for registration as national political parties. Parties are also supposed to show support of about 20% of the people in all districts: UDUB (ruling part), Kulmiye and UCD (opposition parties). The framers of the Constitution learned from the 1960's: 60 parties vying for 123 seats as well as the current Iraqi plethora of parties. Local elections were held for 379 seats on 26 district councils.

The third phase in the transition towards democracy was the presidential election held in 2003. Kahin became the first Somaliland present to be elected in a free and fair election for the first time. However, the margin of victory was only 80 votes. The runner up Ahmed Mohamed Silanyo, the veteran SNM leader, is popular and comes from the majority clan-family. Besides, Kahin was from the Gudabursi clan and worked in Siyad's dreaded security service (the NSS). This reflects the greater political maturity and tolerance manifested by Somalilanders At first Kulmiye rejected the results and resorted to court challenge; very soon however, pressure brought to bear and calm minds prevailed.

The fourth phase of democratization consisted in hosting parliamentary elections. For the House of Representatives (not the *Guurti*, indirectly elected). For the first time on Somali soil since 1969, House of Representatives held election on 29 September 2005. Obviously, this very significant step reflected the formal transition step from clan caucus representation to a modern electoral democracy. All these Somaliland elections were observed by external and internal monitors and were deemed free and fair and impressive. The results of the 2005 parliamentary vote: UDUB 33; Kulmiye 28 and UCID 21 out of a total of 82 for the chamber. Here is a unique case that opposition seats outnumber government seats. It requires discipline and shared notions of common political culture to avoid, for example, flimsy motions of impeachment. This is where the concept of "Loyal Opposition" attains remarkable practical meaning. After the elections, meaningful discussions were held among the three political parties, the NEC and the government aimed at producing a code of conduct to which the parties would adhere during the pre-campaign, election, and post-election periods. This involves internalizing and enhancing the vision and values of a democratic political culture.

What factors account for the disciplining of Somaliland politics? Internal factors above all, are the role of the *Guurti*; also the role of meritocracy based on business and commerce; as apposed to the ascriptive monopolistic elite who funded the Union of Islamic courts. At least 50% of Somaliland income comes from the Somaliland Diaspora – they have stake and they have sent delegations several times to mediate internal problems. Professor Jhazbay of South Africa has a very interesting and relevant reason: the uphill struggles for recognition help to discipline domestic Somaliland politics.

Since 1991, Somaliland has had no partners in Somalia, with whom to conduct meaningful dialogue. The evolving democratic vision and political culture in the north has, for many years, confronted the vacuum of the anarchistic and negative political culture of the warlords; and for a very brief period, the anti-democratic political culture of the Jihadi-Islamists only to be replaced by a regime bent on undertaking the slippery slope towards militaristic despotism. Perhaps the most important historical legacy of Somaliland may prove to be its role as a model for visions and practicalities of democratization. Muslims are often asked to choose between democracy and stability. Somaliland shows that there is a way to promote democratization without causing havoc and anarchy. It is the most democratic country in the Horn of Africa.

References

Bayart, Jean-Francois. *The State in Africa: The Politics of the Belly.* London: Longman, 1993.

Bongartz, Maria. *The Civil War in Somalia* (Current African Issues II, Nordiska Afrikainstitute, 1991).

Chege, Michael. "Remembering Africa." *Foreign Affairs* (Vol. 71, 1992).

Contini, Paolo. *The Somali Republic: An Experiment in Legal Integration.* 1969.

Davidson, Basil. *The Liberation of Guinea.* Baltimore: Penguin Press, 1969.

Drysdale, John. *The Somali Dispute.* New York: Praeger, 1964.

Drysdale, John. *Somaliland: The Anatomy of a Secession.* 1991.

Tom Farer. *War Clouds on the Horn of Africa.* New York: Carnegie, 1976.

Gebre-Medhin, Jordan. *Peasants and Nationalism in Eritrea.* Trenton: Red Sea Press, 1989.

Horn of Africa Volume XIV Numbers 1 (January-March) and 2 (April-June). 1991.

Markakis, John. *National and Class Conflict in the Horn of Africa.* London: Zed Books 1990.

Nzongola-Ntalaja, Georges (ed.). *Conflict in the Horn of Africa.* Atlanta: African Studies Association Press, 1991.

Prunier, Gerard. "A Candid View of the Somali National Movement". *Horn of Africa* (Vol. xiii, No. 3 & 4, July-Sept. und Oct.-Dec.), 1990.

Rajagopal, B. & Anthony Carroll. "The Case for the Independent Statehood of Somaliland". Washington, DC, 1992.

Selassie, Bereket Habte. *Conflict and Intervention in the Horn of Africa.* New York: Monthly Review Press, 1980.

Steiner, Jurg. *European Democracies.* New York: Longman, 1991.

Touval, Saadia. *Somali Nationalism.* Cambridge: Harvard University Press, 1963.

Trevaskis, K.N. *Eritrea: A Colony in Transition: 1941-52.* New York: Oxford, University Press, 1960.

de Visscher, Charles. *Theory and Reality in Public International Law.* Princeton: Princeton University Press, 1968.

CHAPTER 7

SOMALI ISLAM AND POLITICS

INTRODUCTION

This chapter traces the role of Islam in Somali politics and provides a historical context for the manifestations of politicized Islam within the current Somali crisis. Even though Islam epitomizes Somali culture and the Somali experience, Somali historiography is lacking in studies concerning political Islam.

Political Islam has manifested an expansionist as well as a revivalist face. Expansionism involves the spread of religion and the rapid conversion of non-Muslims. Revivalism involves the phenomenon superficially referred to as 'born again' among those who are already converted. In a relatively routine search for personal roots in piety, revivalism reflects an Islamic renewal reformist movement; but revivalism in an angry process of 'rediscovered fundamentalism' implies fanaticism, often spilling over into violence.

On 7 October 1990 the Islamic movement opposed to the military regime headed by Dictator Mohamed Siyad Barre issued a formal manifesto entitled 'The Righteous Call'. An Analysis of this document reveals an Islamic revival and reformist movement. However, pockets of Islamic 'fundamentalists' have continued to surface both during the pre-Siyad and the post-Siyad era. What role has Islam played in Somali politics?

EXPANSIONIST ISLAM DURING THE ERA OF TRADE AND CITY-STATES

It is not often remembered that both Islam and Christianity found homes on the Horn of Africa, almost from their very inception. Certain historical episodes point to the introduction of Islam on the north-east African coast before it became firmly rooted in

Arabia itself; nevertheless, the mass conversions and deepening of Islam among the Somalis seem to have taken place only in the eleventh, twelfth, and thirteenth centuries. Lacking a tradition of political unity achieved through a centralized state, Somali nationalism has historically relied on Islamic cultural nationalism.[1] I. M. Lewis offers us the following summary account of Somali Islam:

Despite their differences in the jurisdiction allowed to the Sharia there is little difference between the nomads and the cultivators in the importance attached to the fundamental principles of Islam. Except for a few tribes who have remained relatively sheltered from Muslim influence, the five 'Pillars of the Faith' – the profession of the Faith; prayers; fasting, somewhat irregularly observed perhaps; almsgiving; and pilgrimage – seem to be universally practiced. Competent witnesses have generally been struck by the devoutness of the Somali tribesman.[2]

Religious associations and rituals, however, tend to be more formal and structured among the settled cultivators and urban populations. Somalis follow sunni Islam and their religious practices have been greatly influenced by Sufism; four Sufi orders are especially influential among the Somalis: Qadiriyya, Ahmadiyya, Salihiyya, and, less significant in terms of followers, Rifa'iyya. Sufism has given Somalis space to incorporate several aspects of their pre-Islamic customs and practices. For example, the rites involving a particularly pious young wife or young children in obligatory prayers for rain reflect non-Islamic elements.[3]

For the most part, rural Somalis, especially the pastorialists, have tended to rely on traditional Somali law (*xeer Soomali)* in regulating most of their lives. At the core of this law is the concept of paying *diya*. The Somalis as a people are divided into five main 'clan families', and each in turn is subdivided into clans, sub-clans, sub-sub-clans… resulting in extended families. Within this kaleidoscopic spectrum of clan affiliations, the most binding and most frequently mobilized loyalty involves the *diya*-paying group. This unit embodies a specific contractual alliance whereby an injury done to any member of the group implicates all those who are a party to its treaty. Thus, if a man of one group kills a man of another, his group as a whole has to pay one hundred camels in compensation (fifty if the victim is a woman).

Somalis are aware that this is contrary to the Islamic stipulation of an eye for an eye; however, they have gone on for hundreds of years expressing their passionate attachment to the Islamic *Sharia* as an ideal while pragmatically sticking to their traditional law. This is, of course, not unusual in Islamic societies and very often there is also a syncretic combination of *Sharia* and traditional custom.

Somali lore divides society into two main groups: the man of religion (*wadaad)* and the warrior (*waranleh,* literally 'spear-bearer'). The *wadaads* devote their lives to religion and in some sense practice as men of God. A *wadaad* who is more learned in religious knowledge is usually referred to as a shaykh. His duties include teaching elements of the faith and the Quran to the young. He is expected to apply the Islamic *Sharia* in conducting marriage ceremonies and in settling disputes pertaining to matrimony and inheritance. He is often called to assess damage for injury in cases in which, as stated above, traditional Somali law is applied for historical and practical reasons. In contrast to the position of religious personalities in Shia Islam and even in other Sunni Muslim countries, Somalia is significant in preferring the separation of the roles of religious leaders from political leaders. Only in very exceptional circumstances would Somalis tolerate the assumption of political power by religious leaders. Ideally, for remaining aloof from politics, men of religion were considered above the rigid bonds of *diya* paying and clan obligations. In many cases in the past, their lives were spared during periods of violent internecine secular rivalry and conflicts. Accordingly, they were often able to play leading roles as mediators in such conflicts.

Somalia's geography has played a crucial role in influencing its history. The Red Sea and the Indian Ocean have facilitated long-distance trade from ancient times. There is some evidence to suggest that Egyptians, Phoenicians, Persians, and others may have come to the Horn of Africa and East African coast centuries before the birth of Christ.[4] The ancient world knew Somalia as the land of Punt, a major source of frankincense and myrrh. From north-east Somalia the chief exports were aromatic gums and spices. In addition, a little coconut oil was exported.[5] From the long Somali coast, frankincense and myrrh, livestock, hides and skins, ivory, ostrich feathers, coffee, furs, and gold from the Abyssinian highlands were exported to Egypt, the Gulf, India, and China. All this indicates that some people at least were living in permanent settlements. Prior to Islam, Somalia became a significant part of the Red Sea-Indian Ocean trading network. Similarly, Arab penetration along the northern and eastern Somali coasts antedates the Islamic period.

Nevertheless, the Islamic epoch produced quantitative and qualitative changes on all such trends with profound consequences. The trend towards settlement and trade is given impetus to such an extent that the Somali coast as a whole is dotted with a series of significant Islamic city-states such as Zeila, Bulhar, Berbera, Mogadishu, Merca, Barawa: Forms of Islamic organization and administration were imported and modified to fit local realities. Islamic commercial laws and regulations, systems of weights and measures, navigation techniques, and security arrangements facilitated trade, including the book trade. Institutes of higher religious learning and cultural contacts and exchanges flourished. Muslim Arabs and Persian settlers became important elements in the developing coastal city-states. Ibn Battuta, considered one of the greatest Muslim travelers of the Middle Ages, visted Zeila and Mogadishu around 1331. He was struck by the informal, consultative nature of rulership in Mogadishu. Elements of traditional Somali 'pastoral democracy'[6] seem to have commingled with Islamic hierarchical structures:

I disembarked with my companions, and greeted the Qadi and his followers. He said to me: 'In the name of God, let us go and greet the Shaikh.' 'Who is the Shaikh?' I asked, and he replied: The Sultan.' For it is their custom here to call the Sultan 'Shaikh' ... [Following prayers at the chief mosque in Mogadishu] the Shaikh went out of the door of the mosque and put his sandals on... and set off on foot to his house, which is near the mosque, everyone else following barefoot.[7]

Though Mogadishu was typical of the string of Islamic city-states, Zeila developed to the point that it became the capital of the flourishing Muslim state of Adal under which at least twenty other Muslim towns flourished in the fifteenth and sixteenth centuries in the Somali hinterland. In a number of such towns urbanized, mixed populations grew that owed no loyalty to clan *diya*-paying groups.

The inland city of Harar developed into a major centre of Islamic learning and culture with a widespread reputation.

Compared with other African peoples, the peoples of the Horn are strikingly similar in many ways. They also have significant differences. The highlanders of Abyssinia (present-day Ethiopia), who follow an early form of Christianity, have developed centralized religious and state institutions and practice agriculture. The coastal peoples, mostly Somalis, have adopted Islam, decentralized polities, and a pastoral way of life. At the same time, the two ecological zones and their peoples complement one another. In normal circumstances the highlanders conduct their trade through the coastal peoples. In time, the crusades entered the history of the Horn. Some of the Christian semi-feudal rulers of Abyssinia dreamt of an expansion in order to have direct access to the sea for trade and the procurement of arms. They appealed to the Portuguese for help: 'We are a Christian island in an Islamic sea.'[8]

In 1415 the Abyssinians invaded the large sultanate of Ifat under which came the state of Adal. They decisively defeated the Muslim armies and chased the sultan, Sad al-Din, to an island off the coast where they killed him in battle. Since he died in holy war, *jihad*, he was later revered as a saint by Somali mystics. The Muslims were avenged by the remarkable leader Ahmed Gurey (or Ahmed Gran, the left-handed) in the second decade of the sixteenth century. He began life as a famous warrior who later assumed the religious title of Imam. His armies pushed deep into the highlands inflicting one defeat after another on those who had shed the blood of Sad al-Din and other Muslims in previous wars. He was defeated eventually and killed in 1542 when the Abyssinian armies were joined by at least 400 Portuguese bearing fire arms.

Ahmed Gurey's *jihad* was the high-water mark but not the end of such *jihads*. In the next three centuries or so they were eclipsed by wars waged by the non-Muslim, non-Christian Oromos in the course of their northward migrations. Oromo migrations drove a wedge between the older crusading antagonists.

ISLAMIC RESURGENCE AND THE ANTICOLONIAL JIHAD

During the fifteenth, sixteenth, and seventeenth centuries Portuguese traders and soldiers landed in the Somali territories and ruled some of the coastal city-states. By disrupting and capturing their trade, they significantly contributed to the decline of not only the Somali but also the Swahili city-states to the south. Worse was yet to come: in the late nineteenth century the British, French, and Italians, as well as a heavily armed Abyssinian state under Emperor Menelik, all moved in to partition and colonize various parts of the Somali territories. Since the turn of the century Somalis have learned to live under Italian Somaliland, French Somaliland (Djibouti), Ethiopian Somaliland, British Somaliland, and the British-administered Northern Frontier District in Kenya.

European imperialism served as a catalyst for Islamic revivalism in several parts of the Muslim world: Emir Abdel Kader in Algeria, the Sanusi in Libya, the Wahhabi in Saudi Arabia, the Mahdi in the Sudan, and the Sayyid in Somalia. From 1899 to 1920 Shaykh Mohammed Abdille Hassan, popularly known as the Sayyid, waged a twenty-year anticolonial *jihad* against British, Ethiopian, and Italian military forces. With messianic zeal he exhorted all Somalis to return to the strict path of Muslim devotion. Shaykh Mohammed traveled widely in East Africa and the Middle East. He came in contact with various trends of Islamic resurgence. He drew inspiration from the Mahdists' holy struggle for freedom in the Sudan. During a pilgrimage to Makka he became a disciple of Mohammed Salih, the founder of the Salihiyya. This order is remarkable for its puritanical precepts. The founder appointed the Sayyid as a deputy and charged him with its propagation among the Somalis.[9]

Around 1987 he began to teach and preach near Berbera on the north Somali coast where he was incensed to witness the activities of the Christian missionaries operating along the coast under British colonial protection. In 1899 he formally declared *jihad* against 'infidel' domination, and in a letter to the British he wrote: 'If the country [Somaliland] was cultivated, or contained houses or property it would be worth your while to fight... If you want wood or stone you can get them in plenty. There are also many ant heaps. The sun is very hot. All you can get from me is war, nothing else.'[10]

The Sayyid was a great poet in a nation of poets, and he was able to convey his appeal to moral regeneration, his call to anticolonial struggles, and his vision of liberation in lines of exceptional poetry. He called his followers the Dervishes and his movement came to be known as the Dervish movement. Saadia Touval offers the following assessment of his movement: 'It was motivated primarily by religious fanaticism and had as its ultimate objective the imposition of the Salihiyah precepts and way of life upon the population. But to attain that objective, political means were necessary. The political struggle inevitably had nationalist ingredients, and the ultimate religious objectives of the movement had certain nationalistic aims as their corollaries.'[11]

Most Somalis admire the Sayyid for his defiance of colonial authorities. They differ widely with regard to his historical legacy. While clan affiliations and loyalties divide Somalis, the Islamic faith and the common cultural and linguistic elements make Somalia one of the few relatively homogeneous nations in Africa. The Sayyid's fanatical attempt violently to impose the minority Salihiyya Sufi order over the other three—which constituted a majority—was a highly divisive strategy. Instead of facilitating peace and binding warring clans, Islam, politicized by the Sayyid, exacerbated conflicts among Somalis. The Sayyid and his Dervishes were allegedly implicated in the murder of the famous Qadiriyya Shaykh Uways in 1909. Shaykh Uways wes devoted to the spread of his order's teaching in the southern interior among nominal Muslims and non-Muslims. Apart from contributing a great deal of devotional poetry in Arabic, he also attempted to translate traditional Arabic hymns into Somali utilizing his own phonetic system. The British took full advantage of the Sayyid's misdeeds to influence the founder of the order, Muhammad Salih, who in 1909 denounced the Sayyid and in essence 'excommunicated' him, though there is no such procedure in Islam.

From 1887 to 1904 the Sayyid gained well-deserved popularity by acting as a 'poor man of God' (as he referred to himself) and mediating in inter-clan and intra-clan disputes among groups in the Burao area who were related to neither his father's nor his mother's clans. In words and in deeds (risking his life as a devout man of religion) he sought to forge alliances in order to redirect internal violence towards external enemies. He continued to succeed in his efforts and for a certain period he drove the British administration from the interior, confining them to a narrow coastal strip. The Dervishes were even able to raid with impunity the colonial capital of Berbera. However, problems with food supplies, the British-Italian coastal blockade on arms, and related factors put pressure on his basically temperamental personality and caused him to handle internal contradictions violently rather than peacefully as he had preached and practiced during the early and middle stages of the movement. He has left a very important even though negative lesson for future Somalis: the violent pitfalls of an embryonic theocratic state founded on a narrow, fanatical, sectarian ideology.

In spite of Muhammad Salih's denunciation and growing defections of his followers,[12] the Sayyid continued to wage wars and to escape from the international coalition of forces ranged against his movement. In 1920 the British took the unprecedented step of introducing airplanes in an African conflict when they bombarded his magnificent fortress at Taleh. The Sayyid escaped, but his forces suffered heavy casualties in the combined aerial and ground assault. Though a defeated man, he died peacefully some time in 1921. Many Somalis feel that his trials and tribulations vindicate the age-old adage: he who holds the holy book should not wield the sword.

THE MODERN NATIONALIST PHASE SUFFOCATES AN ISLAMIC RENEWAL

The word 'modern' in used here purely for convenience. Most of the literature of African nationalism tends to refer to earlier manifestations as forms of early resistance and to label as 'modern' that phase of anticolonial struggle that involves political parties and related types of organizations. The Dervish movement had at least one significant outcome. Colonial authorities felt obliged to keep Christian missionary activities generally out of their Somali colonies. Somalis see this as a positive outcome because today fewer than 1 per cent of all Somalis are Christians.[13] Thus Somalia is spared the problems facing other Muslim societies such as Nigeria and the

Sudan, even Malaysia and Egypt, which have significant Christian or other non-Muslim minorities.

In preserving their religious homogeneity, Somalis missed the opportunity to participate in a colonial schooling system for a considerable period of time. In Africa generally, the state-sponsored school system hardly operated during the first forty years or so of colonialism. During most of that period, missionaries provided schooling as a significant aspect of their Christianizing mission. During the late 1930s and early 1940s Somalis resisted even state-sponsored efforts at providing education. They continued to associate colonial education – public or otherwise – with the propagation of Christianity. In any case, the British government was not too ready to spend money on Somali development, having spent considerable sums waging war against the Dervish movement.

The revolutionary radicalism of the Sayyid was replaced by the cautious reformism of elders who emerged during the 1920s and 1930s. An example of such a new leader was Haji Farah Omar, a former colonial civil servant who became active around 1920.[14] In spite of his Islamic reformist orientation, jittery colonial authorities did not wish to take any chances and he was exiled to Aden. While there, he actively participated in the formation of the Somali Islamic Association, a cultural organization with indirect political implications. In some ways Haji Farah's efforts were similar to those of Ben Badis in Algeria. Ben Badis's reformist movement was able to forge close ties with the nationalist movement. Thus the Algerian nationalist party, the FLN (National Liberation Front), came to reflect an Islamic as well as a secular outlook.[15] And even though the FLN waged a prolonged revolutionary war for independence which led it to adopt, in the past at least, a radical version of socialism as political ideology, the Islamic aspect never faded. In fact it has grown with time to the point where today it has broken away and offers a violent alternative to the secular FLN as a ruling movement. The banishment of Haji Farah and his Somali Islamic Association seems to have contributed to a rupture in linkages between Islamic reformism and secular Somali nationalism that flourished in the 1940s and 1950s.

The main Somali nationalist political party, the Somali Youth League (SYL), grew out of the Somali Youth Club (SYC), established in Mogadishu on 15 May 1943. As a result of Mussolini's defeat during World War II, the British occupied most of the Somali territories, including those in Ethiopia. The British Military Administration supported the SYC and the SYL, hoping that they, in turn, would back Britain's interest to administer ex-Italian Somaliland under a UN Trusteeship. 'There is good reason to believe that it [the British Military Administration] was not merely a benevolent onlooker, but provided during the early 1940's guidance and help to the inexperienced Somali politicians.'[16]

The SYC had thirteen founding members, among whom was Abdulkadir Sekhawe Din, a prominent Mogadishu-based religious figure. His prestige, networks, and unassuming leadership helped to give the SYC firm urban roots during its early, fragile years. However, it does not seem that he was able (or wanted) to exercise strong leadership in matters pertaining to the SYC's ideology and programme. Another prominent Mogadishu religious leader and founding member was Haji Mohammed Hussein whose ideological proclivities lead him to become an ardent supporter of Nasserism and Islamic socialism. Virtually all of the ideological and programmatic inspiration for the SYC came from the forceful personality of Yassin Haji Osman who had himself been influenced by Marxist elements within the defeated Italian community. In fact the original SYC flag was red in colour, bearing an emblem that reflected a blending of Marxist and Islamic symbols. The SYL later toned down some of Yassin Haji Osman's leftwing excesses. Nevertheless, SYC and SYL documents hardly mention the important role of the Islamic religion in Somali life. Paradoxically, they appear much more radically secular than even the formal position of the Algerian FLN, which was compelled to wage a Mao-style guerrilla war for independence.

Perhaps another important reason for the paradox involves the question of education. The SYC founders deliberately chose the word 'youth' to emphasize their 'modernity' and to distinguish themselves from 'traditional elders' (both religious and secular) who had, in their opinion, reacted to colonialism too defensively and rejected indiscriminately even the 'modern' education that comes with European colonialism. For some of the most radical secular leaders of modern Somali nationalism, 'Islam', as Professor John L. Esposito observed in another context, was simply an obstacle to change, an obstacle whose relevance to the political and social order would increasingly diminish.[17] When the SYC changed its name to the Somali Youth League in 1947, it transformed itself into an organized political party with branches throughout all the divided Somali territories. The SYL issued a four-point program during the same year. The first and second points read: 'To unite all Somalis generally, and the youth especially with the consequent repudiation of all harmful old prejudice (such, for example, as tribal and clan distinctions); to educate the youth in modern civilization by means of schools and by cultural propaganda circles.'[18]

By 1939 only twelve Western-style schools provided education for a tiny group of 1776 pupils in Italian Somaliland.[19] Only a handful of individuals had received secondary education. Unlike the situation in several other African colonies, none of the SYC/SYL founding fathers had received a university education. SYL leaders experienced an inferiority complex on this issue and began to discuss the need to 'jet-propel' their people, to paraphrase Kwame Nkrumah's famous words,[20] in order to catch up with education advances made in other parts of Africa during the last fifty or sixty years of colonial rule. Consciously or unconsciously they blamed traditional Muslims for this lag.

The fourth point in the SYL program deals with the need to adopt a script to develop Somali as a written language. The third point deals with the perennial issue in Somali politics: the need to free and unify the Somali people, divided into five parts under four colonial powers (Britain, Italy, France, and Ethiopia). A nationalist party, the Somali National League, in outlook and program very similar to the SYL, established itself in British Somaliland (1951). On 1 July 1960 ex-British and ex-Italian Somaliland obtained political independence and merged to form the Somali Republic. Perhaps another major reason why between the 1940s and 1960s Islam did not figure prominently in Somali politics, as it has done in other Muslim Societies, was the monopolistic obsession most Somalis had on the issue of freedom and unification with the remaining territories: northern Kenya (the NFD) under the British, Djibouti under the French, and, more significantly, the Ogaden region under Emperor Haile Selassie of Ethiopia. Accordingly, irredentist nationalism suffocated Islamic reformism as a significant aspect of Somali nationalism.

CAUTIOUS ISLAM DURING THE ERA OF PARLIAMENTARY POLITICS (1960-1969)

Writing in 1961, Frantz Fanon detected a major weakness in African liberation movement: beyond the political objective satisfied by formal, or in his words 'flag independence', nationalist parties were strikingly lacking in a comprehensive program of authentic development involving the economic, political, social, and cultural aspects of their societies. His simplified, though not simplistic, theory argues that the small, weak pseudo-bourgeoisie that leads the independence movement tries to develop the country through a robot-like imitation of the Western bourgeoisie. When they discover they cannot replicate Western capitalist accumulation, and that they lack economic security based on industrialization, they are unable to maintain liberal bourgeois political systems.

Thus they fall back on dictatorial one-party or military regimes. The nationalist front collapses and the politics of ethnicity, tribes, and clans rears its ugly head and is even able to cause serious setbacks for the pan-African movement that had gathered remarkable momentum during the 1940s and 1950s. Negative consequences appear in the realm of culture and social relations. According to Fanon, neocolonialism represents a major pitfall for uncritical forms of national consciousness.[21] Post-independence Somalia faced many of the problems he described.

Following twenty years of Fascist dictatorship, Italy, by 1950, emerged with a reconstructed parliamentary system under Christian Democrat rule. The UN appointed Italy as a 'trustee' to administer its former colony between 1950 and 1960. Italy took all measures to ensure that an independent Somalia would be governed by an Italian-type 'parliamentary model'. The constitution was written by Italian and American experts. As a result, Islam receives mention as the state religion, but nothing further is said. No attempt was made to develop forms of local democratic institutions that would not only relieve pressure on the 123-member national parliament, but would also facilitate the creative mingling of traditional Somali democratic practices with the demands of a large-scale state. Posi-tive aspects of Islamic culture that bind Somalis across clan cleav-ages were ignored.

Worse, perhaps, was the fact that no effort was made to devise electoral mechanisms that would at least minimize clan loyalties and channel parochial interests towards national objectives. As the years went by, national parties became 'clan' and even 'sub-clan' parties, and some degenerated into one-man 'parties'. Scandalous use of parlia-mentary patronage and the regular exploitation of 'voting power' for purposes of sectional or personal gain created a general atmosphere of cut-throat competition, corruption, incompetence, and irrespon-sibility.

Perhaps no issue demonstrated better the impotence of the Somali parliamentary system than the question of a script for the Somali language. The governments that were elected into power between 1960 and 1969 were unable or even unwilling to resolve it. Apart from Islam, the Somali language constitutes the most prized of all things in the Somali national heritage. In restricted circles the Arabic script had long been in use as a medium for writing Somali. The Sayyid utilized it and his arch rival Shaykh Uways was even able to introduce several technical improvements to this historical legacy.

In 1920 Osman Yusuf Kenadid invented an original script for Somali. SYL cadres used this system of witing, popularly known as Osmaniya, during the heyday of anticolonialism. Gradually, a significant portion of the Somali-educated elite came to prefer the adoption of a modified Latin script for writing Somali. Therefore, both before and after independence in 1960, the question of adopt-ing a standard orthography for Somali was fiercely debated.[22]

With the parliamentary governments unable to provide leader-ship and guidance, various personalities and voluntary organization within Somali's civil society moved to politicize the issue. Among the three who actively advocated an Arabic script for Somali were General Mohammed Abshir, Ibrahim Hashi Mahamud, and Mahamud Ahmed Ali. These men, and the others who supported the Arabic script for Somali, injected notions of political Islam during the parliamentary era. We shall discuss their views briefly to demonstrate the role they played in keeping alive the issue of Islam in Somali politics. At one point in his life General Abshir was considered among the most westernized of the Somali elite. During the mid-1960s he underwent a spiritual crisis and became a born-again Muslim. In 1967, during a public debate on written Somali held in Mogadishu, he argued: '...How can you differentiate between the Muslim identity from the Somali identity? To me, being a Somali and being Islamic are one and the same thing. The terms "Somali" and "Muslim" are synonymous in my mind. Islam provides our code of life. It is our state religion. Hence, the question of a script for our language puts our basic cultural and spiritual values at stake ...'[23]

In a 1963 publication in Arabic, *al-Sumaliyyatu bi-lughati l-qur'an* (*Somali in the Qur'anic Script*), Ibrahim Mahamud hashi offered several arguments in support of the Arabic script for writing Somali: Somalis are Muslims and the Constitution should be taken seriously since it states Islam is the state religion. Due to geographic proximity and comprehensive historical contacts, Somali culture and Arabic culture are closely related. Writing Somali in Arabic characters would facilitate these cultural and religious contacts and strengthen relations between Somalis and the rest of the Muslim world. He cited Pakistan, Iran, and Afghanistan as examples of Islamic non-Arab countries that use Arabic characters to transcribe their languages.

Ibrahim Hashi argued that Arabic ranks high among the major languages of the world and Somalis would have access to qualitative higher education in several countries. Besides, Arabic typewriters and printing presses could be obtained more cheaply and conveniently than if Somalia were to adopt a totally new script such as Osmaniya. Many among Somalia's educated elite have studied Arabic and the general public is to some extent familiar with Arabic letters through elementary Qur'anic instruction.[24] There existed already a crude form of writing in Arabic script 'used by merchants, in business, in letter writing, in the writing of petitions, and in the writing of *gasidas by wadaads*, whence its name is derived ("wadaad's writing")'.[25]

As an interpreter for the British in Burao, northern Somalia, Mahamud Ahmed Ali's father gave him an early interest and opportunity in modern education. However, throughout his life he retained a strong interest in Islam and led a pious Muslim life. He is considered the father of modern Somali education in the north because he helped establish the first primary school in 1938. As the school opened its doors, a rumour spread alleging a British attempt to introduce written Somali in modified Latin characters. Religious fanatics saw in this a deliberate Christian plan to weaken the influence of Islam among Somali youngsters. Disturbances occurred and three Somalis were killed in the northern town of Burao.[26]

Mahamud Ahmed Ali continued his efforts to spread education in British Somaliland despite opposition and antagonisms that sometimes seemed to threaten his very life. To his credit, he devised a curriculum that included a significant amount of instruction in the Islamic religion and the Arabic language and literature. Upon his retirement in the mid-1960s he became even more religious. As a Muslim lay ideologist, he offers an interesting thesis in defence of the Arabic script for Somali.

His arguments reflect an attempt to transform the sixteenth-century violent *jihads* into twentieth-century peaceful coexistence with intensive religious and ideological struggles for hegemony. In his words: 'There are about 3 to 4 million Amharas and about 4 to 5 million Somalis. In between these two, we find about 12 million Oromos. If you are historic minded, you will see that, twenty to thirty years from now, the emerging power on the Horn of Africa would be that power which has the Oromos on her side...'[27]

Historically, Somali *wadaads* and shaykhs have played a key role in the spread of Islam within the Horn of Africa. Mahamud Ahmed Ali felt that Somalis had become too lax and casual in their attitude towards Islam. He called on them not only to revive their faith but actively to expand it. he felt that the adoption of the Arabic script would strengthen Islamic ties and unleash the zeal required for such missionary undertaking. According to professor Ali Mazrui:

In Africa since independence two issues have been central to religious speculation–Islamic expansion and Islamic revivalism. Expansion is about the spread of religion and its scale of new conversions. Revivalism is about rebirth of faith among those who are already converted. Expansion is a matter of geography and populations–in search of new worlds to conquer. Revivalism is a matter of history and nostalgia–in search of ancient worlds to re-enact. The spread of Islam in post-colonial Africa is basically a peaceful process of persuasion and consent. The revival of Islam is often an angry process of rediscovered fundamentalism.[28]

Ahmed Gurey's campaigns represented a militarized form of Islamic expansionism, while the Sayyid's movement manifested a violent form of 'rediscovered fundamentalism'. Most of the arguments in favour of the Arabic script for Somali were based on a revivalist perspective. Dring the 1960s Mahamud Ahmed Ali and a few others tried to argue from the vision of an Islamic expansionism. He felt that the secular nationalist movement had distorted the problem of Somali unification and driven it up a blind alley; he reasoned that the 40 per cent and more Muslims within Haile Selassie's Ethiopian empire offer Muslim Somalis a natural 'Trojan Horse'. The issue, according to him, is Muslim vs. non-Muslim and, by wrongly defining the problem as Somalia vs. Ethiopia, Somalis allow the minority Christian rulers of Ethiopia the opportunity to rally even their dominated Muslim subjects against the Somalis.

The Somali language belongs to the Cushitic family which includes Oromo, Afar, Rendile, Borana, and others within the Horn of Africa. Somali contains about twenty-two consonant phonemes and ten vowel phonemes. The question of how and with what degree of success the Arabic script could be adapted for Somali from a linguistic perspective revolved mainly around the system of representing the relatively large number of Somali vowels which play a decisive role in Somali unlike the fewer vowel sounds in Arabic. In any case the parliamentary regimes were unable to resolve the impasse.

One of the SYC/SYL founders, Haji Mohammed Hussein, broke away and formed an opposition party, the Greater Somalia League. Besides supporting the Arabic script for Somali, his party advocated closer links with radical Arab nationalism under President Nasser. From time to time, members of parliament would speak in favour of joining the Arab League. Somalia joined the World Muslim League, headquartered in Saudi Arabia. Paying lip service to Islam, parliamentary regimes maintained a law prohibiting Somalis from using alcoholic drinks. However, in Mogadishu at least, the law was implemented with great flexibility. Thursday afternoons and all day on Friday were adopted as official days of rest instead of the Saturday and Sunday of the colonial era. During the 1960s then, Islamic politics was tentative and cautious and revolved mostly around the issue of a suitable script for Somali, energetically conducted by the various cultural and educational organizations, publications, and personalities.

ISLAM ON THE DEFENSIVE: THE SIYAD AFRO – MARXIST MILITARY REGIME

Fanon's observation concerning pseudo-parliamentary rule transforming itself rapidly into dictatorial rule as a result of failures in economic modernization needs to be slightly revised to fit the Somali experience. When confronted with the choice between tyranny and anarchy, the former nationalist politicians who manipulated the ineffective parliamentary system opted for anarchy which, some would argue, is more in keeping with traditional forms of pastoral democracy. Obviously the dictatorial system would have to come from other sectors of society and on 21 October 1969 the head of the Somali National Army, General Mohammed Siyad Barre, by means of a coup established a military dictatorship.

Coming as it did after the parliamentary tilt towards anarchy, the military coup signaling a swing of the pendulum towards tyranny was ironically greeted with public relief and approval. During its first months in power, the Siyad regime did not do anything to alarm Somalia's religious strata. However, on the first anniversary of the military coup, Siyad formally proclaimed on behalf of his ruling Supreme Revolutionary Council (SRC) that henceforth Somalia was to become a 'scientific socialist state'. The previous nationalist name, 'Somali Republic', was now transformed into a neo-Marxist version, 'Somali Democratic Republic'.

A number of the SRC members admired President Nasser of Egypt and, therefore, Somali religious leaders thought that Somali socialism might turn out to be another version of Nasser's Islamic socialism after all. It was not long before they became both disappointed and alarmed. Siyad repeated in lecture after lecture that there was only one true, universal 'scientific socialism'; the other versions one encounters on the continent as African or Islamic socialisms were fake and dangerous. 'Islamic socialism had become a servant of capitalism and neocolonialism and a tool manipulated by a privileged, rich, and powerful class.'[29] During the parliamentary era of secular nationalism, the state appeared to bypass Somali Islam, while the Siyad regime seemed bent on a policy of hostility and confrontation.

As a consummate politician and manipulator, Siyad did not let hostilities get out of hand, at least not during the early 1970s. When launching their first Three-Year Plan 1971 – 1973, the new leaders felt compelled to seek the support of religious leaders to implement its socio-economic program. In March the government newspaper proclaimed, 'Who is against scientific socialism is against the only system compatible with our religion.'[30] On 4 September 1971 over a hundred religious leaders were gathered in Mogadishu where Siyad urged them passionately and at length to participate actively in the building of a new socialist society. His speech contained a clear warning: either help us build the scientific socialist society as we have defined it or stay out of politics altogether. On this and other occasions (such as Islamic festivals) Siyad insisted that religion 'was an integral part of the Somali world view, but it belonged in the private sphere, whereas scientific socialism dealt with material concerns such as poverty. Religious leaders should exercise their moral influence but refrain from interfering in political and economic matters.'[31]

Moreover, Siyad's Marxism-Leninism lacked a genuine bourgeoisie to condemn. His attacks were aimed at certain elements or elites of the previous parliamentary regimes. In making such attacks he would often include the established religious leaders and, in his loose, repetitive, rhetorical style of speech making, he would often name names, thereby reducing what was intended as a class analysis to petty personal attacks. What prevented a clash between scientific socialism and Somali Islam at that point? Several reasons may be advanced to explain the lack of concrete public opposition by religious leaders during those years. In spite of rhetorical excesses, scientific socialism in practice turned out to be a series of pragmatic campaigns to eradicate glaring social, economic, and environmental crises afflicting Somali society. A number of the religious leaders felt that, given the indecision and chaos of the parliamentary regime, the new regime should at least be given a period of time to prove itself one way or another. Besides, potential Islamic actors recognize consciously or unconsciously that Somali Islam possesses only loose structures spread out in a relatively expansive land with inadequate transport and communication facilities. It draws on mixed social bases whose members are still strongly influenced by clan loyalties in spite of hundreds of years of Islamic influence. Even though the organization of Islamic activists has considerably improved since then, informal networks and loose Sufi-based associations continue to dominate.

Somali Islam has not developed a tradition for handling Muslims who go astray. The homogeneity of religion and of Islam itself in Somalia has led to a situation of extreme tolerance on matters of religion. The Sayyid's dervish movement was provoked and attained glory in confrontations with foreign infidels. When the Sayyid later unleashed his forces against fellow Muslims, for example, his savage raid against the famous Qadiriyya settlement at Sheikh, many came to interpret his actions as motivated more by clan hostilities than by Islamic Puritanism. In any case Somalia as a whole is more marked by the evolution of a cautious ethic propagated by the main Sufi orders which have avoided direct confrontations with political authorities and fallen back on patience to tolerate the survival of unjust conditions.

Some of the religious leaders were impressed by the Siyad regime's preoccupations with social justice. Moreover, social justice in the Islamic as well as the traditional Somali frame of reference is inseparable from the egalitarian ideal. They were therefore able to support many of the pragmatic socialistic measures with sincerity (at least for a period of time), professing that Islam is not only a spiritual vocation, but also a way of making a living. Those whose motives were basically dominated by material gains supported the radically secular regime out of opportunism. Thus, for example, the Somali press reported that in July 1973 sixty Qur'anic teachers, who had participated in a socialist orientation course, 'accepted the truth of scientific socialism and had promised to pray for its success henceforth'.[32] For many of Somalia's religious elites, especially those descended from communities that lived in the old Islamic city-states discussed above, their toleration of the regime came from a sense of spiritual superiority and historical contempt: 'out of deep-seated feeling that scientific socialism represented only a short-lived threat to their ancient religion'.[33] As it turned out, they were eventually proved right. Even though the regime lasted for twenty-one years and did not renounce socialism formally, strictly speaking the scientific socialist phase lasted for only seven years (from 1970 to 1977 when the Russians were expelled and Somalia waged war to free Somali populations under Ethiopian rule).

In February 1974 Somalia decided to accept an invitation extended earlier to become the Arab League's only non-Arab member. The decision was generally well received by the people, especially the religious elites. On his way home from the Arab League gathering, President Siyad first stopped in the northern regions of the country where people came out in spontaneous demonstrations of support. Somalis and Arabs have strong historical links, Islam providing the most important bond:

> This vibrant devotion to the values and beliefs of Islam has prompted the Somalis, rather like the Hausa of Nigeria, to fabricate and perpetuate an elaborate genealogy tracing their roots to Arabian ancestry. Although most educated Somalis dismiss the claim to Arabian descent as a pious historical fraud, the Somali populace sets much store by it, a circumstance that explains the massive popularity of the 1974 decision to join Somalia to the Arab League.[34]

Perhaps the timing of the decision on Siyad's part had to do with the 1973 world oil crisis and the emerging strength of Arab petro-dollar states. Religious leaders hoped that the Arab League connection would temper and eventually neutralize Siyad's scientific socialism. Around this time Saudi Arabia began offering Somalia aid conditional on its reducing ties and reliance on the USSR. Though the new regime had the closest political and military links with the USSR since its inception in 1969, it was only in July 1974 that, in a less dramatic manner, it signed the Treaty of Friendship and Co-operation with the Soviet Union.[35] The timing had a lot to do with the emerging competition between the Somali and Ethiopian military regimes for the attention and favors of the USSR. The UN declared 1975 International Women's Year and Siyad felt he should make a significant contribution worthy of his new status as an elderly convert to revolutionary Marxism-Leninism. Ever since the heady months following the 1969 revolution up to his election as Chairman of the OAU in 1974, he had come to taste glory on an international scale and did not seem ready to yield the limelight.

Somalia agreed to host the continental pan-African Women's Conference (April 1975) to prepare for the July UN World Conference on Women held in Mexico City. In January Siyad proclaimed a new family law which gave women the right to inherit property equally with men. Religious leaders were outraged: here finally they found tangible evidence that the scientific socialist state wanted to undermine the basic laws and codes of an Islamic society. Utilizing their right to speak within their mosques during Friday noon prayers, twenty-three religious leaders protested. They were arrested, charged with violating state security, and ten of them were publicly executed on 23 January 1975. Even though most religious leaders avoided open protests, this event marked the beginnings of a silent Islamic opposition movement. Somali religious leaders discovered that the post-Arab League honeymoon had lasted for less than a year.

In July 1976 Somalia launched a new, single party – the Somali Revolutionary Socialist Party (SRSP). Originally intended to facilitate mass participation, the SRSP soon came to serve as a complement to the main spying agency, the National Security Service (NSS). It was also charged with the task of political indoctrination through the propagation of the ideology of scientific socialism. The zealots among the party cadres continued to put religious leaders on the defensive. The practice of jailing people for allegedly misusing Islam spread to the regions and increased as time went on. At the Somali National University, for example, some of the lecturers in Arabic and Islamic religion often found themselves in and out of prison, depending on the whims of the party representative to the university.

To rub salt into the wound, Siyad's speeches on religion began to sound blasphemous. He argued that there was no contradiction whatsoever in holding the Qur'an in one hand and the *Communist Manifesto* in the other. He tried to convince his audiences that Marxism-Leninism represents the twentieth-century manifestation of the essence of Islam. Most Somalis simply could not believe that, even after sentencing, he would execute the religious dissenters. The Prophet of Islam, he argued, came at a time when women were highly exploited and he helped improve their condition. In other words, the Prophet's message was a correct socialist response to an exploitative society in Makka which had oppressive class structures. To his religious audiences Siyad was suggesting that the Qur'an may be of human rather than divine origin and indirectly comparing himself with a modern prophet, thus increasing the misunderstanding and hostility between the religious elites and the regime.

The period after January 1975 was marked by masked and sometimes unmasked battles between the regime and Muslim leaders. Following the establishment of the party (SRSP) in 1976, the regime, imitating the Soviet model of societal organization, went on to establish bureaucratic, SRSP-controlled social organizations for women, youth, and students, trade unions for workers, and co-operatives for settled farmers. During this period Siyad also intensified the campaigns against the so-called *wadaad xume* bad-filthy *wadaad*). Applying his usual divide-and-rule tactics, Siyad described the bad religious men as those failing to understand that the true principles of Islam can only be guaranteed by his scientific socialist revolution. He accused them of being instigated and manipulated by foreign powers interested in destabilizing Somalia and derailing the revolution. He never bothered to describe the characteristics of a 'good *wadaad*' (apparently the one who toes the government line or keeps his mouth shut), and therefore all men of religion felt themselves vulnerable. During this period an official who was too punctilious in his religious observance was less likely to win favorable political posting or promotion.

The ideological struggles waged during the later part of the dictatorship phase did not proceed for a long period of time. In 1977 the perennial issue, some may even say the nemesis, in Somali political life radically transformed the situation. Ever since the drought of 1974-5 the issue of Somalis under Haile Selassie's rule once again resurfaced. The Somali army peacefully went into the Ogaden region and brought out victims who were resettled together with others in the programmes mentioned above. Upon the overthrow of the emperor, the regime began to prepare, train, and support the

Western Somali Liberation Front (WSLF) which waged a relatively successful guerrilla war in the region. In 1977 pressures from the army and other strata of Somali society prompted Siyad to send the Somali army in support of the WSLF.

By the end of 1977 most of the Ogaden had been liberated. The city of Jigjiga was in Somali hands, Dire Dawa was controlled by both sides with Somalis gaining the upper hand, and the ancient Islamic city of Harar was under siege surrounded by Somali troops and WSLF guerrillas. The USSR openly embraced the new Ethiopian military regime and put pressure on the Somali government to co-operate with it. Early in 1977 Mengistu Haile Mariam came to power in a coup and the Soviets rushed to sign a treaty of peace and friendship with his government. By September the Somali army was deeply involved in the campaign to back the WSLF, and in November 1977 Siyad abrogated the treaty of peace and friendship signed with the USSR in 1974. In foreign affairs he realigned Somalia with the USA, the Western powers, and the moderate and conservative Arab block. He broke diplomatic relations with Cuba, which sent thousands of troops in an unprecedented Soviet airlift in order to push the Somali army out of the Ogaden by February/March 1978.

Siyad, who had hoped to make a historic contribution to the perennial problem of Somali liberation and unification, lost the war and lost his sense of direction, his ideological bearings. For all practical purposes scientific socialism was dead as a ruling ideology, though Siyad never admitted this publicly. The stage was set for both ideological confusion and growing societal chaos. Following the *de facto* collapse of scientific socialism, Siyad could have attempted to revive the Somali nationalism of the 1940s and 1950s. Instead, he resorted to masked and unmasked forms of clannism and nepotism. As part of his public relations, he sometimes appeared with a religious rosary and made the obligatory pilgrimage to Makka. He ruled out the Numeiri option of resorting to a born-again Islamic political ideology.[36] He has probably done the Islamic opposition movement a great favor by not appropriating their religiously influenced vocabulary, their symbols, and some of their objectives as a substitute for Marxism-Leninism after 1977.[37] During this period his attitudes seem to swing between considering Somali Islam as a paper tiger, to be provoked with impunity, and regarding it as a sleeping giant, to be treated with prudence and caution.

Cultural and social tensions as well as the insecurities brought about by state-instigated clan warfare in rural areas created a sense of profound national crisis. The crisis was exacerbated by a climate of social malaise which people felt but could not define: some called it moral decay–the absence of the rule of law facilitating daily manifestations of corrupt practices, nepotism, clanism, embezzlement of public funds and properties, abuse of authority, and other malpractices. The capital city of Mogadishu, for example, used to be one of the calmest and safest cities in the world during most of its history up to the 1970s it had been transformed into one of the worst in terms of violence and lack of security.

In response to social and economic insecurities, the Islamic reaction adopted various manifestations: (a) a striking increase in religious observances among the people, especially among the urban elites; (b) compared to the early days of the military regime, a marked increase in communal religious practices including pilgrimages to the tombs of local saints; (c) visits to charismatic shaykhs for spiritual healings; and (d) enhanced activities among relatively self-reliant Islamic agropastoral co-operatives. The regime began to claim that elements of the educated, religiously inclined urban elite had started to form an underground Islamic opposition movement. However, there was no evidence of such a movement during this early period; an examination of the existing evidence leads us to conclude that the Islamic opposition movement developed eventually as a consequence of excessive, unprovoked state repression rather than as a deterrent to it.

The tradition in Somalia has been to set aside a small space for public prayers at places of work – office buildings, schools and colleges, ministries, factories, shops, and hotels. Prayer spaces were usually out in the open, next to a water pipe for performing ablutions. Previously one noticed that those regularly praying in such set-aside spaces included messengers, some drivers, and other lower-class members of the civil service. Newcomers included commercial elements as well as middle-sector members of the civil service. Those with higher status prayed in their spacious offices. Relatively speaking, urban Somalis tend to be lax in observing the fast during the holy month of Ramadan; this drastically changed during these years as the observance reflected quantitative and qualitative transformations. Attendance at mosques increased significantly, especially during Ramadan.

Somali women from mixed social bases were very active in organizing Qur'anic reading sessions in various homes, especially on Thursday evenings. The Somali Islamic Movement is essentially a product of internal factors. It has been influenced to some extent, of course, by the world-wide Islamic revival movement. On the question of women this influence is partly manifested. Traditionally, most Somali women do not wear the veil associated with Middle Eastern and other Muslim women. The women of the minority urbanized communities making up the old trading city-states discussed above wore veils. However, among the majority of pastoral and agricultural Somalis the veil was never worn, even when they came to constitute the majority in the historic cities like Mogadishu. In keeping with Islamic modesty, they usually wore a cover over their heads and shoulders, baring their faces and hands. To make a statement, some of the educated women in the university and the civil service began to wear not the black or white veil (ha'ik) but the *hijab*, a semi-*chador* imitated from the Egyptian Islamic movement. As Frantz Fanon demonstrated concerning the veil in colonial Algeria, Somali women adopting a non-Somali, Muslim dress were definitely sending a political, religious message. Use of the *hijab* was a reaction by militant Somali women who felt their social code violated and heavily damaged by a reckless socialist-oriented dictatorship.

Perhaps as a surviving aspect of its ancestor-worshipping Cushitic past, Somali Islam is characterized by a marked degree of pilgrimages to the tombs of local saints, the most prominent being Shaykh Abdirahman al-Zeilawi in the north, Shaykh Uways in Biyoolay, and Shaykh Ali Maye in Merka. Following the earlier discouraging of such religious rituals and festivities, the government reversed its position and routinely approved requests to hold them.

A marked inclination to saint veneration induces a climate of religious rapture at these festivals. Thousands of the faithful from discrete clans and regions congregate in a vast assembly to worship together and to undergo a collective experience of cathartic ecstasy during which many are healed of their physical, emotional, and spiritual anxieties. Therefore, membership in an order, allegiance to its spiritual master, and active involvement in its communal rituals tend to cut across, sometimes to override, tribal allegiance, fostering a widespread awareness of a pan-Somali, multiethnic community unified by a vibrant devotion to common spiritual values. Hence, while ethnicity divides the Somalis through binary oppositions of lineage segmentations, Islam unifies the Somalis under the umbrella of non-tribal mystical associations.[38]

Certain shaykhs are visited during all seasons on account of their reputed powers of healing, including Shaykh Nur whose agropastoral community is situated on the river Juba a few miles north of Kismayu. Given the opportunity to visit his religious commune in November 1981, I was surprised to see the large number of representatives of the 'modern' elite—pilots, including the one who invited me to join him for the trip, doctors, engineers, teachers, traders, administrators—who had come to consult the shaykh for personal reasons. While waiting to meet the shaykh, we were invited to have dinner in one of the numerous hut-like waiting rooms where we met a businessman from Kismayu and a Qur'aric teacher. Reputed to be very rich, the businessman from Kismayu told us that he was extremely depressed; he had lost his peace of mind and could only sleep in peace in Shaykh Nur's compound. He had been there already for three months and planned to stay on for three or four months longer. The Qur'anic teacher came from the border areas where he had lost hope in his attempt to mediate in clan warfare among the neighboring clans he was serving. He was convinced that the wars had little to do with traditional Somali clan conflicts. They were instigated, he believed, by external elements who were providing modern weapons to their respective groups. Had he not come to Shaykh Nur to seek spiritual healing and guidance, he was sure that he would have lost his mind.

A part from, or perhaps in addition to, spiritual healing, Somali Islam has a significant record in establishing agricultural co-operatives called *jamaha*. One of the earliest was established in 1819 by Shaykh Ibrahim Hassan Jebra on land acquired on the river Juba in the south. The Sheikh *jamaha* in the north, at one time raided by the Sayyid, offers another famous example. The post-Sayyid Dervishes have also been important as founders of agricultural communities. At the village of Hallin in the Nugal region, for example, I came across a remarkable farming co-operative of about 150 celibate men under a religious shaykh growing various crops: cabbages, tomatoes, onions, papayas, carrots, and watermelons. They were also experimenting with specimens of spices and lemons.[39] They were cofindent that their success could be easily replicated in that they were part of a chain of co-operatives headed by Shaykh Mohammed Rabbi of the Salihiyya order.

By far the most impressive examples of religious grass-roots development organizations were the one established by Shaykh Mohammed Raghe within a mountainous zone near the town of Gebileh, north-west region, and the one headquartered around the town of Baidoa in the south, founded by Shaykh Abdirahman Mohamud (popularly known as Shaykh Banaaney). Both represent modernized forms of the traditional *jamaha* in which economic productivity received much more attention than in an ordinary *jamaha*. Shaykh Raghe's community, the Eil Berdaleh Co-operative, was spiritually guided by the shaykh who left technical and administrative matters in the hands of the able secretary-general, Mahamud Jama. The latter, who had received agricultural training in England, briefly served as Minister of Agriculture during the parliamentary epoch. The community helped to settle drought victims voluntarily, grew various cash and food crops, and experimented with a variety of crop specimens including coffee (not normally grown in Somalia). Former community members serve as its representatives and marketing agents in Berbera, Djibouti, and Mogadishu.

The Shaykh Banaaney religious co-operative was established in 1959. The founding shaykh later visited Eil Berdaleh in the north to learn from its agricultural, marketing, organizational, and spiritual experience. As of June 1987 the religious co-operative cultivated 22, 525 hectares in three religious/economic centres situated in two regions south of Mogadishu. It owned about 10,000 head of livestock, of which about 2500 were camels and 4000 cattle. Beginning with the simple tools of an average Somali farmer, the co-operative through self-reliant efforts came to possess four small tractors, one bulldozer, four diesel water pumps, one oil-pressing machine, and a large truck. Religious co-operatives which I observed began with poor communities; the resources mobilized through religion employed skilled, semi-skilled, and unskilled labor around three main settlements which were located between three and five hours' drive from each other. In 1984 OXFAM America donated three solar pumps to the community. The community took several loans from the Somali Development Bank and, unlike most of the bureaucratic government-sponsored co-operatives, has paid its debts regularly and punctually. Its crop-production activities involved experimenting with several species, growing a variety of vegetables and such crops as sorghum, maize, sesame, groundnuts, beans, sunflower, and bananas. Each co-operative family devoted part of its labor time to collective activities; the rest was used in private plots.[40]

Paradoxically, while the old ruling elites tried to develop Somalia as a miniature Western society with competitive party elections and parliamentary paraphernalia, and the new military dictatorship tried to transform the country, in the shortest possible time, into an Eastern socialist society complete with a vanguard party and controlled social and mass organizations, a remarkable group of rural religious elites was experimenting with indigenous voluntary grass-roots models based on Islam. It is also remarkable that they made significant progress at a time when the military state had put Somali Islam on the defensive.

THE HAWKS AND THE DOVES: ISLAMIC AND OTHER OPOSITION MOVEMENTS

In spite of his Western alliances, Siyad refused to permit multi-party politics. Accordingly, opposition to his rule took on an armed clandestine form. On 9 April 1978 a group of officers from one Somali sub-clan hurriedly launched a coup attempt following the Ogaden war defeat. Among the thirty-six arrested, seventeen were executed by firing squad in October. One of the plotters, Colonel Abdullahi Yusuf, escaped to Addis Ababa, where he established an external armed opposition group with the help of Ethiopia and Libya. Mengistu's Ethiopia placed a radio transmitter at the disposal of the Somali Salvation Democratic Front (SSDF) which continued to draw its support from Majerteyn (Darod) sub-clans. For various reasons beyond the scope of this chapter, the SSDF came to suffer internal conflicts and lose its earlier impact. Two cells of Somali Marxist elements defected during this period. Perhaps the most effective of the externally based opposition forces has been the Somali National Movement (SNM), formed in London in April 1981.[41] The SNM quickly developed an effective guerrilla army and strategy allowing it to overrun the main cities like Hargeisa and Burao in northern Somalia during 1988-9. Deriving most of its support from northern Isaq clans and sub-clans, the SNM continued to hold on to most of the rural areas until Siyad was finally overthrown.

A mass movement signifying an increase in religious practices and rituals picked up momentum during the mid-1980s. It elicited contradictory responses on the part of the exhausted military dictatorship. Born-again members of the educated elite, including girls dressed in the *hijab*, were harassed and intimidated. A number of female students were expelled from the university for wearing Muslim symbolic dress. A number of male students who had formed Qur'anic study circles were also expelled and some of their leaders jailed. They were accused of belonging to a subversive 'Muslim Brotherhood' cell. By 1987 relations with the religious elite took a turn for the worse and a number of religious leaders in Mogadishu were arrested, charged with destabilizing the regime, and sentenced to death. Aware of his growing weakness, Siyad decided not to carry out the sentences but to let the accused suffer in jail.

Official provocations led to religious riots and government massacres which took place in 1989 and 1990. The murder of the Italian Bishop Salvatore Colombo gave the government an excuse to arrest several religious leaders. Somali opinion charged the government with cynically murdering the bishop to win Western support as a secular bulwark against Iranian-type fundamentalism. Muslim leaders organized protests calling for the release of their jailed leaders. Over a thousand lost their lives in street killings, night round-ups, and executions.[42] In May 1990 former politicians issued a manifesto condemning the regime.[43] On 7 October 1990 the Islamic opposition movement issued its formal document, the Islamic Call.[44] It offered an outline history that viewed Ahmed Gure's expansionist *jihads* in a positive light; the Sayyid's name was omitted, while the document indirectly acknowledged his radical revivalist movement. As discussed earlier on, this represents Somali ambivalence towards the Somali Dervish movement.

The Islamic Call began with a general endorsement of the previous Manifesto, proclaimed by former Somali parliamentary leaders. Both internal opposition movements espoused non-violence in calling for a dialogue to achieve a peaceful settlement of the civil wars; however, signatories of the Islamic Call traced the origin of the problem to secular nationalism and blamed not only the Siyad regime, but also the parliamentary system, for having led Somalis astray. Obviously they reserved particularly harsh condemnation for Siyad's scientific socialist regime. Islamic Call accepts democracy as the general objective but insisted on an Islamic *(shura)* parliamentary democracy. Islamic Call signatories included several faculty members of the Somali National University, engineers, lawyers, doctors; the document lists sixty-seven individuals bearing the religious title 'shaykh', seven with the title 'Haji', and eleven with the title 'Maalim' (Islamic teacher). The Islamic movement in Somalia, as elsewhere, does not represent a marginal stratum of the elite. The active presence of intellectuals and professionals among them shows that catalytic actions are not led by frustrated lecturers in Arabic and Islamic studies as is often assumed. Lay ideologists have considerably helped the movement to develop and mature. An analysis of the Islamic Call and its leading personalities indicates its mainstream, Islamic-renewal aspirations. Its rejection of violence is but one aspect of its opposition to radical Islamic 'fundamentalism'.

THE POST-SIYAD ERA AND ISLAMIC GROUPS

The Islamic Call movement could have played a significant role in normal society-state circumstances. Its non-violent approach marked it for a reformist path. However, its leaders suffered a set-back when the Cairo reconciliation conference was aborted. Clan-based militias of the United Somali Congress (USC) finally chased Siyad out of Mogadishu on 27 January 1991. A number of the armed opposition volunteers – north and south – wore white arm or head bands with

'Allahu Akbar' ('God is Great') in green Arabic letters. Some felt that Islam would gain more respect and prestige in the new Somali order. Unfortunately, for key parts of Somalia including Mogadishu, what ensued was militarism and anarchy barring the immediate possibility of reconstructing a new Islamic-inspired order. Here and there, as groups of Islamic renewalists became eclipsed by chaotic events, pockets of Islamic 'fundamentalists' began to emerge.

Siyad and his remaining forces drove south to Kismayu and west to his clan homeland near the Ethiopian and Kenyan borders. Weeks later, his forces launched attacks from Kismayu in a major effort to recapture Mogadishu. They were beaten back and forced to flee into Kenya. From his home base Siyad continued to raid the intervening Rahanwin territories in spoiler efforts to destabilize Mogadishu. USC military leader General Mohamed Farah Aydid fought back all such raids at tremendous cost to the lightly armed Rahanwin agropastoralists surrounding the regional capital of Baidoa. Famine deaths peaked at 1700 a week in Baidoa in mid-1992, dropping to around 500 or fewer when President Bush launched Operation Restore Hope (ORH) under a United Nations mandate in December 1992.

As soon as the USC captured Mogadishu, an open split occurred between its military wing headed by General Aydid and its Manifesto wing headed by hotel owner Ali Mahdi Mohamed. Ali Mahdi had his faction name him 'Interim President', but this action was condemned not only by General Aydid, but also by other opposition groups – the SSDF, SPM, and the SNM in the north. Military confrontations between Aydid's Habar Gedir clan and Mahdi's Abgal clan (both Hawiye) followed. Mogadishu, especially between September 1991 and December 1992 when ORH intervened, became another Beirut in a civil war that created a so-called green line between Ali Mahdi's northern sector and Aydid's southern Mogadishu. Prior to such military confrontations, a loosely organized group of Islamic elements attempted to restore order during the months of February-April 1991.[45] Instead of emphasizing law and order and civil behavior at least in the initial phases, they prioritized the Islamic moral (Sexual) code that ran counter to the behavior of the gun-toting youth recruited under various clan militias. The religious elements retreated and organized their efforts into controlling and administering the newest Mogadishu zone called Medina, to the south and by the ocean. Even though many of them were Abgal (Hawiye), their Islamic politics kept them aloof from the Mahdi-Aydid military confrontations.[46]

The SNM in the north hosted a popular congress in Burao in April-May 1991. This congress, and a much larger one held in the non-Isaq town of Borama from January to May 1993, included sultans and chiefs from various regions and clans, religious leaders, businessmen, former politicians and military officers, intellectuals and prominent ex-civil servants. The Burao congress declared the former British Somaliland a new Republic of Somaliland with SNM leader Abdirahman Tuur its first President. The Borama congress continued the process of grassroots clan reconciliation, adopted guiding principles of a new constitution, and went on to elect former 1960 independence premier Ibrahim Mohamed Egal as the new President of the Somaliland Republic. Besides problems enumerated above, Somalia has also to confront an Eritrea-type problem of self-determination in the north.

The relatively democratic process in the north (Somaliland) has helped to ease not only clan tensions but also potential religious tensions. The SNM, like the other armed opposition movements, has had pockets of Islamic fundamentalists among its militia and some of its leaders. Early in 1993, for example, a group of fanatics stoned five women to death in Hargeisa on the charge that they were prostitutes. Official and public reaction went against them and they vanished from the scene. The SNM has encouraged various Islamic factions – orthodox Somali Sunni Shaykhs, Islamic revivalists, and 'fundamentalist' – to participate in pro-Islamic deliberations. Following the 1987 SNM congress, for example:

The Islamic fundamentalist wing got its share with the 'General Principles' of SNM constitutions: 'The Constitution shall be based on Islamic Sharia' (Art. 1), Somali traditional law will apply except when 'contrary to the Islamic Sharia' (Art. 3), the SNM flag will bear as an inscription the first surat of Quran in Arabic (Art. 10).[47]

There are more women waring *hijabs* in Burao – the seat of a popular shaykh – than in Hargeisa and western Somaliland. Shaykh

Ali was educated in Saudi Arabia and has been an 'ambassador-at-large' of the loose *Ittihad* Islamic 'fundamentalist' movement. He conducts regular visits to Mogadishu and other Islamic centres in the south where he is received with popular enthusiasm.[48] The movement's political stand is based on a fundamental proposition: Somalia has tried a Western parliamentary system as well as an Eastern scientific socialist system and both have proved to be dead ends; it is about time to introduce an Islamic state: 'Allah willing, we will not accept another deviation from the right path.'[49]

Moving east of Burao, one enters north-eastern Somalia where the SSDF has had violent confrontations with Islamic 'fundamentalists'. During the mid-1980s, and SSDF suffered an internal crisis, one wing opting to stay rebellious within Ethiopia, another defecting to join Siyad's side in the civil wars. Upon the fall of Siyad the rebellious wing returned and took control of the north-east regions – Bari, Nugal, and a part of Mudug. Colonel Abdullahi Yusuf emerged as Minister of Defense as the movement also welcomed former Police Commander General, now Imam, Mohamed Abshir Musa as the new SSDF Chairman. One of the more prominent Somali 'fundamentalist' groups, the *Ittihad al-Islami* (Islamic Unity), has strong leaders and followers in these regions. It first succeeded in bringing order to the port of Bosaso. When chaos broke out as private militias were hired to protect private properties, the *Ittihad al-Islami* took charge, providing efficient service, security, and law and order at minimal cost. They also used part of the funds raised at the port to invest in Islamic charity undertakings. They sponsored a well-organized non-governmental organizations, al-Falah, which maintained and improved services at Bosaso hospital.

As they gained popularity and influence, they reportedly began to buy and store large quantities of arms. Their multiclan following included supporters from other parts of Somalia. One of its leaders in 1992 was Shaykh Ali Warsame. Others included Mohamed Shaykh and Hussein Abdulle.[50] As their popularity and strength increased, tensions between them and the SSDF began to rise. The killing of the first UN medical expert in north-east Somalia was blamed on the *Ittihad al-Islami*. Movement supporters claim that the assassination was the work of the old regional leaders who had been replaced by the former SSDF exiles. It is alleged that these leaders did it in order to turn the conflict into an SSDF-*Ittihad* struggle.[51] SSDF Chair Imam Abshir, incidentally, is an Islamic renewal leader who served as one of the most prominent signatories to both the Manifesto and the Islamic Call documents. The *Ittihad* leader in the Garoe area was called Abdulkadr Gacami, while the leader in the Las Anod area preferred to camouflage his identity by adopting a PLO-type name, Abu Muhsin. Probably, the most charismatic leader was Hassan Dahir Aweys. The SSDF claims that the *Ittihad al-Islami* used radio communications to plan a simultaneous takeover involving Garoe, Qardo, and Bosaso. Fighting broke out in June 1992, and for a few weeks the *Ittihad* had the upper hand, but they were heavily outnumbered by the clan-recruited militias supported by Ethiopian troops invited by Abdulahi Yusuf.

During the June-August 1992 military confrontations it is estimated that between 400 and 600 people lost their lives.[52] The remaining *Ittihad* forces retreated to the port of Las Khore in Somaliland; reports indicate that they have since left the port and were based in a smaller nearby settlement. Supporters of the movement claim that it is an essentially indigenous movement that wants to install an Islamic state and Islamic law (*Sharia*) in Somalia. They intend to respect the rights of non-Muslims; they want to promote better understanding with the West.[53] They have received external assistance in the form of Islamic books and scholarships as well as help to construct or repair mosques. Their opponents charge that their external links involved arms, money, and training besides charity and scholarships. They singled out a foreign visitor from Saudi Arabia for indirectly assisting the revolt. They believe that radical Islam in Somalia has diverse sources of arms, finance, and training: the Sudan, Iran, Egypt, Yemen, Afghanistan, Iraq, and even Saudi Arabia.[54] Following military defeat, the movement is alleged to have changed tactics, concentrating on gaining power and influence through commerce, educational institutions, health, and religious activities. Pockets of radical Muslims controlled dispersed 'islands' within Somalia: Las Khore and some villages in the north-east, the Medina section of Mogadishu, Merca, and, more significantly, the Lugh areas in south-west Somalia where they operated an Islamic mini-state amids surrounding chaos and anarchy. It is too early, however, to be able to obtain a comprehensive assessment of the role of Islamic 'fundamentalism' in contemporary Somalia. The mini-state in the Lugh/Gedo area was also confronted by Ethiopian troops.

Islamic renewal and 'fundamentalist' positions have gained followings among Somali refugees and exiles in various countries including the USA, Canada, the United Kingdom, Italy, France, Germany, Scandinavia, Egypt, Saudi Arabia and the Gulf States, Ethiopia, Djibouti, Uganda, Kenya, and Tanzania. A 'fundamentalist' supporter based in the USA recently argued that it was a mistake for the Bosaso group to have attempted to capture state power violently.[55] He argued that the movement needs a long-range historical perspective. Given the clan and chaotic nature of Somali society, the radical Islamic movement can only come to power through education and persuasion. Islamic 'fundamentalists' have to win a hegemony within civil society before they can hope to conquer the Somali state. According to their external supporters, they should seek strategic influence in educational, health, economic, and cultural institutions. They should also seek to play dominant roles within the voluntary humanitarian and development organizations, including the Islamic co-operatives discussed above. They should pay particular attention to the role of the media.[56] Some of their supporters felt that the Islamic movement in Somalia need not reject Western modernity *in toto:* development strategy, they claim, would be based on selective enclosure – the erection of certain barriers to permit a discriminating approach to modernity similar to the movement promoting appropriate technologies.

Operation Restore Hope lasted from December 1992 till May 1993. Under the acronym UNOSOM II, the United Nations took charge of Somalia and very soon fell into a destructive war with General Mohamed Farah Aydid and his allies.[57] Aydid's militia was alleged to have killed twenty-four Pakistani UN troops on 5 June 1993, and Admiral Howe, head of UNOSOM, backed by Boutros Boutros Ghali, declared war on Aydid and his supporters as they sought to arrest him. From June till October 1993 this UN-sponsored and US-backed manhunt put a hold on most of UNOSOM's reconciliation and reconstruction tasks. In October American helicopters were shot down and, in one street fight alone, eighteen American soldiers were killed, one was captured, and over seventy-five wounded. This act prompted President Clinton to shift policies back to diplomacy and politics as he ordered an end to the manhunt. These events also caused the United States to ask the UN to reverse policies.[58] Among other things, these destructive engagements postponed the critical task of demobilizing Somalia's clan militias.

During the engagement Aydid's ally Omar Jess visited the Sudan, Iran, and other Islamic countries. Aydid's opponents claim that he received financial and military assistance from these countries. The truth of this claim has not been established conclusively one way or the other. Aydid, through his radio broadcasts, tried to appeal to Islamic groups to support his struggles. It appears that ultimately he won only the fanatical support of his clan, the Habar Gedir. This incident and the ones in the north-east show that clan consciousness and clan politics continue to be a potent factor overshadowing Islamic politics. Perhaps this is also the case in countries like Afghanistan where tribal and clan divisions hide behind sectarian Islamic conflicts. Another constraint is that the Islamic 'fundamentalists' do not have, as yet, a paramount charismatic leader able to unite the various factions and command the respect of many in the divided Somali society. Islamic politics in Somalia would also have to be flexible enough to respect traditional Somali law (*xeer*), especially in rural areas where attitudes do not support notions of an eye for an eye. Somali women traditionally do not wear veils (except by choice) and they are vocal and organized enough to obtain significant concessions at the various peace and reconciliation forums. A female supporter of Islamic movements stated: "If properly and flexibly implemented, there is no conflict between an Islamic state and Somali women ... The question is: will it be properly and flexibly implemented?"[59]

The transitional period is to oversee the crafting and adoption of a new constitution, to be followed by a new era of multiparty politics – if all goes according to publicized statements and agreements. Some of the Islamic movement supporters feel that the various Islamic tendencies might be able to vie for power through multiparty elections. Their hopes for influence would increase if they are able to form effective coalitions after such elections. The rules of the electoral process possibly may ask them to choose party names that do not monopolize the title 'Islamic' in a country where practically everyone is a Muslim. Unlike during the nationalist, parliamentary, and military-rule epochs, Islam is today poised to play a more prominent role in Somali politics: the issue is how much and what kinds of Islam are compatible (or necessary) for political development in Somalia's future.[60]

The options that seem open for political Islam include:

1. The Civil Society strategy: Among other things, this involves efforts to exercise hegemony in education, health and social services, commerce and financial markets; business, cultural and religious activities. The idea is to influence politics indirectly rather than directly. This is the strategy pursued by the traditional Somali Sufi non-governmental organizations such as Ahlu-Sunna wal-Jama'a and Majma. Waxda emerged in the north at one point in time in support of the SNM, with a vision of evolving and developing Muslim society in the long run by influencing by example via mosques, schools, clinics, charitable work, trade etc. Indonesia is probably the best example of Islamic civil society influencing the political arena. Many traditional NGOs emphasize non-violence to differ from the radicals.

2. The Islamic Court movement: Somalia is probably unique in creating Islamic (Sharia) courts with armed militia. This option developed both as a backlash to the anarchy of Somali wardlordism and a yearning for a new era of law and order. The Islamic NGO's that have emerged in dialectical opposition to Siyadism, have enabled the rise of Islamic courts by creating a conducive environment. The movement began with separate sub-clan courts with their own militia. This pragmatic response led to the establishment of subclan courts, the mobilization of court militia and eventually a federation (UIC). By 2004/2005 they decided to amalgamate into the Union of Islamic Courts (UIC). The UIC is in fact an umbrella organization for a broad range of socio-economic, commercial, political and clan interests. In June 2006, the UIC vanquished the coalition of warlords armed and financed by the US in its war against terrorism. The UIC came to confront the UN sponsored Transitional Federal

Institutions (TFI). "For many of the Courts' Hawiye supporters, the primary aims of the "uprising" have already been achieved: the removal of the warlords, restoration of peace and security, unification of the region under a single administration, and the opening of the port and airport. From this perspective there is no need for further expansion or confrontation with the TFIs and their Ethiopian guardians. Instead, the Courts and TFIs should negotiate security and power sharing arrangements for an interim period until a permanent national government can be established" (Matt Bryden, 2006).

Like other such disparate movements, the UIC had two opposed factions – the moderates in the above quotation and the radicals described below. The moderates are often called reformists. They tend to be more receptive to new ideas, practices, and institutions. They have a vision of Islam and democracy with its principles of limited government, public accountability and rotation of leaders, separation of powers and checks and balances. They believe that Islamic sharia needs to be reinterpreted according to the changing needs of modern society. Therefore, there is a clash of visions with the radicals or jihadists who despise democracy as the rule of humans as opposed to Islamism, which they believe is rule of God.

3. The Jihadist option: This implied aiming at and capturing state power (as in Iran) and installing an Islamist State. They intend to use any means necessary and tend to glorify violence including political suicides. They reject the power sharing vision of the moderates.

The nonviolent moderate "thinking is anathema to the ultra-nationalist elements within the Courts, especially the *Shabaab*, whose membership is drawn from a broad cross section of Somali clans. Public statements by *Shabaab* leaders and their UIC allies assert that the Somali jihad will continue until it reaches every corner of the Somali Republic. Sheikh Hassan Dahir Aweys, to whom much of the Court membership looks for guidance, has also implied that the UIC could legitimately take an interest in the welfare of Somalis in eastern Ethiopia. Such statements appear to set the Courts on a collision course with the governments of Puntland and Somaliland, as well as Ethiopia. However, UIC nationalists probably do not envision military expansion, so much as encouraging sympathizers within each of these areas to take the lead in challenging the established authorities." (Ibid). By October 2006, it became clear that the Somali jihadists have captured the whole movement.

4. The Democratic/constitutional approach: The implication of this option involves power sharing and the willingness to participate in democratic, multi-party electoral politics and hopefully accept constitutional limitations. Turkey is perhaps the best example of this approach. This option, however, was aborted in Algeria in 1992. The window of opportunity to negotiate a power sharing constitutional system was missed between June and December 2006. In the Khartoum negotiations between the UIC and the TFG, the moderates within the UIC led by Sheikh Sharif appeared willing to accept the principle of multiparties and elections. From the TFG side, this reconciliation effort was headed by the speaker of the TFG parliament Sharif Hassan Sheikh. Unfortunately, it soon became clear that both sides were conducting false negotiations. From the UIC side, the jihadist minority in ascendancy would not give up their vision of an Islamist state imposed by any means necessary. The militarists within the TFG were encouraged by Ethiopia's readiness and willingness to impose the TFG on the Somali people via military force.

The US global policy of counter-terrorism provided Ethiopia with both diplomatic cover and military assistance, an enabling environment. Within such an atmosphere, the talks and negotiations were doomed from the start. Inviting and relying on Ethiopian troops has posed an insurmountable obstacle to the Transitional Federal Government's ability to gain the support and trust (legitimacy) of the Somali people due to the perception within Somalia regarding foreign troops, especially those from neighboring countries which may be biased towards one or more elements of the Transitional Federal Government. The majority moderates within the UIC and the constitutional elements with the TFG, have both lost to the minority jihadists (UIC) and minority militarists (TFG). This proves the saying that the people who are moderate are not effective and the people who are effective are not moderate.

Had the constitutional approach succeeded, one could speculate about the checks and balances within Somali society that might moderate the harsh and radical elements within political Islam. Most of these are "foreign Islamic" elements imported by the jihadists. Somalia does not have a history of radical Islam with exception of the Dervish movement at the turn of the 20th century. The majority rural population – the pastoral and agropastoral communities – are attached to both Islam and traditional law (xeer), without noticing any contradictions. They will probably resist attempts to impose strict Shariah laws on their age long traditions. The will and capabilities of the business elite (some of whom have funded the Islamist movement), to reign in the radicals and steer the movement toward Islamic moderation. One may surmise that Somali civil society – both at home and in the diaspora – would, with some exceptions, tend to favor a moderate brand of Islam. Many Somali women will continue to struggle to protect and promote the human rights they gained during many years of struggle. They will also encounter the resistance of the youth who resent the banning of khat, movies, TV and sports. In addition, the majority of the traditional Sunni religious leaders practice a more tolerant form of Islam, and would prefer the civil society strategy. The violent resistance that would emerge as a result of the politicization of clan emotions – clanism remains the most potent force within Somali politics and society. There is also international powers that would also support moderate Somali Islam. These indigenous checks and balances could only be effective when aggressive foreign troops are ruled out. Instead of supporting and encouraging such indigenous checks and balances, counter-terrorism obsession believes that military repression is the best way to prevent Islamism from growing as a threat to the US and Ethiopia.

Notes

1. I. M. Lewis, the Modern History of Somaliland (London: Weidenfeld and Nicolson, 1965), 16.

2. Id. , 'Sufism in Somaliland: A Study in Tribal Islam', reprinted from the BSOAS 17:3 (1955) and 18:1 (1956).

3. B.W. Andrzejewski, 'Drought as Reflected in Somali Literature', Savanna, 2:2 (December 1973), 140-1.

4. Neville Chittick, 'The Coast before the Arrival of the Portuguese', in B.A. Ogot (ed), *Zamani– A Survey of East African History* (London: Longman, 1974), 100.

5. Ibid. 103.

6. I.M. Lewis, *A Pastoral Democracy* (London: Oxford University Press, 1991).

7. G.S.P. Grenville Freeman, *The East African Coast—Select Documents from the First to the Earlier Nineteenth Century* (London: Oxford University Press, 1962), 28-9 and 30.

8. Tom J. Farer, *War Clouds on the Horn of Africa:* A crisis for Détente (New York: Carnegie Endowment for International Peace, 1976), 9.

9. D. Jardine, *The Mad Mullah of Somaliland* (London: Herbert Jenkins, 1923), 36-8.

10. Quoted in John Drysdale, *The Somali Dispute* (New York: Praeger, 1964), 32.

11. Saadia Touval, *Somali Nationalism* (Cambridge, Mass.: Harvard University Press, 1963), 55-6.

12. In April 1982 I had the opportunity to interview Abdi Dheer, an ex-Dervish general, in the north-eastern town of Erigavo. Abdi Dheer idolized the 'early Sayyid' but felt the 'later Sayyid' deviated from the straight religious path and reintroduced the evils of clan loyalties and politics.

13. Harold D. Nelson (ed.), *Somalia: A Country Study* (Washington, DC: United States Government, 1982), 105.

14. Touval, op. cit. 65.

15. Jean-Claude Vatin, 'Popular Puritanism versus State Reformism: Islam in Algeria', in James Piscatori (ed.), *Islam in the Political Process* (Cambridge: Cambridge University Press, 1984), 86.

16. Touval, Op. cit. 86.

17. John L. Esposito, *Islam and Development* (Syracuse, NY: Syracuse University Press, 1980), ix.

18. Cited in Lewis, op. cit. (1965), 123.

19. Touval, op. cit. 73.

20. Kwame Nkrumah, *Ghana—The Autobiography of Kwame Nkrumah* (New York: International Publishers, 1971).

21. Frantz Fanon, *The Wretched of the Earth* (New York: Grove Press, 1968), 148-205.

22. Hussein M. Adam, 'A Nation in search of a Script' (M.A. Thesis, University of East Africa, Kampala, 1968), iv.

23. Ibid. 75. General Abshir, who suffered as a political prisoner for many years under Dictator Siyad, emerged as Imam Abshir, serving leader of the north-eastern regions of Somalia for several years.

24. Ibid. 62-3.
25. Lewis, cited in ibid. 80.
26. Ibid 64.
27. Ibid. 66.
28. Ali A. Mazrui, 'African Islam and Competitive Religion: Between Revivalism and Expansion', in a special issue dedicated to 'Islam and Politics', *Third World Quarterly*, 10:2 (April 1988). 499.
29. Nelson (ed.), op. cit. 115.
30. Ibid.
31. Ibid. 116.
32. Ibid.
33. Ibid.
34. David Laitin and Said Samatar, *Somalia: Nation in Search of a State* (Boulder, Co.: Westview Press, 1987), 44.
35. Ibid. 82.
36. See Alexander S. Cudsi, 'Islam and Politics in the Sudan', in Piscatori (ed), op. cit. 36-55.
37. According to several Somalis who have held intimate conversations with him on matters of religion, deep down Siyad did not really believe in any religion. He somewhat believed in 'Scientific Socialism', which he considered, in his half-educated mind, as a sort of 'magic wand' that would solve problems of state power and societal transformations.
38. Laitin and Samatar, op. cit. 45.
39. Hussein M. Adam (ed), A Preliminary Survey of the Nugal Region (Mogadishu: SURERD Publications, 1982), 52.
40. Mohamed Hassan Farah, 'Sheikh Banane Cooperative Developments', a mimeographed paper prepared for the International Relief/Development Project; Harvard University, 1989.
41. Farer, op. cit.95-6.
42. Robert M. Press, 'Rebels Close in on Somalia Capital', *The Christian Science Monitor,* 24 December 1990, 4; also Helene Jean, 'Barre's Clan Seeks to Keep Power in Somalia', *Guardian Weekly,* 6 January 1991, 12.
43. See 'Somali Manifesto I', published by the *Horn of Africa,* 13:1 and 2 (1990), 110.
44. In December 1991 Mohamed Hassan Farah and I translated this important mimeographed document from Somali into English.
45. An interview with Abdirahman Osman Raghe in Mogadishu, 3 August 1991.

46. Another interview with A. O. Raghe in Worcester, 5 December 1993.

47. Daniel Compagnon, 'The Somali Opposition Fronts: Some Comments and Questions', Horn of Africa, 13 (1990), 43.

48. Interview with A. O. Raghe, 5 December 1993.

49. In interview with Ahmed Farah Ali, Hageisa, 2 July 1991.

50. Interviews with Mohamed Hassan Barre and Osman Barre in Qardo, Bari Region, 28 March 1994.

51. Interview with radical Islamic movement supporter and hotel owner Dahir Gufure in Qardo, Bari Region, 31 March 1994.

52. Based on the interviews conducted as reported above.

53. Interview with Dahir Gufure.

54. Interview with Mohamed Hassan Barre.

55. Osman Sultan Ali, publisher of *Horn of Africa* journal, in a presentation at the Fifth International Congress of Somali Studies, College of the Holy Cross, Worcester, MA, 2 December 1993.

56. Ibid.

57. John Drysdale, *Whatever Happened to Somalia? A Tale of Tragic Blunders* (London: HAAN Associates, 1994).

58. Ibid. 211.

59. Ms Halima Awale in a presentation at the Fifth Congress of Somali Studies, 2 December 1993.

60. A paraphrase of a question by Michael C. Hudson in John Esposito, *Islam and Development,* 5.

References

Adam, Hussein M. "A Nation in Search of a Script"(M.A. Thesis, University of East Africa, Kampala, 1968), iv.

Adam, Hussein M (ed). A Preliminary Survey of the Nugal Region (Mogadishu: SURERD Publications, 1982), 52.

Ali, Ahmed Farah. Personal Interview. Hargeisa: 2 July 1991.

Ali, Osman Sultan. Presentation. Fifth International Congress of Somali Studies, College of the Holy Cross, Worcester, MA: 2 December 1993.

Andrzejewski, B.W. "Drought as Reflected in Somali Literature". *Savanna*, 2:2 (December 1973), 140-1.

Awale, Ms. Halima. Presentation. Fifth Congress of Somali Studies. 2 Dec. 1993.

Barre, Mohamed Hassan. Personal Interview. Qardo, Bari Region: 28 March 1994.

Barre, Osman. Personal Interview. Quardo, Bari Region: 28 March 1994.

Chittick, Neville. "The Coast before the Arrival of the Portuguese." In B.A. Ogot (ed), *Zamani–A Survey of East African History*.(London: Longman, 1974), 100.

Compagnon, Daniel. "The Somali Opposition Fronts: Some Comments and Questions". *Horns of Africa*, 13 (1990), 43.

Cudsi, Alexander S.. "Islam and Politics in the Sudan". In Piscatori (ed.), *Islam in the Political Process*. Cambridge: Cambridge University Press, 1984) 36-55.

Drysdale, John. *The Somali Dispute*. New York: Praeger, 1964. 148-205.

Drysdale, John. *Whatever Happened to Somalia? A Tale of Tragic Blunders*. London: HAAN Associates, 1994.

Esposito, John L. *Islam and Development*. Syracuse, NY: Syracuse University Press, 1980) ix.

Fanon, Frantz. *The Wretched of the Earth*. New York: Grove Press, 1968.

Farah, Mohamed Hassan. "Sheikh Banane Cooperative Developments". For the International Relief/ Development Project. Harvard University, 1989.

Farer, Tom J. *War Clouds on the Horn of Africa: A Crisis for Détente*. New York: Carnegie Endowment for International Peace, 1976), 9.

Freeman, G.S.P. Greenville. *The East African Coast – Select Documents from the First to the Earlier Nineteenth Century*. (London: Oxford University Press, 1962), 28-9 and 30.

Gufure, Dahir. Personal Interview. Quardo, Bari Region: 31 March 1994.

Hudson, Michael C. Paraphrase of a Question. In J. Espisito, *Islam and Development*, 5.

Jardine, D. *The Mad Mullah of Somaliland*. (London: Herbert Jenkins, 1923), 36-8.

Jean, Helene. "Barre's Clan Seeks to Keep Power in Somalia." *Guardian Weekly*. (6 January 1991) 12.

Laitin, David and Samatar Said S. *Somalia: Nation in Search of a State*. (Boulder, CO: Westview Press, 1987), 44.

Lewis, I.M. *A Pastoral Democracy*. London: Oxford University Press, 1961.

Lewis, I.M. *The Modern History of Somaliland*. London: Weidenfeld and Nicolson, 1965, 16.

Lewis, I.M., "Sufism in Somaliland: A Study of Tribal Islam"

Mazrui, Ali A.. "African Islam and Competitive Religion: Between Revivalism and Expansion", In a special issue dedicated to 'Islam and Politics', *Third World Quarterly*, 10:2 (April 1988) 499.

Nelson, Harold (ed.). *Somalia: A Country Study.* Washington, DC: United States Government, 1982), 105.

Nkrumah, Kwame. *Ghana – The Autobiography of Kwame Nkrumah.* New York: International Publishers, 1971.

Press, Robert M. "Rebels Close in on Somalia Capital." The Christian Science Monitor. (24, December 1990) 4.

Raghe, Abdirahman Osman. Personal interview. Mogadishu: 3 Aug. 1991.

Raghe, Abdirahman Osman. Personal interview. Worcester: 5 Dec. 1993.

Touval, Saadia. *Somali Nationalism.* Cambridge: Harvard University Press, 1963.

Vatin, Jean-Claude. "Popular Puritanism versus State Reformism: Islam in Algeria." In James Piscatori (ed.), *Islam in the Political Process.* Cambridge: Cambridge University Press, 1984) 86.

INDEX